THOMAS HEYWOOD

A STUDY IN THE ELIZABETHAN DRAMA
OF EVERYDAY LIFE

BY

OTELIA CROMWELL

ARCHON BOOKS
1969

SBN: 208 00767 9
Library of Congress Catalog Card Number: 69-15681
Printed in the United States of America

TO THE MEMORY OF

MY PARENTS

JOHN WESLEY CROMWELL

LUCY McGUINN CROMWELL

CONTENTS

INTRODUCTION

This study of Thomas Heywood is an effort to form an
estimate of the poet's contribution to one phase of Elizabethan drama, namely, the plays presenting in plot, characterization, or general atmosphere, Elizabethan England. The
contrast between the realism of Heywood's most widely read
play, *A Woman Killed with Kindness,* and the idealism, for
instance, of Shakespeare's *As You Like It* is sharp and
immediately apparent. What is more provocative of discussion is the point of view and purpose and method of the
writers of plays essentially realistic, but marked by a wide
range of differences in tone and manner. Ben Jonson,
Middleton, Dekker, Heywood, William Rowley, and Brome
alike hold up the mirror to the passing show of their day;
their dramas, however, conform to no one pattern in the
richly varied coloring of their realism. Among these productions Heywood's plays are not indistinctive. They offer
prevailing characteristics of their own. Moreover, I feel
that the poet was inspired by a purpose, a constant, conscious
impulse animating and guiding the spirit of his work, and
that his dramatic art, even in its limitations, was not inadequate for the expression of this purpose. It has been my
object to indicate what Heywood's aim was, how, and to
what extent he realized it.

The main facts of Heywood's life have been pointed out
by Miss Katherine Lee Bates in her Introduction to the
edition of *A Woman Killed with Kindness* and *The Fair
Maid of the West I,* published in the Belles-Lettres Series.
My only reason for presenting any biographical material is
to show how Heywood's dramatic purpose and the achievement of it are explained in the poet's life and character. To
Miss Bates I am especially indebted for her bibliography.
Naturally, my conclusions are based upon my own reading,

but Miss Bates's list served as a point of departure for further investigation and certainly saved me much expenditure of time. The questions of the authorship and chronology of the few doubtful plays have formed the subject of several investigations and some controversy: notably, the discussions of Miss Hibbard and Mr. Aronstein on the authorship of *The Fayre Mayde of the Exchange,* the contributions of Professor Andrews and Professor Martin to the solution of the problems relating to the collaboration of *The Late Lancashire Witches,* and the claims made by Professor Adams for Heywood's authorship of *A Warning for Fair Women, How a Man May Choose a Good Wife from a Bad,* and certain scenes of *Captain Thomas Stukely.* In reaching my decisions concerning these vexed problems I have examined carefully the evidence submitted by these critics of Heywood and, although I have not been able to accept every deduction submitted, the obligation of the last reader in the class to those preceding him is mine. Particularly have I been helped by the wealth of detail submitted by Professor Adams in his sympathetic appreciation of Heywood.

It is a pleasure to express my gratitude for personal encouragement and direction. I refer to the suggestions of Miss Eva Porter, instructor of English in the Emma Willard School, who read my manuscript, to the interest shown in my work by Miss Margaret Corwin, executive secretary of the Graduate School of Yale University, and to the stimulating teaching of Professors George H. Nettleton, Robert J. Menner, and Tucker Brooke of Yale University. Most deeply am I indebted to Professor Brooke. Professor Brooke directed my attention to Heywood as a subject for investigation. For his helpful, friendly counsel and scholarly criticisms I am sincerely grateful; studying under him has been, indeed, a privilege and an inspiration.

THOMAS HEYWOOD

CHAPTER I

HEYWOOD'S DRAMATIC CAREER

In 1612 there was published in London a book, whose title-page reads: "An Apology for Actors. Containing three briefe Treatises. 1. Their Antiquity. 2. Their ancient Dignity. 3. The true use of their Quality. Written by Thomas Heywood. Et prodesse solent et delectare. London. Printed by Nicholas Okes 1612."[1] The customary dedicatory epistles prefixed to writings of the period are not lacking: there are a dedication to the Earl of Worcester and an address to the reader signed, respectively, "Thomas Heywood" and "T. Heywood," while similar prefatory remarks to the actors of the city appear over the initials "T. H." Following these introductions are more than a half dozen complimentary poems to the author: contributions by one Arthur Hopton; John Webster, the dramatist; John Taylor, the Water Poet; and Richard Perkins, Christopher Beeston, and Robert Pallant, members of the Queen's company of actors.[2] Each of these writers except the first named refers explicitly to the author of the appended tract as "Thomas Heywood."

That this "Thomas Heywood" was connected with the stage goes without saying. By Perkins, Beeston, and Pallant he is called "fellow."[3] The strongest evidence, however, is in the nature of a great part of the contents of the *Apology* itself, which bespeaks most unquestionably the

[1] *An Apology for Actors.* In three books by Thomas Heywood. From the edition of 1612 compared with that of W. Cartwright. With an introduction and notes, by J. P. Collier. London: Reprinted for the Shakespeare Society, 1841. Title page.

[2] The Malone Society, *Collections IV-V*, 1911. No. V, pp. 270-271.

[3] *An Apology for Actors,* pp. 8-11.

author's background of stage experience. Indeed, there has never been raised the slightest shadow of doubt that this "Thomas Heywood" was an actor of the Queen's company, the actor-author of the published plays bearing the same title-page motto, the "Et prodesse solent et delectare" of the *Apology for Actors,* the prolific writer, according to his own account, who "had either an entire hand, or at the least a maine finger" in two hundred and twenty plays.[4]

The *Apology for Actors* is a respectable piece of literary criticism. Its subject is dramatic history and dramatic art. Following closely the outline of contents inscribed upon the title-page, *Part One* and *Part Two* constitute a running commentary upon the ancient dramatists; while *Part Three* presents the poet's position upon the ethics of the stage, the utility of the theatre, and the nature of dramatic art. In tone, the *Apology* is uniformly serious indicating nothing so much as the lofty moral intention of the writer. It is a defense of the stage; its arguments, however, are unequivocally and wholly for players and plays of the better kind:

"I also could wish, that such as are condemned for their licentiousnesse, might by a generall consent bee quite excluded our society; for, as we are men that stand in the broad eye of the world, so should our manners, gestures, and behaviour, savour of such government and modesty, to deserve the good thoughts and reports of all men, and to abide the sharpest censures even of those that are the greatest opposites to the quality. Many amongst us I know to be of substance, of government, of sober lives, and temperate carriages, housekeepers, and contributory to all duties enjoyned them, equally with them that are rank't with the most bountifull; and if amongst so many of sort, there be any few degenerate from the rest in that good demeanor which is both requisite and expected at their hands, let me entreat you not to censure hardly of all for the misdeeds of some, but rather to excuse us, as Ovid doth the generality of women."[5]

[4] *The Dramatic Works of Thomas Heywood,* 1874, Vol. IV. *The English Traveller.* Prefatory address to the reader.
[5] *An Apology for Actors,* p. 44.

Here are the unmistakable convictions of a man whose high ethical standard imposes a strict moral code upon the actor. Yet he reveals a wise and kindly tolerance. Feeling personally responsible for the reputation of actors, Heywood was sensitive toward adverse criticism levelled against the profession. He wrote the treatise in defense of the group to which he belonged. He made it plain, though, that in no respect was he the champion of immorality. Heywood's actor must himself be clear in his conduct.

Equally direct is his language as to the aim of the theatre. One need not believe, indeed, as Philipp Aronstein interprets it, that Heywood's chosen motto—his adaptation of Horace's

Aut prodesse volunt aut delectare poëtae[6]

indicates literally the poet's unfailing intent, and that to him the theatre was, narrowly speaking, a "volkshochschule."[7] Moreover, Heywood's position, as to the underlying aim of poetry, was neither original nor unique. The Renaissance critics, we recall, were divided upon the question of the function of poetry, wavering between the utilitarianism of Horace and the broader aesthetic view of Aristotle; a goodly number of these writers: namely, Daniello, Minturno, Giraldi Cinthio, Varchi, Scaliger accepted the theory of the Latin poet. At the end of the sixteenth century Heywood's contemporary, Sir Philip Sidney, wrote in his answer to Gosson's *School of Abuse* (1579) that "Poesie is therefore an arte of imitation . . . with this end to teach and delight."[8] Of lesser note than the author of *An Apology for Poetry* (1583-1595) are other Elizabethan critics, Lodge, Webbe, Nash, Puttenham, who also justify the art upon moral and utilitarian grounds. Heywood's claim to distinction, however, rests in

[6] *Ars Poetica,* 333.

[7] "Thomas Heywood" by Philipp Aronstein. *Anglia* XXXVII-XXXVIII, 1913, p. 191.

[8] *An Apology for Poetry,* Sir Philip Sidney. In *Elizabethan Critical Essays,* edited by G. Gregory Smith, 1904, Vol. I, p. 158.

the minuteness of his analysis of the scope of the drama, in the concreteness of the suggestions he offers to actors, and in the consistent simplicity of his method of attacking the problem. As to the purpose and benefit of the stage, he says:

> First, playing is an ornament to the citty . . . Secondly, our English tongue, which hath ben the most harsh, uneven, and broken language of the world—is now by this secondary meanes of playing continually refined, every writer striving in him selfe to adde a new florish unto it; so that in processe, from the most rude and unpolisht tongue, it is growne to a most perfect and composed language . . . Thirdly, playes have made the ignorant more apprehensive, taught the unlearned the knowledge of many famous histories, instructed such as cannot reade in the discovery of all our English chronicles; . . being possest of their true use, for or because playes are writ with this ayme, and carried with this methode, to teach their subjects obedience to their king, to shew the people the untimely ends of such as have moved tumults commotions, and insurrections, . . . If a morall, it is to perswade men to humanity and good life, to instruct them in civility and good manners, shewing them the fruits of honesty, and the end of villany. . . . . . and these are mingled with sportfull accidents, to recreate such as of themselves are wholly devoted to melancholly which corrupts the bloud, or to refresh such weary spirits as are tired with labour or study, to moderate the cares and heavinesse of the minde, that they may returne "to their trades and faculties with more zeale and earnestnesse, after some small, soft, and pleasant retirement.
>
> Briefly, there is neither tragedy, history, comedy, morall, or pastorall, from which an infinite use cannot be gathered. I speake not in the defence of any lascivious shewes, scurrilous jeasts, or scandalous invectives. If there be any such I banish them quite from my patronage; . . We present men with the ugliness of their vices to make them the more to abhorre them;—"[9]

At this point we must remember that Heywood's discussion of the drama did not end with his making a case for the plays. In addition to his wholly unambiguous theory of the function of plays, he offers some very con-

[9] *An Apology for Actors*, pp. 51-54.

structive criticism as to the presentation of plays and as to methods of acting. To repeat, plays are "to provide amusement," "to polish the English tongue," and "to instruct." But the actor himself must appreciate the value of rhetoric, he must be taught how to speak, to use gestures properly, to feel the relation between word and action. In a word,

> "A delivery and sweet action is the glosse and beauty of any discourse that belongs to a scholler. And this is the action behoovefull in any that professe this quality. Not to use any impudent or forced motion in any part of the body, nor rough or other violent gesture, nor on the contrary to stand like a stiffe starcht man, but to qualifie everything according to the nature of the person personated; for in overacting trickes and toyling too much in the anticke habit of humors, men of the ripest desert, greatest opinions, and best reputations, may breake into the most violent absurdities."[10]

But we discern again the note of modesty:

> "I take not upon me to teach, but to advise, for it becomes my juniority rather to be pupil'd myselfe, then to instruct others."[11]

Thus Heywood has outlined the aim of the drama and the means of accomplishing it. Loyalty and good faith, courage and kindliness, manners and morals are to be presented through the sober or amusing incidents of whatever material the poet can command. To write plays of the kind proposed, the poet must, perforce, be familiar with the chronicles of his country and the legends and tales gleaned from the storehouse of fact and fancy; he must be a man of varied experiences and broad sympathies; most of all, he must be willing to conform to the principles of poetic justice, for the ultimate judgment of the play, as hinted by the *Apology,* will give the palm to a sound, wholesome, moral issue rather than to the artistic triumph of sheer cleverness or sharp practice over virtue or ignorance. In the light,

[10] *Ibid.,* p. 29.
[11] *Ibid.,* p. 30.

then, of Heywood's own words, two questions naturally arise:

I. What qualities did Heywood himself bring to the prosecution of his dramatic career? In other words, did his experiences and associations furnish him with opportunities to see life in the complexity of its relations; and, granted that he had seen much, what may be inferred, of his prevailing mood and general attitude toward life? And

II. In what respect, if at all, may his plays be considered an expression of his theory of the stage?

A considerable body of information about Heywood's activity is at hand. This material consists of entries in Philip Henslowe's *Diary,* items in contemporary records of the dramatic companies playing in London and in the counties of England, further items in the Registers of the Stationers' Company, the references to Heywood made by his associates, the dedications to his plays, and the recent discoveries of Miss Bates in the Clerkenwell Parish Register[12] and in the Probate Registry of Somerset House.[13] From this evidence one may gather some important facts of Heywood's life and not only construct a fairly complete outline of the poet's long career of dramatic activity but gain a clearly defined impression of the man himself.

Thomas Heywood was born, probably, between 1570 and 1574. A later birth date would hardly be in harmony with the poet's own reference to himself at a period not later than 1635:

"Further to expect any new conceits from old heads is as if a man should look for greene fruit from withered branches. But as Time, the producer of all things, though he be aged Himselfe, is every houre begetting something new, so we on whose heads he hath cast such a snow, as no radicall or naturall

---

[12] *A Woman Killed with Kindness* and *The Fair Maid of the West,* edited by Katherine Lee Bates, 1917. Introduction, XLIV.

[13] *Ibid.* Introduction, XLVIII.

heate can melt, in imitation of him . . . will never suffer our braines to leave working, till our pulses cease beating."[14]

Turning now to Henslowe's *Diary*, we find, in the list of plays presented by the Admiral's men at Newington Butts, this entry: "ye 19 of Julye 1594 ne Rx at 2 pte of godfrey of bullen."[15] Fleay's identification of "godfrey of bullen" with *The Four Prentices of London*[16]—and this conjecture appears a happy one—permits us to accept 1594 as an approximate date for the beginning not only of Heywood's connection with Henslowe but of his theatrical career. Very few productions could have antedated a play alluded to by the author as having been written in "my infancy of judgment" and "my first practice."[17] This "first practice," *The Four Prentices of London,* was not the exercise of a boy in his teens. The author could not have been much younger than twenty years of age. On the other hand, we cannot believe that Heywood, in 1594, had passed his twenty-fifth year, unless we assume that he was actively engaged in the labors of city poet[18] when he was well beyond the age of seventy.

Heywood may have been born in Lincolnshire, as his reference to a certain Sir George Saint Poole of Lincolnshire as "my countryman"[19] suggests. Further, there is no internal evidence conclusively incompatible with his having been reared in the country. It is entirely true, as Miss

---

[14] *The Hierarchie of the Blessed Angells.* Dedication.

[15] *Henslowe's Diary,* edited by W. W. Greg, 1904. Part I, F 9^v, p. 18.

[16] *A Biographical Chronicle of the English Drama,* Frederick Gard Fleay, 1891. Vol. I, pp. 282-283.

[17] *The Dramatic Works of Thomas Heywood,* Vol. II. *The Four Prentices of London.* Prefatory Epistle.

[18] *History of Lord Mayor's Pageants,* Frederick W. Fairholt, 1843, p. 58.

[19] *Pleasant Dialogues and Drammas von Tho. Heywood,* W. Bang, 1903, p. 253.

Bates says, that the single reference to Sutton's Windmill[20]
as against numberless allusions to places in London indicates
a long residence in the city. As we read Heywood, we are
conscious of a bareness of imagery of country life. We
miss pictures of the familiar aspects of eternal nature. The
urban background of the plays may be attributed, I believe,
to the poet's temperamental indifference to what is commonly
called the "beautiful" in nature and to his uncompromising
fidelity to the relation between atmosphere and plot, rather
than to utter ignorance of the topography of Lincolnshire,
or to unfamiliarity with the out-of-doors world. The hawking scene, in the sub-plot of *A Woman Killed with Kindness,*
not to mention, from the same play, the presentation of a
consistent and vivid coloring of Elizabethan manor house
life, bears witness to an experience that must have been
gathered beyond the confines of London. Unlike persons
exclusively city bred, to whom an occasional trip into sub-
urban districts affords a glimpse of regions remembered
often afterwards as realms of mystery and delight, Heywood is singularly unaffected by the simple charm of the
country. He is not stirred by the lure of the unknown to
construct an artificial, Arcadian background of the simple
situations of everyday life because, in all probability, he had
seen much of rusticity. At most, however, this experience
of country life was brief as contrasted with the longer years
spent in the city; doubtless it was limited to the years of
Heywood's boyhood; for from 1594 to 1639 there is an
almost unbroken chain of data furnishing proof of his residence in and about London for the period of time between
these dates.

We are in greater certainty about Heywood's education.
A university training must account for the nature of his

[20] *A Woman Killed with Kindness* and *The Fair Maid of the West,*
edited by Katherine Lee Bates. Introduction, XLVIII.

reading and his intimate knowledge of classic lore. The five plays—*The Golden Age, The Silver Age, The Brazen Age, The Iron Age (I, II)*—all based upon classic legend; the translations from Greek and Latin poets; the quotations and adaptations from the philosophers and the church fathers, forming the framework of *The Hierarchie of the Blessed Angells;* all these attest the schooling offered by the universities of the time. Moreover, this mass of internal evidence, too vast in extent to be disregarded, is supplemented by the poet's own words about himself and the tributes of his associates. Contemporary opinion of Heywood is voiced in the direct testimony of those composing prefatory verses to certain of his works, and in the casual allusions to him scattered here and there in other writings. Although these numerous references differ in tone as we should expect the appreciations of friendship to be unlike impersonal criticism, yet, our ears become attuned to a recurrent note never silent —the tribute to Heywood's erudition. As much as we are impressed now by Heywood's indefatigable industry and learning—the explanation, indeed, for the extraordinary number of his plays—these qualities seem to have singled him out in his own day. Webster naming the poets says: "and lastly (without wrong last to be named) the right happy and copious industry of Master Shakespeare, Master Dekker, and Master Heywood; wishing what I write may be read by their light."[21]   Richard Braithwait in his *Survey of History* barely mentions Homer because his "Judicious Friend Master Tho. Heywood hath taken in hand (by his great industry) to make a Generall (though Summary) description of all the Poets lives."[22]   And Heywood's friends, Shakerley Marmion and two others, who sign them-

[21] *The Works of John Webster*, edited by Alexander Dyce, 1859. *The White Devil*. (Address.) To the Reader.
[22] *A Survey of History: or A Nursery for Gentry*, by Richard Braithwait, 1638, p. 114.

selves respectively "D. E." and "S. N." in prefatory verses to the *Pleasant Dialogues,* give due honor to our poet's store of learning as well as his industry. The first-named writes:

> "Heywood, when men weigh truly what thou art,
> How the whole frame of learning claimes a part
> In thy deepe apprehension; and then see
> To knowledge added so much industry."[23]

To "D. E." Heywood is "the learned author Master Thomas Heywood"[24] and "S. N." alludes to Heywood's "learned pen."[25] One Samuel King, in lines appended to *The Wise Woman of Hogsdon,* praises "the learned author Mr. Thomas Heywood," adding

> "Was now Macaenas living, how would hee
> Support thy learned wit? Whose industry
> Hath purchas'd such a knowing skill, that those
> Who read admire thee;"

Even the ironic strain of William Hemminge's ridicule of Heywood in *On the Time-Poets*[26] is softened by the conceded "Heywood Sage." At Cambridge Heywood evidently studied,[27] but at what particular college we cannot say.

---

[23] *The Dramatic Works of Thomas Heywood,* Vol. I.

[24] *Ibid.*

[25] *Ibid.*

[26] *On the Time-Poets,* cited as an anonymous poem by Halliwell in the *Shakspere Society Papers* (Vol. III, 1847, p. 173), is, in reality, only a fragment, the entire poem entitled *Mr. Thomas Randolph the poet, his finger being cut off by a riotous gentleman, his friend Mr. William Hemming made this elegy on the same.* The complete version discovered in a Bodleian Ms. (Ashmolean Ms. 38, art. 34) was first printed by Professor John J. Parry in an article, "A Seventeenth Century Gallery of Poets," appearing in the *Journal of English and Germanic Philology,* xix, No. 2, 1920, pp. 270-277. A little later Professor G. C. Moore Smith, not knowing that Professor Parry had preceded him, printed the same poem in a book entitled *William Hemminge's Elegy on Randolph's Finger, Containing the Well-Known Lines "On the Time-Poets" now first published with an introduction and Notes . . .,* Oxford, 1923.

[27] *An Apology for Actors,* p. 28.

Peterhouse has been suggested. Perhaps he did study there; but the evidence for this assumption is principally the statement of William Cartwright, the publisher of a garbled edition of the *Apology for Actors* (c. 1658), and the words of Sencer, a character in *The Wise Woman of Hogsdon*.[28] From these two sources, however, satisfactory conclusions can scarcely be drawn. Cartwright, guilty of the unscrupulous methods of editing displayed in his edition of the *Apology,* cannot inspire the reader's confidence in his unsupported statement. The dialogue of the comedy is vague in meaning and uncertain as to its reference. Our safest source of information is Heywood himself when speaking in his own person. Writing in 1612 in the *Apology for Actors,* he declares: "In the time of my residence in Cambridge, I have seen tragedyes, comedyes, historyes, pastorals, and shewes, publickly acted, in which the graduates of good place and reputation have been specially parted."[29] More specific reference to his university residence has yet to be discovered. The declaration as quoted from the *Apology* may not tell us all that we should know, but it is absolutely unequivocal; then too, it is of the utmost significance as shedding light upon the poet's early interest in the stage. From the detailed enumeration made by him of the classes of plays, we perceive that, while he was a student, he was a close observer of the theatrical shows at Cambridge, if he did not take an active part in the performances. It is not at all unlikely that these academic entertainments awakened an interest in stage plays, which sent him, with or without a college degree, to London, where he began the apprenticeship for his life's work.

In London Heywood undoubtedly was in 1594. Just when he arrived we do not know. If he was born between 1570 and 1574, his university residence was hardly prolonged

[28] *The Dramatic Works of Thomas Heywood,* Vol. V. *The Wise Woman of Hogsdon,* p. 321.
[29] *An Apology for Actors,* p. 28.

after 1590 or thereabouts. Between the time of the departure from Cambridge and 1594, the date, possibly, of the beginning of Heywood's dramatic career, there falls in our narrative a gap of several years. Without attempting to construct a chronological table of his activity, one would like to account for the employment of these pivotal years. We may hazard one or two guesses. Heywood may have been engaged as actor or as actor-playwright, getting his stride while working over or composing plays more or less indifferent in value. Such plays may have been rejected as too crude for performance. Perhaps, at this time he was working over old plays or engaging in other kinds of hack work for the Admiral's men or the Earl of Worcester's company, groups of actors associated subsequently with Heywood. A workshop period productive of little in which the playwright had a major part is not an impossibility; neither is it unlikely that for a year or two the apprentice actor may have been used in parts too insignificant to have been noted. There remains another theory, which we need not reject summarily. Again turning to the *Apology for Actors*, we note these words:

> "the king of Denmarcke, father to him that now reigneth, entertained into his service a company of English comedians, commended unto him by the honourable the Earle of Leicester; the Duke of Brunswicke, and the Landgrave of Hessen retaine in their courts certain of ours of the same quality."[30]

A page or two further in the same book, reference is made to a company of English comedians that travelled in Amsterdam and gave performances of *The Four Sons of Aymon*.[31] What may have reference to this "company of English comedians" is an item transcribed from the town records of Leyden by Mr. John Tucker Murray in his history of the English dramatic companies of the Elizabethan age. The item shows that all or part of the Earl of Worcester's com-

[30] *Ibid.*, p. 40.
[31] *Ibid.*, p. 59.

pany visited Holland in the summer or fall of 1590. Commenting upon the circumstances proved by the record, Mr. Murray writes:

"During 1591 the Earl of Worcester's Company acted at Faversham, Norwich, Coventry, Leicester, Marlborough, Gloucester, Shewsbury, and Southampton. Toward the end of this year, or the beginning of 1592, Robert Browne and Richard Jones planned to go abroad with the company. From a passport granted the actors on Feb. 10, 1592 by Charles Howard, Lord Admiral, we learn that their names were: Robert Browne, John Bradstreet, Thomas Saxfield (i. e. Sackville), Richard Jones. We also learn that they intended playing in Zealand, Holland, Friesland, and Germany. . . . ."[32]

Heywood's name does not appear among those granted the passport on February 10, 1592, but he may have crossed the Channel beforehand with the Earl of Worcester's men in 1590, or he may have joined Browne and his fellows later when they travelled on the continent for the performances at Frankfort, Cologne, and Nürnberg.[33]

After 1594 we walk on firmer ground. From this date, to the end of the fourth decade of the seventeenth century, for a period of well-nigh fifty years, when Heywood was between the ages of twenty and seventy, he led an active public career. During the first thirty years of this time, he was engaged in the busy life of actor and playwright. After 1623 or 1624, he devoted himself more largely to writing and to the publication of his productions.

The bare facts of the first stage are many and, within certain prescribed bounds, varied. For the period between 1594 and 1596 there are in Henslowe's *Diary* entries pertaining to many plays, certain ones of which have been identified as Heywood's. Fleay was the first to note the fact that the designations used by Henslowe for these plays, as well as the stage properties mentioned in the *Diary* for

---

[32] *English Dramatic Companies, 1558-1642*, by John Tucker Murray, 1910, pp. 50-51.
[33] *Ibid.*, p. 52.

some of them, suggest plots or characters of plays known to be Heywood's. Reference has already been made to the apparent connection between the "godfrey of bullen" of 1594 and *The Four Prentices of London.* Other identifications made by Fleay are the "seleo & olempo"[34] of March 5, 1594 as *The Golden Age,* the "firste pte. of herculous"[35] of May 7, 1595, as *The Silver Age,* the "2 p of hercolas"[36] of May 23, 1595 as *The Brazen Age,* and the "troye"[37] of June 22, 1596 as *The Iron Age.*[38] Dr. Greg agrees, in the main, with Fleay's inferences, but in commenting upon the "sege of London."[39] of December 26, 1594, he says: "This play may very likely underlie those scenes (I-X and XV) which deal with the besieging of London, by the Bastard Falconbridge in *I Edward IV* . . . Unlike Fleay, I regard *Edward IV* on internal evidence as unquestionably Heywood's."[40]

It is possible, then, that Heywood had produced for the Admiral's men between 1594 and 1596 not less than six plays—*The Four Prentices of London, The First Part of Edward the Fourth, The Golden Age, The Silver Age, The Brazen Age,* and *The Iron Age.* Such an amount of work would not only show the industry of the poet, but presume a fixed relation between him and the Admiral's men, the company presenting the plays. This surmise is not weakened by the entries in the *Diary* for the next two years. The "haywodes bocke"[41]—the fourth item in a series of loans

[34] *Henslowe's Diary,* edited by W. W. Greg, Part I, F 11ᵛ, p. 22.

[35] *Ibid.,* F 11ᵛ, p. 22.

[36] *Ibid.,* F 12ᵛ, p. 24.

[37] *Ibid.,* F 21ᵛ, p. 42.

[38] *A Chronicle History of the London Stage,* pp. 114-116. This hypothesis is not necessarily inconsistent with the judgment of Professor J. Q. Adams (*Modern Language Notes,* June, 1919) that the plays of the *Four Ages,* in the form in which we now have them, "were certainly the product of Heywood in 1610-12."

[39] *Henslowe's Diary,* Part I, F 11, p. 21.

[40] *Ibid.,* Part II, p. 173.

[41] *Ibid.,* Part I, F 23, p. 45.

made by Henslowe to four members of the Admiral's men in October 1596, the "oserycke"[42] for which receipts are entered in February 1597 and which is referred to in 1602 as Heywood's "Bocke of oserecke,"[43] as well as a group of his *Dialogues and Dramas*[44] entered in April 1597 as "V playes in one"[45] record the continuation of Heywood's activity with the Admiral's men. It is not, however, until later that the *Diary* becomes quite explicit as to Heywood's connection with Henslowe. In 1598 appears the following most interesting entry:

> "Mdo. that this 25 of marche 1598 Thomas hawoode came & hiered himesealfe with me as a covenante searvante for II yeares by the Recevenge of II syngell pence accordinge to the statute of winchester & to begine at the daye above written & not to playe anywher publick abowt london not whille these II yeares be expired but in my howsse yf he do then he dothe forfett unto me by the Recevinge of this IId fortie powndes & wittnes to this.

> <table>
> <tr><td>Antony Monday</td><td>Wm. Borne</td></tr>
> <tr><td>Gabrell spencer</td><td>Thomas dowton</td></tr>
> <tr><td>Robart shawe</td><td>Richard Jonnes"[46]</td></tr>
> <tr><td>Richard alleyn</td><td></td></tr>
> </table>

Here is proof positive of Heywood's services as an actor with the Admiral's men from 1598 to 1600. On the other hand, the possibility of his becoming a shareholder later is less evident. If he was a shareholder, he succeeded in holding himself singularly aloof from the financial transactions of the company. In contrast to the men, who witnessed his covenant, together with others, whose names were from time to time affixed as witnesses to the acknowledgments of indebtedness retained by Henslowe upon his making loans to actors, Heywood is not mentioned as a medium for trans-

[42] *Ibid.*, F 26, p. 51.
[43] *Ibid.*, F 116, p. 182.
[44] *Biographical Chronicle of the English Drama*, Vol. I, p. 286.
[45] *Henslowe's Diary*, Part I, F 26, p. 51.
[46] *Ibid.*, F 231, p. 204.

mitting advance payments upon plays or for making partial
payments upon unfinished plays. In 1600 he was evidently
no shareholder, for we miss his signature among the names
subscribed to a statement of the company's complete indebtedness to Henslowe at the time. The document reads:

> "So that the full some of all the debts wch we owe Mr.
> Henshlowe this Xth of July *1600* comethe to Just the some of
> (   ) three hundred pounds whiche some of three hundred
> pounds we whose names are here under written, doe acknowledge
> our dewe debt and doe promyse payment: (out of our pt)

J Singger	Robt Shaa
Thomas Downton	Thomas towne
Humfry Jeffes	W birde
Anthony Jeffes	Edward Jubye
Charles massye	Richard Jones"[47]
Samuell Rowley	

Moreover, as actor, he evidently did no borrowing himself.
As we have his own testimony to the fact that he spent
rather prodigally in his youth,[48] he must have been in
circumstances affluent enough, at least, to have rendered him
independent of the credit system established by Henslowe
for that astute broker's benefit if not for the advantage of
the impecunious actor. Payments for his own plays, though,
our poet did not reject. On December 6, 1598 he received
through Robert Shaw, Henslowe's advance agent for the
moment, three pounds as first payment for a play "ware
w^{th}owt blowes & love w^{th}owte sewte";[49] on February 10,
1598 through Thomas Dowton three pounds for another
play, "Jonne as good as my Ladey."[50] Neither of these
plays is extant.

From 1600 to 1602 Heywood's name is not on the pages
of the *Diary*. It has been noted that he was not one of the

[47] *Ibid.*, F 69, 70, pp. 12, 123.
[48] *Hierarchie*, Bk. IV, pp. 208-9.
[49] *Henslowe's Diary*, Part I, F 52^v, p. 100.
[50] *Ibid.*, F 53, p. 102.

eleven men signing the document of July 10, 1600. Neither does it seem that he continued with Henslowe as an actor, a "covenante servant" under the old agreement of 1598. In 1600 he may have been playing with a company, of whose history we have as yet no information; or perhaps he was travelling abroad with a group of actors; or, as Miss Bates infers from lines in Heywood's elegy on King James, he may have been attached to the household of the Earl of Southampton.[51] The title page of *Edward the Fourth* (1600) bears this statement "As it hath divers times been publikely acted by the Right Honourable the Earle of Derbie his servants." As Mr. Chambers explains, this company was not the Earl of Derby's company which afterwards became the Chamberlain's company, including Shakespeare among its members, but was a second Earl of Derby's company organized possibly under the patronage of the successor of Ferdinando Stanley, the patron of Shakespeare's company, and playing frequently from 1594 to 1618 in the provinces.[52] Heywood had evidently sold *Edward the Fourth* to the Earl of Derby's company, and it is not improbable, also, that he played with that company between 1600 and 1602.

From August 17, 1602 to March 16, 1603 Heywood was with the Earl of Worcester's company playing at the Rose. That he took a more prominent part in the activities of the Earl of Worcester's company than he had taken in the Admiral's from 1598 to 1600 is evidenced from certain entries in the *Diary* for this time. With the actor John Duke, Heywood negotiated with Henslowe for a loan of forty shillings to Chettle and Day for "a playe wherein shores wiffe is writen." (Date not given.)[53] Once, but once only, he even borrowed from Henslowe two shillings

[51] *A Woman Killed with Kindness,* edited by Katherine Lee Bates. Introduction, LXXXIX.

[52] *The Elizabethan Stage,* by E. K. Chambers, 1923. Vol. II, pp. 126, 127.

[53] *Henslowe's Diary,* F 121, p. 190.

sixpence for a pair of silk garters![54] From time to time
sums are mentioned for the purchase of properties for his
plays: September 3, 1602, eight shillings for "IIII Lances
for the comody of thomas hewedes & Mr. smythes;"[55] September 4, 1602, fifteen shillings "to bye things for thomas
hewode playe & to lende unto dick syferweste to Ride downe
to his felowes;"[56] November 3, 1602, twenty-seven shillings
"for the mackynge of the sewte" for Osericke;[57] November 9,
1602, thirty-eight shillings eightpence for "calleco sewtes
and II buckerom sewts,"[58] December 9, 1602, four pounds,
ten shillings for "II peces of changable taffetie," both for
the play *Christmas Comes but Once a Year,*[59] February 4,
1603, twenty-two shillings "for vellvet & satten for the
womon gowne of black vellvet,"[60] February 5, 1603, six
pounds thirteen shillings for "a womones gowne of blacke
velvett,"[61] March 7, ten shillings "unto the tayller,"[62] all of
these last named items pertaining to *A Woman Killed with
Kindness.* These details as to expenditures not only throw
light upon the cost of certain kinds of stage properties, but
testify especially to the regard in which Heywood's work
was held. If there had been the shadow of a doubt as to
the probable success of the forthcoming presentation of
A Woman Killed with Kindness, six pounds thirteen shillings would hardly have been risked as outlay upon a single
costume. Of equal significance are the other entries relating
to Heywood's activities with Worcester's men. Omitting
Oserick, first presented in 1597,[63] and the *Overthrow of the*

[54] *Ibid.,* F 114, p. 178.
[55] *Ibid.,* F 115ᵛ, p. 180.
[56] *Ibid.,* F 114, p. 178.
[57] *Ibid.,* F 117ᵛ, p. 184.
[58] *Ibid.,* F 118ᵛ, p. 186.
[59] *Ibid.,* F 118ᵛ, p. 186.
[60] *Ibid.,* F 119ᵛ, p. 189.
[61] *Ibid.,* F 119ᵛ, p. 188.
[62] *Ibid.,* F 120ᵛ, p. 190.
[63] *Ibid.,* F 25, p. 50.

Rebels, also an earlier composition,[64] we note the names of eight new plays, a busy record for the five months extending from September 3, 1602 to February 5 of the same year. It is true that in writing five of these plays Heywood collaborated with others: *Albere Galles* (September 4, 1602),[65] in all probability the unnamed play of September 3, 1602,[66] was the work of "Thomas hewod & Mr. Smyth;"[65] "harey Chettell Thomas deckers thomas hewode & Mr. Smythe & Mr. Webster" wrote *Lady Jane* (October 15, 1602);[67] "Thomas hewode & John Webster," as may be noted in one entry, "hareye chettell & thomas deckers," according to another, wrote *Christmas Comes but Once a Year* (November 2, 1602);[68] the *London Florentyn* (December 17, 1602) is the joint production of Heywood and Chettle,[69] as is an unnamed play of January 14, 1603.[70] Although Heywood's share in each instance of this collaboration may have been inconsequential, his industry during this brief time cannot be questioned. To the credit of his unassisted efforts there remain *A Womon Kylled wth Kyndnes* (February 5, 1603),[71] *Cuttyng Dicke* (September 20, 1602),[72] and *The Blind Eates Many a Flye* (November 24, 1602).[73] Of this total output of eight plays, all are lost except *A Woman Killed with Kindness.*

During the winter of 1602 (1603), the company had the honor of appearing at Court. For how many performances we are uncertain; the records, however, found in the Council Register and in the Accounts of the Treasurer of the

---

[64] *Ibid.,* F 25, p. 50.
[65] *Ibid.,* F 115^v, p. 180.
[66] *Ibid.,* F 115^v, p. 180; F 115^v, p. 181.
[67] *Ibid.,* F 117, p. 183.
[68] *Ibid.,* F 117^v, p. 184; F 118, p. 185.
[69] *Ibid.,* F 108^v, p. 172.
[70] *Ibid.,* F 119, p. 187.
[71] *Ibid.,* F 119^v, p. 188.
[72] *Ibid.,* F 116, p. 181.
[73] *Ibid.,* F 118, p. 185.

Chamber, as reported by Mr. Chambers, include two dates for
the Earl of Worcester's company: January 3, 1602 (1603),
and February 14, 1602 (1603). Representing the company
in these recorded items are the names of William Kempe
and Thomas Heywood.[74] This is significant as further
evidence of Heywood's complete participation in the interests
of the Earl of Worcester's men.

After James I ascended the English throne, the principal
theatrical companies came under royal patronage. By the
favor of the new monarch, the old Lord Chamberlain's men
became the King's company, the Earl of Worcester's the
Queen's, and the Earl of Nottingham's (Admiral's) became
Prince Henry's.[75] The patent for the King's company,
recorded in the Patent Rolls for 1603, is dated May 19.[76]
The legal status of the Queen's men is implied by an undated
draft for a patent. This document, as has been pointed out,
must have been prepared between December 1603 (the Earl
of Worcester's company was acting in Leicester in October
and December of that year) and March 15, 1604, when
the company had already passed under the patronage of the
Queen.[77] Among the ten names of actors specified as of the
Queen's company, occurs our poet's name, appearing third
on the list. He is also mentioned with the other Queen's
men, who marched in the triumphal coronation procession,
brave in his apportioned four and a half yards of red cloth.[78]

From 1604 until the death of Queen Anne on March 2,
1619, the Queen's company played in London intermittently
and in the provinces. Abundant proof of Heywood's continuous membership is at hand. In the license of April 15,

[74] "Court Performances," by E. K. Chambers. *The Modern
Language Review*, Vol. II, 1906-7. October, 1906, 1-13.

[75] *Time Triumphant*, by Gilbert Dugdale. Printed in *Nichol's
Progresses*, Vol. I, p. 413.

[76] Malone Society, *Collections, Part III*, 1909, p. 264.

[77] *Ibid.*, pp. 265-267.

[78] *Transactions of the New Shakspere Society*, 1877-9.

1609, authorizing the company "to use and exercise the arts and faculty of playing comedies" and other plays in the Red Bull and certain theatres in London and in any town halls in the provinces,[79] Heywood's name occurs. When the company visited Norwich on May 6, 1615, March 30, 1616, and May 31, 1617, a copy of the patent of 1609, dated January 7, 1611 and bearing the same names, was presented as credentials.[80] Two entries in the Mayor's Court Books of Norwich—May 6, 1615 and March 30, 1616 —contain Heywood's name among the others seeking license to play in the town.[81] He is also among the actors of the Queen who on October 2, 1617 entered a petition to the court for their defense against the charge of not repairing the roads near the Red Bull theatre.[82] Finally, we note that he is one of the actors receiving each an allotment of four yards of black cloth for Queen Anne's funeral on May 13, 1619.[83]

Whether Heywood continued his stage career after the death of Queen Anne is a mooted question, the point at issue, on the one hand, arising over the interpretation of a phrase in a legal document of 1623. To retrace our steps for a moment. In August 1612, Thomas Greene, a member of the Queen's company, died. His will, which had been witnessed on July 25, 1612, by several members of the company, including our poet,[84] may be considered with a series of documents shedding additional testimony upon Heywood's membership in the Queen's company. These are the papers of the lawsuit brought by Susan Baskerville, Thomas Greene's widow, who had remarried, against the Queen's

[79] Malone Society, *Collections, Part III*, 1909, pp. 270-271.
[80] *English Dramatic Companies*, Vol. II, p. 340; 341; 343.
[81] *Ibid.*, Vol. II, p. 340; 341.
[82] *Ibid.*, Vol. I, p. 194.
[83] *History of English Dramatic Poetry to the time of Shakespeare and Annals of the Stage to the Restoration*, by J. P. Collier, 1879, Vol. I, p. 397.
[84] *A Chronicle History of the London Stage*, p. 194.

company for its failure to pay to her certain sums of money accrued from Greene's share in the company's earnings. Now, although this suit was instituted in 1617, it lingered in Chancery for several years, Heywood's being among the other names of the company in the various documents filed from time to time in the proceedings.[85]   As late as June 1623, he is again included with his fellow actors, described as "all fellowes and sharers of the said Companie, and now comme or shortlie to comme from the said Playhouse called the Redd Bull to the Playhouse in Drurie Lane called the Cockpit, by their deed indented bearing date on or about the third daie of June in the fifteenth yeere of the raigne of our new soveraigne Lord King James over England."[86]   It is clear that the first reference is to the entire group as of 1617; and it seems probable that all, except those specifically noted as deceased, are of the company *"now* comme, or shortlie to comme" from the Red Bull to the Cockpit.   If this be the correct interpretation of the words, Heywood was acting or at least he was a shareholder in the company in 1623.   The argument, on the other hand, for Heywood's retirement from the stage after 1619 rests on the fact mentioned by Mr. Murray that Heywood's name does not appear in the records of any of the companies playing in London or in the counties after 1619.[87]   Too much, though, should not be made of this fact.   In the Appendix to the Malone Society *Collections, Part III,* are reprints of two drafts for licenses which as yet have not been traced.   The first one, dated February 1624 and recorded in the Docket Book of the Signet Office, is a draft for a license for an unnamed company, presumably the Queen's as that company by reason of the death of the queen was without a patron, and as Robert Lee, one of the leading actors of the old Queen's company, is named.   The second one, referring to the same

[85] *Ibid.,* 272-297.
[86] *Ibid.,* 285.
[87] *English Dramatic Companies,* Vol. I, p. 256.

company and of the same date, mentions "Robert Lee and Nicholas Longe with the rest of their Companies." In the same group of documents is included an entry of November 1622, a warrant for Robert Lee, Richard Perkins, Ellis Worth, Thomas Basse, John Blany, John Cumber, and William Robbins, late comedians of Queen Anne deceased "to organize and direct a children's company." As the offices of these two companies were not necessarily connected, it is entirely possible that Heywood may have retained his membership in the company represented in the Docket Book of the Signet Office by the names of his associates Robert Lee and Nicholas Longe, but may not have been affiliated with the group directing the children's company.

Allusions to presentations of Heywood's plays, other than those mentioned by Henslowe, are not lacking. Of two specific references to the poet by name, the first is in the Revels account book for 1604-05. It reads: "1604. By the Queens Ma^tis plaiers. On Sunday ffollowinge (Innocents Night) A plaie cald How to Larne of a woman to wooe. Hewood."[88] The rôle of the second Luce in *The Wise Woman of Hogsdon* supports Fleay's assertion that *How to learn of a Woman to Woo* was Heywood's *Wise Woman of Hogsdon*.[89] The second reference, of date twenty years later, appears in Sir Henry Herbert's official record of plays licensed in 1624. From this account, it is learned that on September 3, 1624, the Cockpit company was given permission to produce a new play, that was evidently Heywood's *Captives*.[90] This is, of course, a suggestion that Heywood was connected with the Cockpit theatre as late

[88] *Extracts from the Accounts of the Revels at Court in the Reigns of Queen Elizabeth and King James I*, by Peter Cunningham. Printed for the Shakspere Society, 1842, p. 204. *The Elizabethan Stage*, Vol. IV, p. 171.

[89] *Biographical Chronicle of the London Stage*, Vol. I, p. 292.

[90] *The Dramatic Records of Sir Henry Herbert*, by Joseph Quincy Adams. *Cornell Studies in English III*, 1917, p. 29.

as 1624. Other records cite the *Silver Age* and *Lucrece* as presented at Greenwich in 1612,[91] and the revival of *Lucrece* at the Cockpit in 1628[92] and of *If You Know Not Me You Know Nobody* at the same theatre when the play was "above one and twenty."[93] *Love's Mistress* was "three times presented before their two excellent Maiesties within the space of eight days" at the Phoenix (Cockpit) between 1625 and 1636.[94]

Between 1630 and 1640 Heywood occupied the position of city poet, a post involving the labor of writing the pageants produced annually upon the occasions of the inauguration of the Lord Mayor of London. The very titles, given by our poet to these shows, indicate the esteem, the love he had for his London. In the list of pageants described by Fairholt, the following ones are ascribed to Thomas Heywood: *London's Jus Honorarium* (1631), *Londini Artium et Scientarum Scaturigo, or London's Fountain of Arts and Sciences* (1632), *London Imp. or London Mercator* (1633), *Londini Sinus Salutis or London's Harbour of Health and Happiness* (1635), *Londini Speculum: or London's Mirror* (1637), *Porta Pietatis, or The Port or Harbour of Piety* (1638), *and Londini Status Pacatus, or London's Peaceable Estate* (1639).[95] As Fairholt notes, the city pageant of 1639 is the last one recorded before the Parliamentary Wars interrupted civic festivities. It must be admitted that in the writing of these shows Heywood was lamentably uninspired, but to be judged fairly such productions should be seen in the elaborate setting of their original

[91] *Extracts from the Accounts of the Revels at Court,* p. 211.

[92] *A Chronicle History of the London Stage,* p. 333.

[93] *The Dramatic Works of Thomas Heywood,* Vol. I. *If You Know Not Me You Know Nobody.* Prologue reprinted from *Pleasant Dialogues and Drammas.*

[94] *The Dramatic Works of Thomas Heywood,* Vol. V. Title page of *Love's Mistress.*

[95] *Lord Mayors Pageants . . .* by Frederick W. Fairholt. Printed for the Percy Society, 1843, 54-62.

presentations. Heywood himself makes fitting acknowledgment, at the close of the pageants, of the artistic skill in
design and construction of the master workmen who constructed the "Triumphall Models."[96] It appears that during
Heywood's term of office the mechanical side of the presentation was entrusted to the members of one family: "that
kind Maister Gerard Christmas" who "spared neither cost
nor care, either in Figures or ornaments" and Master
Gerard's two sons, John and Mathias, following the calling
of their father. As city poet, Heywood is perhaps the target
of Glapthorne's shaft, one of the characters in *Wit in a
Constable* saying:

. . . . "or perchance
You may arrive to be the Citty Poet
And send the little moysture of your braine
To grace a Lord Maiors festivall with showes
Alluding to his trade, or to the company
Of which he's free, these are the best preferments
That can attend your learning!"

(Act 1, sc. 1)

Doubtless there was in this gibe a double thrust, allusions
to the literary defects of the pageants and to Heywood's
assumption of the cause of the English tradesman.

Heywood himself published or witnessed without his
sanction the publication of the following plays: *The First
and Second Parts of King Edward the Fourth* (1600), *If
You Know Not Me You Know Nobodie* (1605), *The Second
Part of, If You Know Not Me You Know Nobodie* (1606),
The Rape of Lucrece, A True Roman Tragedie (1608),
The Golden Age (1611), *The Brazen Age* (1613), *The
Silver Age* (1613), *The Four Prentices of London* (1615),
The Fair Maid of the West, Or, A Girle worth Gold (1631),
The Iron Age (1632), *The English Traveller* (1633), *The
late Lancashire Witches* (in collaboration with Richard

[96] *The Dramatic Works of Thomas Heywood*, Vol. V, pp. 274,
374-375.

Brome) (1634), *A Pleasant Comedy, Called a Mayden Head well lost* (1634), *A Challenge for Beautie* (1636), *Loves Maistresse: Or, The Queens Masque* (1636), *The Royal King and Loyall Subject* (1637), *Pleasant Dialogues and Drammas* (1637), and *The Wise Woman of Hogsdon* (1638). *Fortune by Land and Sea* (in collaboration with William Rowley) was not published until 1655.

Aside from this steady output of plays, Heywood produced a quantity of non-dramatic work. These writings are listed simply to attest his indefatigable industry and the catholicity of his taste. They include one quasi-epic, *Troia Britanica* (1608), *An Apology for Actors* (1612), *A Funeral Elegie upon the death of the most hopefull and illustrious Prince Henry of Wales* (1612), an *Epithalamium* (1613) for the marriage of the Princess Elizabeth, *Gunaikeion or Nine Books of Various History Concerning Women* (1624), *A funeral elegie upon the much lamented death of the Tres-puissant and unmatchable King* (1625), *England's Elizabeth Her Life and Troubles During her Ministrie, from the Cradle to the Crowne* (1631), *Philocothonista, or, The Drunkard, Opened, Dissected and Anatomized* (1635), *The Hierarchie of the blessed Angells, their Names, Orders, and Offices, The Fall of Lucifer with the Angells* (1635), *The Wonder of this Age: or The Picture of A Man Living who is One Hundred Fifty two yeeres old, and upward* (1635), *The Three Wonders of this Age* (S. R. April 8, 1636), *A True Description of His Majesties Royall Ship, built this yeare 1637, at Woolwitch* (1637), *A Curtaine Lecture* (1637), *A New Book of Mistakes, Or, Bulls with Tales, and Buls without Tales, But no lyes by any meanes* (1637) and *The Exemplary Lives and Memorable Acts of Nine the most Worthy women of the world* (1640). To this list must be added the undated *Life of Merlin, Sirnamed Ambrosius, his Prophecies, and Predictions interpreted; and their truth made good by our English Annalls. Being a Chronographicall History*

*of all the Kings, and memorable passages of this Kingdome,
from Brute to the Reign of our Royall Soveraigne King
Charles,* some translations of Sallust, and varied occasional
verse inspired by the fortunes of the poet's friends.[96a]

So much for the bare record of Heywood's dramatic
achievements and activity as a writer upon general subjects.
This array of talent and industry, however, concerns us only
as it sheds light upon the personality and interests of the
poet.

The facts, as we have them, are proofs of a stage career
of prolonged activity. But it may be assumed that Heywood's theatrical relations were broader and deeper and
richer than the records attest. As the years came and went,
they offered to the poet, indeed, forced upon him innumer-
able opportunities for seeing life; for no one, connected
continuously with the theatre may remain a consistent
recluse. The mere extent of time, though, is just a hint
of the entire story. Heywood's perspective was by no means
confined to the walls of the Red Bull and the Cockpit
theatres or to the comparatively commonplace audiences that
frequented these places of amusement. As a member of
the Queen's company—Her Majesty's players—he belonged
to a group of actors who were called upon at times to appear
at Court. Although it must be conceded that the Queen's
company never attained the prominence at Court enjoyed by
its rival, the King's men—we remember that Shakespeare
was identified with the latter company—nevertheless the
Accounts of the Court Revels of the time show that the
second company was included in the royal entertainments.
Besides the entries already cited, those bearing Heywood's
name, there are frequent allusions to the Queen's company,
chiefly as recipient of payments made to it through some of
its members; "John Duke one of the Queenes M^{ties} players,"
"Thomas Greene for himselfe and his fellowes the Queenes

[96a] Titles compiled from Miss Bates' List.

Ma^{ts} Servauntes."[97]   From records of receipts, we see that
the company was at Court regularly for the Christmas
season from 1603 through 1615, omitting the years 1606
and 1607.[98] The appearance of the company at the times
specified was not limited to the presentation of single plays
or to solitary performances. The Revels' Accounts read:
"Thomas Greene one of the Quenes players . . . . . for
three severall playes" (1610) ;[99] there is evidence also for
four court performances by the Queen's company during the
year 1611-12.[100] Unfortunately, the titles of the plays are
not usually noted in the Accounts, but of those plays specified by name in the items for the Queen's company, all, with
the one exception of *The City Gallant,* are Heywood's.[101]
Coming into Court circles at regularly recurring occasions,
our poet touched the life of the higher classes frequently
enough to see it in many phases. Had he not made friendships among the nobility, had he come and gone in an
impersonal relation only, these annual visits alone, extending
over so many years, must have made him familiar with the
atmosphere surrounding him. Even though he may not
have been in sympathy with what he had ample opportunity
for observing, he gained an insight into conditions, which,
offering a strong contrast to the life of the country gentry
and that of the London apprentice, made him see the latter
in sharper outlines. That he maintained his unperturbed
sense of values is abundantly proved by the manly tone of
his address to his honored patron, the Earl of Worcester.
Heywood is nothing if he is not patriotic, and the loyalty

[97] *Extracts from the Accounts of the Revels at Court.* Introduction.
[98] *Ibid. The Elizabethan Stage,* Vol. IV, pp. 118-130; 168-183.
[99] *Extracts from the Accounts of the Revels at Court.* Introduction XI. *The Elizabethan Stage,* Vol. IV, p. 176.
[100] *Extracts from the Accounts of the Revels at Court.* Introduction XII, XIII, p. 211. *The Elizabethan Stage,* Vol. IV, p. 178.
[101] *Extracts from the Accounts of the Revels at Court. The Elizabethan Stage,* Vol. IV, pp. 168-183.

of which patriotism is but a part he feels keenly; but his flattery—being an Elizabethan he could not utterly escape the custom of his age—is not excessive, and he never grovels. To the Earl of Worcester he brings the gratitude due the patronage bestowed by a noble name; but his references to the favors bestowed upon him by the Earl bespeak a personal acquaintance if not friendship, transcending the conventional relation between patron and poet. The tone of this dedication is in marked contrast to that of the preface to *Love's Mistress,* addressed to the Earl of Dorset. In the latter case Heywood's words, while losing none of the poet's customary dignity, are rather perfunctory; in his characteristic simplicity he frankly states that he has been impelled to dedicate *Love's Mistress* to the Earl of Dorset because the play had pleased the Queen. In respect to the Earl of Worcester, Heywood's attitude is more personal. As a member of the Earl of Worcester's company for nearly two years, he had profited personally from the Earl's protectorship, and probably it is in acknowledgment of an obligation that the dedications to *An Apology for Actors, Gunaikeion, Troia Britania,* and *A Funerall Elegie upon the death of the most hopefull and illustrious Prince Henry of Wales* are to this nobleman. The dedication to *Gunaikeion* deserves quoting—

> "I was (my Lord) your creature, and (amongst other of your servants) you bestowed me upon the excellent Princesse Q. Anne (to whose memorie I have celebrated in these Papers the zeale of a subject and a servant) but by her lamented death your Gift (my Lord) is returned againe into your hands, being stil yours either to keepe unto your selfe, or to conferre where your noble disposition shall best please. However, as I have ever beene an admirer of your vertues, so my prayers still are, they may not only continue you a lasting Honor here upon Earth, but purchase you an everlasting Glorie reserved for you in Heaven.
> Your poore, yet faithfull servant,
> Tho. Heywood."

As concrete evidence of other personal relations between Heywood and those moving in high circles may be con-

sidered the dedication of *The English Traveller* "To the
Right Worshipfull Sir Henry Appleton, Knight Baronet."
Here Heywood speaks of "that alternate Love, and those
frequent courtesies which interchangeably past betwixt your-
selfe and that good old Gentleman, mine unkle (Master
Edmund Heywood) whom you pleased to grace by the Title
of Father." In this same address he refers to another
titled friend "that worthy Gentleman your friend, and my
countryman, Sir William Elvish whom (who for his
unmerited love many wayes extended towards me,) I much
honour"; other indications of Heywood's associations exist
in the group of occasional verses found in *Pleasant Dialogues and Drammas*. Names connected with these poems
are the "Sir George Saint Poole" already alluded to, "Sir
Philip Woodhouse Knight Baronet,"[102] "Sir Thomas Coventry Lord Keeper of the great Seale,"[103] "Sir Henry Carey,
Lord Hunsden, Earle of Dover,"[104] "Sir Ranoulphe Crewe,
once Lord Chiefe Justice of England,"[105] "Sir Paul
Pindar,"[106] the "Lady Anna Carre, sole daughter to the
right Honourable Robert Earle of Somerset, Knight of the
Garter,"[107] and Frances Longe, "a young sweet vertuous
Gentlewoman."[108] These verses including three to unnamed
gentlewomen presuppose relations more or less close between
Heywood and those whom the lines commemorate. Whether
these connections were formed as an outgrowth of Heywood's presence at Court—there are other reasons of course
for the friendship with Sir Henry Appleton and Sir Henry
Elvish—is not relevant. The significant facts are that for a
number of years the company to which he belonged gave

---

[102] *Pleasant Dialogues and Drammas*, p. 255.
[103] *Ibid.*, 263.
[104] *Ibid.*, 264.
[105] *Ibid.*, 265.
[106] *Ibid.*, 267.
[107] *Ibid.*, 265.
[108] *Ibid.*, p. 260.

performances at Court and upon some of these occasions he saw his own plays presented; that he stood in pleasant relationship with several of the nobility; that he had a circle of titled acquaintances, if we may not use the word "friends"; and that he himself was styled "gentleman."[109] All this goes to show that he had at least touched the fringe of gentility, and, in all probability, had mingled in the inner life of the upper classes. When we recall Heywood's university training, his philosophic and meditative bent, we can easily see that fewer opportunities than he undoubtedly had for moving among the gentry would have been more than enough to give him a clearly visualized picture of social conditions in the higher circles.

But Heywood's vista of life embraced more than what his urban experiences, rich and varied as they undoubtedly were, afforded. In the Mayor's Court Books, Collectors' and Receivers' Accounts, Chamberlains' Accounts of the towns of England, exists an enormous amount of data concerning the visits of the theatrical companies to the provinces during the Elizabethan age. To Murray's exhaustive researches we are indebted for reprints of official entries and detailed accounts of the recorded visits of the several companies to every town covered by his inquiry. Reference has already been made to the name of Thomas Heywood in the Norwich records respecting the visits of the Queen's company to Norwich in 1615, 1616 and 1617.[110] These entries, we remember, noted the original date of the company's royal patent and contained the names of the actors comprising the company. There are, however, over sixty other entries not carrying the names of actors, but specifying the sums of money paid the company as gratuities as it travelled mainly in the midland counties and in the south

[109] *Annales or A Generall Chronicle of England Begun by John Stow.* Continued and Augmented, etc., by Edmund Howes, 1631, p. 812.
[110] *Vide supra,* p. 21.

of England. The success of the itinerary is indicated by the return visits to certain towns; fifteen visits to Leicester between 1605 and 1617, eight to Dover between 1605 and 1616, seven to Coventry between 1605 and 1616, six to Norwich between 1609 and 1616, six to Marlborough between 1608 and 1616, with fewer visits to other places.[111] Of the twenty-five towns reported by Mr. Chambers, twelve were revisited.[111] It is quite obvious that Heywood must have accompanied his associates, sharing in their vicissitudes, and, what is of special import, learning more of life. Blind, indeed, he must have been, had he not returned to London, after these frequently repeated excursions into the provincial towns, with fresh impressions gathered from the associations of village taverns and marketplaces, townhalls and castles. Unfortunately, these visits were hurried; they afforded the poet scant opportunity to make prolonged studies of personalities; what he observed was an ever changing panorama, sketches, as it were, of different aspects of human existence, that served to bring into sharper outline his London experiences and to intensify his appreciation of social values.

Under these conditions then—the associations of theatrical companies playing, generally, to audiences of the less-favored sort, participation in Court entertainments occurring at infrequent but fairly regular intervals extending over several years, acquaintances if not friendships enjoyed among people of all classes, and travel in the provinces—Heywood found adequate opportunities to study Elizabethan life. With such a background, in addition to his university training and the possibility of his having travelled also upon the Continent, he must have known the England of his day.

If we can believe the testimony of Heywood's associates, he brought to this knowledge of Elizabethan life temperament and conviction exactly suited to portray what he knew. The greatest importance of the tributes mentioned, viz., the prefatory verses to the *Pleasant Dialogues* and *An Apology*

[111] *The Elizabethan Stage,* Vol. II, pp. 233-234.

for Actors, rests on their uniform spirit of genuine good will and friendship. This is indicated by the cordiality of the salutations, "To my loving friend and fellow," "To my good friend and fellow," "To his beloved friend," "To my approved good friend . . . .," the unaffected simplicity and directness of the sentiments, and the entire lack of effusive flattery or exaggerated eulogy. It seems that the friendship between Heywood and his associates was too securely established to be in need of elaborate protestation, that the relation precluded the studied epithet of praise or even the suggestion of empty compliments. Sincerity is the tone of these voices. Good comradeship, too, marks the spirit of a tangible form of affection shown Heywood, toward the end of his career. Then it was that several of his associates united to contribute sums to defray the cost of illustrating the *Hierarchie*.[112] Considered together, these simple expressions of esteem signify nothing quite as much as they do Heywood's entire worthiness of friendship, his possession of the qualities that draw and keep for the possessor the good will of associates. Nor was he indifferent; his was the spirit that responded to affection, that cherished the informality born of good fellowship. In gentle satire, he resents the familiar names that clung to the playwrights, the "Kit," "Will," "Robin" that no dignity or worth could live down; but as for himself the diminutive is preferred:

> Nor speak I this, that any here exprest,
> Should thinke themselves lesse worthy than the rest,
> Whose names have their full syllable and sound:
> I for my part
> (Thinke others what they please) accept that heart
> Which courts my love in most familiar phrase,
> And that it takes not from my paines or praise,
> If anyone to me so bluntly com
> I hold he loves me best that calls me Tom.[113]

[112] *A Woman Killed with Kindness* and *The Fair Maid of the West*, edited by Katherine Lee Bates. Introduction.
[113] *Hierarchie*, Bk. II, p. 206.

Turning to the opposite side of the picture, to the Heywood who is the occasional butt of contemporary satire, we do not discern much or anything that is essentially at variance with the commendations of the friends. We discover slight, good-humored thrusts directed mainly at facts: his long, doubtless prolonged, period of activity,[114] his championship of the city tradesmen,[115] the uninspired lines of the Lord Mayor's Pageants,[116] his attempts to dramatize classic myths,[116] the short duration of his fame,[117] and his straitened pecuniary circumstances.[114] He himself deplores the poverty of his old age:

> It grieves us now, although too late at last,
> Our Youth in idle Studies to have past:
> And what a folly 'tis, we now have found,
> To cast our Seed in an unfaithfull Ground:
> That in our Youth we have layd up no store,
> Which might maintaine us when our heads be hore;
> And that our shaken Vessel torne and thin,
> Can finde no easie Port to harbor in.[118]

In these lines one does not read remorse for follies of a misspent, extravagant youth, but the whimsical regrets of the humorist regarding his own simple faith. Reversing the mirror upon himself, he contemplates the worldly losses of the scholar, who, dedicated to learning, has disregarded prudence and material gain. Even less than this was said by Hemminge in the allusion to Heywood's poverty in *On the Time-Poets;* and Hemminge, together with the others indulging their wit at Heywood's expense, shows no animosity. Heywood seems to have passed through life making

[114] "A Seventeenth Century Gallery of Poets," by John J. Parry. *Journal of English and Germanic Philology,* XIX, No. 2, 1920, pp. 270-277.
[115] *Wit in a Constable,* by Henry Glapthorne. Act I, sc. 1, p. 171.
[116] Prefatory verses by J. Berkenhead. First Folio, Beaumont and Fletcher.
[117] *A Satire Concerning Poetry,* John Oldham, 1698.
[118] *Hierarchie,* Bk. IV, p. 209.

few, if any, real enemies. At a time when he was playing with Henslowe and was writing vigorously for the stage, he escaped the entanglements of the War of the Theatres, a controversy involving Dekker, Ben Jonson, Marston; he is not mentioned in *The Return from Parnassus* with Marston, Marlowe, Ben Jonson—"the wittiest fellow of a bricklayer in England"—and Shakespeare;[119] and he is not recognized as the object of ridicule in the allusions to plays and players in other plays of the period. There seems to be no evidence suggesting, even remotely, that Heywood was quarrelsome or that he became implicated in personal difficulties. The indications are that he was good-natured, even-tempered, withal modest and unpretentious; kindly, genial, and unselfish.

To appreciate fully the depth and fineness of Heywood's spiritual nature and the sanity of his philosophy of life, one must turn to the poet's own writings: the frank revelations of self and his aspirations, as found in his non-dramatic productions, and the utterances in the plays. The latter, although more or less open to question when regarded as personal allusions, are of moment when they are in harmony with the unequivocal statements of the non-dramatic writings. Heywood, as we know, wrote several bulky volumes. Of his two longest works, the *Hierarchie of the Blessed Angels* and *Gunaikeion,* there is much that is quotation, adaptation, compilation, translation, and the simple retelling of what another has said. Scattered, however, amidst the mass of borrowed material and original reflections, appears now and then in the author's straightforward and simple language, much autobiographical matter. In like manner, the *Apology for Actors*, a shorter but far more original work, suggests, in its expressions of dramatic theory, something of Heywood's own nature; and

---

[119] *The Return from Parnassus, or The Scourge of Simony.* Act I, sc. 2, p. 10.

additional insight into his character is obtained from the dedications and prologues that are attached to his plays.

Despite the monotony and almost unvarying dullness of the *Hierarchie,* the work lives up to the promise of its title, both in length and in the nature of its contents. Throughout, it is serious, pious in tone, an exposition of its prefixed motto: "Vita scelesta vale, caelica vita veni."

Here are reflections that reveal the writer's serious intent and his undeniably grave, religious nature:

"But men for the most part now in their prosperitie so stupidly forget them [the Divine Powers] that in ther extremitie they can hardly find the way unto them."[120]

"The same [Thales] being asked, whether the Actions of men could passe without his knowledge! he answered, No, nor their very thoughts. Intimating, that we ought not onely to keepe our hands cleane, but mindes pure also: since we are to beleeve that the Divine Power is interested in the secrets of our hearts."[121]

"All the Earth calls for Truth; Heav'n doth proclaime
Her blessed; all things tremble at her name.
For Truth no unjust thing at all can doo:

. . . .

She knowes no diffrence, what is just she loves,
But what's impure and sinfull she reproves,
And all men favor her good works, because
Her judgements are upright, and just her lawes.
She's the Strength, Kingdome, Power, Dignitee,
And of all Ages Sov'raigne Majestie;
Blest be the God of Truth."[122]

Written when Heywood was rapidly approaching old age, the *Hierarchie* may suggest the thoughts of one who has outlived the prevailing tendencies of youth. Nothing, however, of Heywood's earlier years, has as yet been discovered that is contradictory to the spirit of these sober reflections.

[120] *Hierarchie,* Bk. II, p. 73.
[121] *Ibid.,* Bk. II, p. 103.
[122] *Ibid.,* Bk. IX, p. 567.

With the *Hierarchie* one should not contrast the dialogue of the plays, that naturally grows out of the characters and the plot, not to mention the influence of Elizabethan standards of taste, but writings that are as frankly subjective as the *Hierarchie*. In lieu of a similar work from the earlier period of Heywood's life, the *Apology* may be considered. Of course, one acknowledges the wide gap between the author's purpose in writing the one book and the aim of the other. A striking similarity, however, between the two is fundamental. The serious tone of the *Apology* has already been pointed out. What forecasts more definitely the pious spirit of the *Hierarchie* is the nature of Heywood's argument for "modest recreations." His appeal is based upon the fact that theatres are not proscribed by either the *Old Testament* or the *New Testament*. In the light of such sentiments expressed again and again in his treatises, the Biblical quotations of the plays, and the numberless but always reverential allusions to the Deity, the simplicity and sincerity of Heywood's orthodoxy cannot be ignored. What one likes especially to remember is Heywood's appreciation for the inner meaning of religion, his fine insistence upon the supremacy of the truth that transcends the conventions of creed and dogma.

An expression of this utter simplicity and sincerity is Heywood's frankness. Consistently silent about his private life, withholding details that would enable us to picture him definitely in the relations of his immediate family, as regards his profession he takes a different attitude. Then it is that he is almost naïve. Habitual modesty may explain the ambiguous words written in 1612: "Loath am I (I protest) being the youngest and weakest of the nest wherein I was hatcht, to soare the pitch before others of the same brood, more fledge, and of better winge than myselfe . . ."[123] It is more likely that in this statement, as elsewhere, Heywood

---

[123] *An Apology for Actors*, p. 16.

is simply speaking frankly as to what he considered a fair estimate of his power, an estimate singularly in accord with that given him by his critics. He is equally direct where false modesty might have tied his tongue. In the prologues and prefatory addresses of several of his plays—to be exact, ten plays of the twenty-four[124]—he makes a direct appeal to readers for the newly published play by recalling its popularity when acted or by naming the personages whom the play had pleased. In doing this, Heywood does not appear to be resorting to what in another might be a shrewd way of praising oneself. The reader is taken absolutely into the author's confidence: "Nor neede they (I hope) much fear a rugged and censorious brow from thee."[125] "I presume the reading thereof shall not proove distastefull unto any."[126] "This . . . . . I presume may be freely read without distaste."[127] Heywood wishes his plays read; at hand he has what seems to him the most effective recommendation to readers; this he used without any ado. But, entirely single in motive and guiltless of studied effort, he is content with the simple statement of fact. Beyond that he is not tempted to go. Heywood's characteristic sincerity and modesty have been so widely acknowledged that one finds it difficult to understand the position of one critic, Theodor Eichhoff. Eichhoff contends that Heywood "keine offene, ehrliche Natur ist (ebensowenig wie die meisten seiner Kollegen),"[128] calling the poet "überall unwahr,"[129]

---

[124] *The Golden Age, The Iron Age (I, II), If You Know Not Me You Know Nobody (1), Love's Mistress, The Rape of Lucrece, A Maidenhead Well Lost, The Four Prentices of London, The Fair Maid of the West (1)*.

[125] *The Dramatic Works of Thomas Heywood,* Vol. II. *The Fair Maid of the West (1),* "To the Reader."

[126] *Ibid.,* Vol. III. *The Iron Age (1),* "To the Reader."

[127] *Ibid.,* Vol. IV. *A Maidenhead Well Lost,* "To the Reader."

[128] *Der Weg zu Shakespeare,* von Theodor Eichhoff. Chapter II, p. 45.

[129] *Ibid.,* p. 50.

a "Krämerseele,"[130] one guilty of "mehr oder weniger offenbaren und vorsätzlichen Lügen."[131] For his thesis that Elizabethan plays were not illegally published through stenographic reports, he bases his assertions upon Heywood's complaint, in the "Prologue of the *Play of Queen Elizabeth*," of the garbled edition of the play, upon the dedication of the *Iron Age* to "Thomas Mannering," upon the statement in the *Apology* concerning the youth and inexperience of the author, and upon the language in general of the prologues and dedications. Because one has been unable to trace the identity of the poet's patron, it seems rash to conclude that the patron "niemals gelebt hat."[132] The other charges against Heywood are founded upon a narrow interpretation of the words of the poet; the critic misses entirely the spirit of the writings and he has failed to take into consideration what can be learned of Heywood from the great body of his writings and from the testimony of his friends.

In his long stage career Heywood experienced the effect of changes in the taste of the playgoing public. During the last years of Elizabeth's reign and at the beginning of the Jacobean era, when he was simply striving to attain the maturity of his powers, he remained apparently undisturbed by the overpowering genius of Shakespeare and the art of Ben Jonson. This was due, first and chiefly, to the fact that no one was more conscious of Heywood's own limitations than he himself, and to the success that he was attaining in his own chosen field, the realm of unaffected realism. Although the Globe on the Bankside and later the Blackfriars attracted the more fashionable audiences, the Red Bull and the Cockpit had their crowds; Heywood could hold his own with Dekker and he was not completely outdistanced by Middleton. In his declining years, however, unable, on the one hand, to cope with the romantic drama of Beaumont

---

[130] *Ibid.*, p. 36.
[131] *Ibid.*, p. 37.
[132] *Ibid.*, p. 45.

and Fletcher, and, on the other, outranked in cleverness by
Shirley and Brome, he saw himself clearly out of joint with
his times. Often and again in the modesty of tone in which
he was wont to allude to what concerned him closely, he
voices his feelings about two things: one, a custom of the
Elizabethan Age; the other, an experience, through which
in its varied aspects every one that survives youth must pass.
As an author, he resented the piratical publishing of his
plays, although he had virtually renounced his acting rights
in selling the plays to the companies for production. As a
man in middle age or approaching maturity, he writhed
under the changes of a newer age, "these more exquisite and
refined Times,"[133] "these more Censorious dayes"[134] demanding that "accurateness both in Plot and Stile"[135] beyond his
reach. Sensitive by temperament, he shrinks from the
adverse comment of the newer age—perhaps some of the
harmless ridicule already cited—but not without a word of
retaliation against what he believes to be the attacks of
untutored critics: How comes it (ere he know it)

A Puny shall assume the name of Poet;
And in a Tympa'nous and Thrasonicke stile,
(Words at which th'Ignorant laugh, but the Learn'd smile
Because Adulterate) and Undenizen'd, he
Should taske such Artists as have tooke Degree
Before he was a Freshman . . . . .

It was not so of old; Virgil the best
Of Epicke Poets, never did contest
Gainst Homer. Ovid was so far from hate,
That he did rather strive to imitate,
Than malign others: . . . . .

I spare to speake of those that live: I embrace
Their loves, and make them Umpires in this case;
Who would, to curbe such insolence (I know)

---

[133] *The Dramatic Works of Thomas Heywood*, Vol. II. *The Four Prentices of London.* Prefatory Address.
[134] *Ibid.*
[135] *Ibid.*

Bid such yong boyes to stay in Jericho
Untill their Beards were growne, their wits more staid;
And not to censure others, till they 'ave made
Works to exceed theirs; to abide the test
Of rough censorious Browes; Better the Best;
To attract the eares and eyes of Princes. When
They have done this (as some they envy) then
They may be admitted Free-men, and so strive
By industry, how in that way to thrive.[136]

Barring the words of resentment against those responsible
for the spurious editions of his plays, and a certain "Austin"
accused by him of plagiarism,[137] this passage from the
Hierarchie seems to furnish the sole instance of Heywood's
allowing himself the indulgence of retaliation. If it is true,
as we have tried to show, that Heywood was singularly
unmolested by the taunts of unfriendly criticism, naturally,
he had little to resent. However, it is a satisfaction to note
that our poet could be roused to an expression of indignation
uttered in his personal defense. Doubtless the words must
be interpreted as the exception, proving the rare equanimity
of Heywood's disposition.

But the character of Heywood in its completeness may not
be read from the occasional tributes of friends, from a group
of isolated lines gathered here and there from his more
serious writings, and from what may be considered the
personal reflections of the plays. Pointed though these
citations be, they are but faintly suggestive indications of
what one learns of Heywood in the underlying spirit of his
work, in his aims, thought, feeling, and general style. In
the atmosphere, thus, of his work considered as a whole he
reveals unquestionably the traits of character mentioned:
directness, modesty, a beautiful sense of loyalty and gratitude, a seriousness tinged with piety, and an absorbing

[136] *Hierarchie of the Blessed Angells*, Bk. IV, p. 209.
[137] *The Dramatic Works of Thomas Heywood*, Vol. III. *The Brazen Age*, "To the Reader."

reverence for truth in thought, word, and action. Sensitive by nature, he resented injustice, but his writings are characterized by the uniformly kindly tone of his genial temperament. Frank to a fault, he was as unbiassed regarding his own merits and shortcomings as he was in his attitude toward others.

This was the real Heywood, the man beneath the playwright and actor, who was drawn to portray the everyday life of his time. Because of his having been a member of the select circle of Cambridge University, because of his intimate associations with his fellow actors at the Rose, the Red Bull, and the Cockpit theatres and the audiences frequenting those resorts, because of his varied experiences at Court, and in the manor houses, inn, and town halls of the country, he knew life of many kinds. That he was attracted to certain types of this life is due partly to force of circumstances—the development of domestic drama in the last decade of the sixteenth century, partly to the fact that among these types he recognized a vitality of human emotions and human problems that challenged his frank and unaffected nature, and partly to his theory of art. Because of his character—the qualities already mentioned—he brought to the presentation of every-day Elizabethan life no warped or cynical nature, no biassed or onesided judgment. He was able to see clearly; he could portray faithfully. If he erred, it was on the side of sympathy and good-humored tolerance. His figures would be pictures, not caricatures. It requires no imagination to see that while Heywood's audiences were being amused by these wholesome studies of his times, they were also being incited to worthy ideals of loyalty and patriotism, valor and honor.

CHAPTER II

To Thomas Heywood are generally ascribed twenty-four extant plays—the twenty-three of the Pearson edition and *The Captives*. Of this number, seven—*The Golden Age, The Silver Age, The Brazen Age, The Iron Age (1, 2), The Rape of Lucrece,* and *Love's Mistress*—are based upon stories taken from mythology or classic legend. The seventeen remaining plays may be said to represent more essentially Heywood's original genius. Of these, fourteen—*The Four Prentices of London, Edward the Fourth (1, 2), If You Know Not Me You Know Nobody (1, 2), The Wise Woman of Hogsdon, The Fair Maid of the Exchange, A Woman Killed with Kindness, Fortune by Land and Sea, The Fair Maid of the West (1, 2), The English Traveller, The Captives,* and *The Late Lancashire Witches*—present in plot, general atmosphere, or spirit, some phase of contemporary English life. Such a proportion, fourteen out of seventeen, indicates unmistakably the poet's preference as to theme. Of course, conjecture as to the nature of the lost plays of the "two hundred and twenty" is hazardous; but the titles of those recorded by Henslowe, *Joan as Good as My Lady, Cutting Dick, The London Florentine, The Blind Eats Many a Fly, Christmas Comes but Once a Year,*[1] suggest subjects not dissimilar to those of the plays at hand. Again, it must not be forgotten that in view of Heywood's total extant literary output—plays and non-dramatic writings—his share in many of the undiscovered or unidentified plays must have been relatively slight. Beyond doubt he made some contributions to the productions, else he would not have mentioned the fact, but it is safe to conclude that the plays

---

[1] *Supra,* pp. 16, 19.

that we know are the bulk of Heywood's independent dramatic work. The significance of the quantity of this output is that it must represent not the poet's "left hand," a casual interest merely, but a deliberate choice, and that is the portrayal of contemporary manners.

Little question has been raised as to Heywood's authorship of the fourteen plays under consideration, external evidence existing for all except *The Fair Maid of the Exchange* and *Edward the Fourth*. If, for the present, these are eliminated, there remain eleven plays of contemporary life, nine of which were written by Heywood alone. These nine constitute an adequate number for study in our attempt to form an estimate of the poet's distinctive characteristics. The facts concerning the plays, about which no doubt as to Heywood's authorship has been raised, may be summarized briefly:

THE FOUR PRENTICES OF LONDON

The title page of the earliest extant edition of this play reads "The Four Prentises of London. With the Conquest of Jerusalem. As it hath bene diverse times Acted, at the Red Bull by the Queenes Maiesties Servants. Written by Thomas Heywood, for I. W. 1615."[2] An edition of 1632 bears also the name of the author, the same theatre, and the same actors' company, with the added information that the "newly revised" play had been received "with good applause."[3]

This play was entered upon the Stationers' Register August 2, 1630 as "4 London Prentises" in a transfer of right from Nicholas Okes to John Okes.[4]

[2] *A List of English Plays Written before 1643 and Printed before 1700.* By W. W. Greg, 1900, p. 52.

[3] *Ibid.*

[4] *Transcript of the Registers of the Stationers' Company.* By Edward Arber. Vol. IV, p. 240.

Prefixed to the edition of 1615 is an address "To the Honest and High-spirited Prentices, the Readers" signed "Thomas Heywood." Because of the bearing of this dedication upon the date of the play and upon the personality of the author, it must be quoted almost entire:

> "No one but to you (as whom this Play most especially concernes) I thought good to Dedicate this Labour, which though written many yeares since, in my Infancy of Judgment in this kinde of Poetry, and my first practice: Yet understanding (by what meanes I know not) it was in these more exquisite and refined Times to come to the Presse, in such a forwardnesse ere it came to my knowledge, that it was past prevention, and then knowing withall, that it comes short of that accuratenesse both in Plote and Stile, that these more Censorious dayes with greater curiosity acquire, I must thus excuse. That as Playes were then some fifteene or sixteene yeares agoe it was in the Fashion. Nor could it have found a more seasonable and fit publication then at this Time, when, to the glory of our Nation, the security of the Kingdome, and the Honor of this Renowned Citty, they have begunne againe the commendable practice of long forgotten Armes, the continuance of which I wish, the Discipline approve, and the encouragement thereof even with my soule applaude. . . ."

Published then in 1615, during the poet's lifetime, bearing his name with that of the actors' company on the title page, prefixed by the signed dedication, and ascribed to Heywood by all the critics and booksellers,[5] *The Four Prentices of London* may be accepted as unquestionably Heywood's. This play is considered one of the poet's earliest compositions, if

---

[5] Kirkman, 1661 (List affixed to Edition of *Tom Tyler*); Phillips, 1675; Winstanley, 1687; Langbaine, 1688, 1691; Mears, 1718; 1726; List affixed to Whincop's *Scanderbeg*, 1747; Chetwood, 1749; Theophilus Cibber, 1753; Baker, *Biographia Dramatica; Companion to the Playhouse,* 1764; *Playhouse Pocket-Companion,* 1779; *Biographia Dramatica,* Reed, 1782; Egerton's *Theatrical Remembrancer,* 1788; Barker, 1803; Jones, *Biographia Dramatica,* 1812; *Retrospective Review,* vol. XI, part I, 1825; Halliwell-Phillipps, 1860; Ward, 1875; Fleay, 1891; Hazlitt, 1892; Greg, 1900; Schelling, 1908; Creizenach, 1909; Singer, 1913.

not the first. There was evidently an edition published earlier than 1615. The suggestion for this supposition lies in the words of the Grocer's Wife in *The Knight of the Burning Pestle* (c. 1611):

> *Cit.* Will it so sir? you are well read in Histories; I pray you what was sir Dagonet? was not he prentice to a Grocer in London? read the play of The Four Prentices of London, where they tosse their pikes so.[6]

To Fleay again we are indebted, he being the first to point out the evidence for the conclusion that this earlier edition appeared, probably, in 1610 and that the play itself was presented as early as 1594.[7] In detail, Fleay's argument is this: Heywood himself says specifically that the play was written fifteen or sixteen years earlier than an historical event named as occurring almost simultaneously with the publication of the play. This historical event, the resumption of the practice of arms in the Artillery Gardens, actually took place in 1610.[8] If the play was printed about that time, it was written as early as 1594 or 1595. Fleay then identifies it with the "godfrey of bullen" already referred to.[9]

The plot had its source, undoubtedly, in the romantic career of Godfrey of Bouillon, but it is not certain that Heywood received his inspiration from Tasso's *Il Goffredo*. Even though the evidence for the early date of the play (1594-5) be rejected and we assume that it appeared after the first complete English translation of *Il Goffredo* (1599), nothing would be proved. Indeed, whether or not Heywood had even read Tasso is irrelevant. Neither from Tasso nor

---

[6] *The Knight of the Burning Pestle* by Beaumont and Fletcher. Edited by Herbert S. Murch, 1908. Introduction, XIII.

[7] *A Biographical Chronicle of the English Drama.* Vol. I, pp. 282-283.

[8] *Annales, or A Generall Chronicle of England, Begun by John Stow, Continued and Augmented—by Edmund Howes,* 1613, pp. 995-996.

[9] *Supra,* p. 7.

from the recorded facts of history did the English poet get the authority for placing the hero of the First Crusade as an exile in London with three brothers apprenticed to London tradesmen. The indebtedness to the epic could not at most involve more than the romantic circumstances of Godfrey's part in the siege of Jerusalem, the name of Eustace transferred from Godfrey's younger brother to one of the four sons of the play, the personages of Robert of Normandy, Tancred of Italy, and the Soldan of Babylon, and suggestions for the miraculous feats of combat between the opposing forces. Hints for these details may have been received from Richard Carew's translation of the first five books of *Il Goffredo* (1594), from the entire poem read in the Italian original, or from a sixteenth century chronicle of the First Crusade. *The Four Prentices of London* in its mingled romance and realism is in spirit a frank exaltation of the valor of English apprentices. Its motive was not to delineate the details of London shop life, which form no part of the background, but rather to express the poet's enthusiasm for England and his faith in the essential virtues of the English tradesman.

IF YOU KNOW NOT ME YOU KNOW NOBODY

The popularity of this double play is attested by the number of editions through which it passed during the lifetime of the poet. Between 1605 and 1639 at least nine editions of *Part I* appeared.[10] Of these early printings of *Part I* the title is invariably the same: *If You Know Not Me You Know Nobodie or the troubles of Queen Elizabeth*. *Part II* exists in four seventeenth century editions, those of 1606, 1609, 1623 (?), and 1632,[10] the title of the 1609 edition adding *"Doctor Paries treasons"* and *"With the Humors of Hobson and Tawny-cote"* to the already voluminous phrasing of the title of the other editions. *Part I* was entered upon

[10] Greg's *List of Plays*, pp. 45-50.

the Stationers' Register as of July 5, 1605[11] and *Part II* as of September 14 of the same year.[12] Both parts are in the name of Nathaniel Butter, the publisher of all of the editions except one, the 1610 edition of *Part I* appearing for Thomas Pavier.[13] In 1639 Nathaniel Butter surrendered his title to both parts of *If You Know Not Me You Know Nobody* to one "Master fflesher."[14]

Although Heywood's name is not on the title page of these early copies of *If You Know Not Me You Know Nobody,* the play may well be included among those bearing the author's name. Inserted among a number of prologues and epilogues written for sundry occasions but printed together in Heywood's *Pleasant Dialogues and Drammas* is a *Prologue to the Play of Queen Elizabeth, as it was last revived at the Cock-pit, in which the Author taxeth the most corrupted copy now imprinted, which was published without his consent.*[15] Now the collection of verses called *Pleasant Dialogues and Drammas* not only bears Heywood's name followed by the familiar motto "Aut prodesse solent, aut delectare," but contains a dedication to the Earl of Dover and an address to the reader, both signed by "Tho. Heywood." In speaking of the *Play of Queen Elizabeth,* Heywood was doubtless alluding to *If You Know Not Me You Know Nobody,* the theme of which not only suggests the queen's name as title, but presents a treatment almost identical with that of Heywood's acknowledged treatise *England's Elizabeth.* Moreover, this title, the *"Play of Queen Elizabeth,"* was the designation used for *If You Know Not Me You Know Nobody* in the earliest catalogues, the double title

[11] *Transcript of the Registers of the Stationers' Company,* III, p. 295.

[12] *Ibid.,* III, p. 301.

[13] Greg's *List of Plays,* p. 49.

[14] *Transcript of the Registers of the Stationers' Company,* IV, p. 466.

[15] *The Dramatic Works of Thomas Heywood,* Vol. I. *If You Know Not Me You Know Nobody,* Prologue.

appearing in the editions of *Part I* published during the poet's lifetime, but not again until after 1691 when it was used regularly by the chroniclers. Characteristic of Heywood is the mildly resentful language of the Prologue against the piratical printing of the play. As a matter of fact, the protest seems to be a direct reference to the unfinished technique of *If You Know Not Me You Know Nobody (1)*, if not an apology for it:

> "Some by Stenography drew
> The plot; put it in print: (scarce one word trew:)
> And in that lameness it hath limp't so long
> The Author now to vindicate that wrong,
> Hath tooke the paines, upright upon its feete
> To teach it walke, so please you sit, and see't.[16]

Perhaps, the immediate object of the poet's complaint was the 1610 edition of *Part I*.

The reference in *If You Know Not Me You Know Nobody* to *Joan's as good as my lady*,[17] the Heywood play recorded by Henslowe as early as February 1598,[18] places the production of *If You Know Not Me You Know Nobody* between 1598 and 1605, the latter year being the date of the appearance of the first edition. Fleay assumes that the play was produced in 1604; Professor Schelling, 1604-1605.[19] Because of the looseness of structure an earlier time nearer 1594 is Aronstein's conjecture.[20] The date 1604-05 seems late, for, although it is difficult to arrange Heywood's plays chronologically on the principle of structure alone, one can hardly imagine *If You Know Not Me You Know Nobody* being written after *A Woman Killed with Kindness* (1603).

[16] *The Dramatic Works of Thomas Heywood*, Vol. I. *If You Know Not Me You Know Nobody*, Prologue.

[17] *Ibid.*, p. 314.

[18] *Supra*, p. 16.

[19] *Biographical Chronicle of the English Drama*, Vol. I, p. 292; *Elizabethan Drama*, Vol. II, p. 575.

[20] "Thomas Heywood." Philipp Aronstein in *Anglia* XXXVII, p. 200.

Part I of the former play is a chronicle play of the simplest type, a mere narrative of historical events in dramatic setting, conventions of dramatic technique being subordinated to a presentation of events according to historical order and importance. During the last decade of the sixteenth century, the years of the highest development of the chronicle play, Heywood would have been more apt to resort to this popular form than later, but there arises the question as to whether a play on Queen Elizabeth would have been presented during her lifetime. With the external evidence in favor of a date later than 1598, the utmost that can be concluded is to place the time of composition between 1598 and 1605, the dramatic structure pointing to the earlier date, the nature of the theme—a panegyric upon Queen Elizabeth —suggesting an occasion after the Queen's death. If the play was produced just before 1605, it must have been written hastily for a presentation at short notice or it was an earlier draft which the poet lacked opportunity to complete in finished form.

For the source of the main incidents of both *Parts I* and *II* Heywood has used, in the language of the *Apology*, "the chronicles of England." The persecutions of the Princess Elizabeth at the hands of Queen Mary and the queen's zealous agents, the theme of *Part I,* as narrated by Holinshed and Stow, are presented with little or no changes from the chronicles. Likewise, the main theme of *Part II,* the Gresham story, adheres closely to the recorded historical fact. For the character of Hobson and the humor of the subordinate action of *Part II,* Heywood has borrowed the story told of old Hobson, a London haberdasher, whose virtues and escapades form the theme of an Elizabethan story, one version of which was printed in 1607.[21] Hey-

---

[21] *The Pleasant Conceits of Old Hobson The Merry Londoner,* A. D. 1607. Edited by James Orchard Halliwell, Percy Society, 1844.

wood must have laid under contribution an earlier narrative of the same personage, evidently a popular character. The story as told in the 1607 edition furnishes the minutest details of Heywood's subplot, our poet's only claim to originality being in his linking the Hobson story with the Gresham story by making Hobson's agent the nephew of Gresham. For the character and rôle in general of young Gresham one discerns clearly an indebtedness to Plautus.

A WOMAN KILLED WITH KINDNESS

This, the best known of Heywood's plays, is not entered upon the Stationers' Register. The two editions that have come down to us are of the years 1607 and 1617 respectively.[22] As the 1617 edition is called "The third Edition," the 1607 edition may be either the first or the second printing of the play. Reference has already been made to the items concerning *A Woman Killed with Kindness* recorded in Henslowe's *Diary*. It will be recalled that these details form part of a group of entries for the Earl of Worcester's company. It was to "Thomas hewode" that six pounds thirteen shillings were paid on the fifth of February, 1603 "for a womones gowne of blacke vellvett for the playe of a woman kylld wth kyndnes";[23] "unto thomas Hewwod" on the twelfth of February 1603, three pounds as part payment for "his playe called a womon kylled wth kindnes";[24] likewise "unto Thomas Hewode" on the sixth of March, 1603, three pounds in fulle (p) payment for his playe called a womon kyld wth kindness."[25] Although the other entries for the play, those of February 4, 1603 and March 7, 1603, do not mention Heywood but the tailor having direct charge, possibly, of the properties,[26] the three specifying Heywood as writer of the

[22] Greg's *List of Plays*, p. 50.
[23] *Henslowe's Diary*, F 119^v, p. 188.
[24] *Ibid.*, F 120, p. 189.
[25] *Ibid.*
[26] *Ibid.*, F 120^v, p. 190.

play are enough to attest the authorship, the date of composition, and the company presenting the play. That *A Woman Killed with Kindness* was a well-known play is, as Miss Bates says, clearly proved by an allusion to it in Middleton's Black Book.[27] It is true that neither of the early editions contains the signed dedication or epistle customarily affected by Heywood and that the edition of 1617 does not bear the name of the acting company; but the unequivocal statements of the *Diary* place *A Woman Killed with Kindness* among the plays that may be considered unmistakably Heywood's own.

Sources for *A Woman Killed with Kindness* have been indicated (1) by Professor Koeppel,[28] who has pointed out the similarities between Heywood's main-plot and the fifty-eighth novel of the first book of Painter's *Palace of Pleasure;* and, (2) by Professor Robert G. Martin,[29] who, admitting that Heywood is indebted to the fifty-eighth novel for the broad outlines of the action, argues that many minor hints are derived from the forty-third novel of the first book. The two tales, narratives based upon the unfaithful-wife motive, have been traced through their various retellings. Painter's fifty-eighth novel, a free translation of the thirty-sixth novel of the *Heptameron* of Queen Marguerite of Navarre, appears as novella thirty-five of *Part I* of Bandello's *Tragical Discourses.* The forty-third novel, which Painter has derived directly from Boaistuau, was originally told by Bandello, novella twelve of *Part II;* it likewise, as novel thirty-two, forms a part of Queen Marguerite's collection of stories. In lieu of external evidence to the contrary, it may be assumed that Heywood used the English version of the tales rather than the foreign

---

[27] *A Woman Killed with Kindness* and *The Fair Maid of the West.* Edited by Katherine Lee Bates. Introduction.

[28] *Quellen—Studien zu den Dramen Ben Jonson's, John Marstons und Beaumont, und Fletchers,* von Emil Koeppel, 1895, pp. 136-7.

[29] "A New Source for A Woman Killed with Kindness." Robert G. Martin, *Englische Studien,* Vol. XLIII, pp. 229-233.

sources and parallels; but this dependence of the play upon
the two tales mentioned does not seem to involve more than
the idea of the theme—marital infidelity—and some details
of situation. The wife presented in the forty-third novel
is a wanton, who, bored with the dullness of country life,
makes advances to a neighboring squire and deliberately
plans to deceive her husband. Upon discovering the deception, the husband, a man much older than his wife, inflicts
upon the lovers diabolic punishment: in the presence of
assembled servants the wife with the assistance of the old
woman, her go-between, is forced to strangle her lover and,
then, is doomed to solitary confinement until she perishes
in the room where the corpse hangs. The action of the
fifty-eighth novel is that also of a young wife with an old
husband, and she, too, chooses for her lover a young clerk,
an inmate of her household. Led by a trusted servant to the
door of the room in which the guilty pair are, the husband
determines to avenge his wrongs while preserving to the
outside world his sense of dignity. Having entered the
room alone, he thrusts the terrified clerk into a closet; then
the loyal servant is conducted into the room only to be
told that his suspicions were groundless. To make amends,
however, the master presents the deserving man with wages
for several years in advance and then dismisses him with
instructions to leave the neighborhood. After the man has
departed, the guilty ones are denounced for the enormity of
their wickedness; in abject fear they receive the command
to keep silence as to their wrongdoing. Their apprehen-
sions, however, are soon quieted, for the husband seems to
forget his injuries, making no further references to the
occurrence and giving the lovers every opportunity to meet.
But their respite is for a few days only: the clerk is then
banished to a distant country, the wife is secretly poisoned,
and the shrewd husband, satisfied with the execution of his
neat plot of revenge, escapes both contempt and suspicion.
Barring the mainspring of action, the adultery motive, and
the similarities in externals pointed out by Professor Koep-

pel and Professor Martin, Heywood's drama is essentially
different from the two tales, although he evidently used them
as source material. Utter wantonness and implacable revenge
devoid of any restraints of obligation, on the one hand, or
of human sympathy, on the other, are the incidents furnishing the framework of the original narratives. In their
development they present little else. Heywood had the
instinct to center his appeal in the emotional crises of the
main incidents and the supremacy of selflessness in the
falling action. That the play is sentimental tragedy rather
than pure tragedy is due to the fact that Heywood could
not develop great character nor sustain vigorous action from
initial motivation through the complexities of situation to the
climaxes of success or failure. This weakness in dramatic
technique has no bearing, however, upon the relation of the
play to its sources and the poet's conception of the plot. The
Frankfords, newly married, have every prospect of happiness. As their friend, Sir Charles Mountford says to them
at the wedding feast:

> Lord sir, in what a happy state live you!
> This morning, which (to many) seemes a burthen,
> Too heavy to beare, is unto you a pleasure.
> This Lady is no clog, as many are;
> She doth become you like a well-made suite.
> In which the Tailor hath us'd all his art:
> Not like a thicke Coate of unseason'd frieze
> Forc'd on your backe in summer; shee's no chaine
> To tie your necke, and curbe you to the yoake,
> But shee's a chaine of gold to adorne your necke.
> You both adorne each other, and your hands
> Methinkes are matches; there's equality
> In this faire combination; y' are both Schollers,
> Both young, both being descended nobly.
> There's musicke in this sympathy, it carries
> Consort, and expectation of much joy.
> Which God bestow on you, from this first day,
> Untill your dissolution, that's for aye.
>   W. K. K. (II, 95)

Handicapped by no disparity in years, social rank, or culture, these two look forward to a rosy future, but the pitiably weak wife does not know how to withstand the advances of her husband's disloyal friend, but, even at the moment of her fall, she is overwhelmed with remorse. When the husband is told of her error, with staunch faith in her virtue he recoils from the unwelcome news; and, when he may not reject the evidence of his senses, he suffers not on account of vanity but for the fall of a cherished idol. It is in the spirit of righteous indignation tempered with mercy that he subordinates his personal resentment to the call of a higher mood and inflicts the punishment that may not be withheld. It is in sorrow and grief that he banishes his wife from her home. And, after all, it must not be forgotten that the distinctive appeal of the outline of the plot rests in the nature of Frankford's revenge. The circumstances leading to its motivation, Mrs. Frankford's infidelity, offer nothing that is striking or original. It is the judgment of the husband that raises the plot out of the hackneyed, and no suggestion for this was received from Painter.

It is barely possible that Heywood may have received a hint from tale fifty-five of *Gesta Romanorum* for Frankford's essential mood of reaction to his wife's guilt. The narrative of a king's son, married to a princess of rare beauty, runs, in part, in this way:

"At this time there was in the court a servant whom the king's son principally trusted, and to whom he had confided the care of one of his provinces. This man, in return for the benefits accumulated upon him, seduced the lady, and wasted the country over which he was placed. When the husband, therefore knew of his wife's infidelity, he was overwhelmed with sorrow, and repudiated her with the loss of every honour. Thus circumstanced, she fell into extreme poverty; and, reduced to despair by the wretchedness of her condition, walked from place to place begging her bread, and wishing for death that came not to her relief. But at length the husband, compassionating her distress, sent messengers to recall her to his court. . . . ."

Although we appreciate the divergences between the plots of the story and the play, we are forced to note one parallel. The grief of the king's son—we recall that "he was over-whelmed with sorrow"—is a detail suggestive of the initial scene of the falling action of the play. The conclusion of the play seems to be entirely Heywood's own.

In the sub-plot Heywood follows more closely its apparent source, the thirtieth novel of the second book of the *Palace of Pleasure*. To Professor Koeppel again we are indebted for pointing out the relation between the sub-plot and the English version of the original. This, too, Symonds had already noted as a novella by Bernardo-Illicini of Sienna.[30] In external incidents and in spirit the drama repeats the plot of the story except for one or two details. In the story the origin of the trouble was not personal enmity as between Sir Francis and Sir Charles of the play, but a family feud growing out of a boar hunt and intensified by the increasing poverty of the Montanines, the last descendants of whom were the brother and sister, Charles and Angelica; Angelica was from the first beloved by Anselmo Salembeni, the proto-type of Sir Francis Acton, the lovers being separated by the family feud only; and it was not Anselmo that was respon-sible for Charles' being in prison, but a citizen, who, wishing to secure the farm of the Montanines, had Charles imprisoned upon a trivial pretext. From this point the play parallels the story, barring, of course, the motives actuating Sir Francis Acton, who is more brutal than Anselmo. The story, unlovely it is true, is in part redeemed by the quasi-dignity of family pride sustaining a time-honored feud and by the romance of the lovers. Heywood, desiring, perhaps, to effect relief from the pathos and intensity of the emotional crises of the main action, has selected for his sub-plot features offering the sharpest contrast to the mainsprings

[30] *Shakespeare's Predecessors in the English Drama*, John Adding-ton Symonds, 1900, p. 368.

of the principal action. His presentation of the hunt, a lively, realistic scene vivid in color and pulsating with action, raises the sub-plot out of the ordinary.

THE WISE WOMAN OF HOGSDON

The one early edition of this play is dated 1638,[31] Heywood's name is on the title page. In the entry in the Stationers' Register, also of 1638, the license is for "a Play called the wise woman of Hogsden by Thomas Heywood."[32] Although *The Wise Woman of Hogsdon* appeared with neither dedication nor address to the reader, there is affixed to the play a complimentary epistle by "Samuel King" "to his chosen friend, the learned author Mr. Thomas Heywood." This personal mark of esteem justifies the assumption that the writer thereof had reasonable grounds for thinking the play to be Heywood's. Here, then, are three bits of external evidence, which, considered together, are of sufficient weight to indicate Heywood's main, if not sole, authorship of the play in question. We confess that the play is not a production written entirely in our poet's distinctive style, but in several phases of its theme and structure it suggests Heywood's hand. May we not conclude that the slight points of dissimilarity between *The Wise Woman of Hogsdon* and the plays characteristically Heywood's bear testimony to the poet's versatility of talent?

The date 1604 has been assigned to the play chiefly on Fleay's assumption that the Heywood play acted at Court in 1604, "How to learn of a woman to woo," was *The Wise Woman of Hogsdon* and that the latter contains allusions to several plays produced around 1660.[33] Of no little significance as to the time of the production of the play are some

[31] Greg's *List of Plays*, p. 53.
[32] *Transcript of the Registers of the Stationers' Company,* Vol. IV, 411.
[33] *A Biographical Chronicle of the English Drama*, Vol. I, 292.

words of Chartley, the scapegrace of the comedy. In rebuking his sweetheart and her father for their tears at his faithlessness this young rascal says:

> Peace foole, wee shall else have thee claime kindred of the Woman kill'd with kindnesse.[34]

As this seems an unmistakable reference to *A Woman Killed with Kindness* (1603), there is basis for placing *The Wise Woman of Hogsdon* after 1603. On the ground that these words could be a satirical thrust at the sentimentality of Mrs. Frankford, they have been cited frequently as evidence of another's authorship rather than of Heywood's. We know, though, that Heywood is habitually frank, even to the point of naïvete. Such an allusion to one of his plays is in direct line with what we believe to be his nature. The play was produced between 1602 and 1605.

No direct source for *The Wise Woman of Hogsdon* has been discovered. It is a clever comedy of intrigue, the center of action being the "wise woman" of Hogsdon (Hoxton), a charlatan whose prototype may well have been an actual London figure. The passage in Jonson's *The Devil is an Asse,*

> Or some good Ribbe, about Kentish Towne
> Or Hogsden, you would hang now for a witch
> Because she will not let you play round Robbin,

> (Act I, sc. 1, 11.16-18)[35]

may refer to Heywood's play or to familiar characters of Kentish Town or Hoxton. In spirit, incidents, and certain characters, the action suggests Plautine comedy, but it cannot be traced directly to any known play of Plautus.

[34] *The Dramatic Works of Thomas Heywood,* Vol. V. *The Wise Woman of Hogsdon,* p. 316.
[35] *The Devil is an Asse.* Edited by William Savage Johnson, *Yale Studies in English,* 1905.

THE FAIR MAID OF THE WEST

The Fair Maid of the West, Or, A Girle worth Gold, a double comedy, was published in 1631.[36] The author identifies himself solely by the initials "T. H." on the title page, but the play is described "As it was lately acted before the King and Queen, with approved liking. By the Queens Majesties Comedians." The entry in the Stationers' Register of June 16, 1631, for Richard Rayston describes the play as "a Comedy called the fayre mayde of the west: 1st and 2ᵈ parte."[37]

The initials "T. H." on the title-page of the 1631 edition of *The Fair Maid of the West* are supplemented by Heywood's complete signature appended to each of the dedications, to "John Othow Esquire, Counsellour at Law in the noble society of Graies Inne" and "Thomas Hammon, Esquire, of Graies Inne." Both of these letters, warmly personal in tone, voice Heywood's esteem for his patrons, his gratitude for "the much love and many courtesies" of which he acknowledges himself the recipient. Characteristically, the strain of sycophancy is lacking. The language to John Othow, Esquire—"let it passe under the title of my love and respect, long devoted unto you; of which, if I endeavor to present the world with a due acknowledgment without the sordid expectation of reward, or servile imputation of flatterie, I hope it will be the rather accepted"—foreshadows the pride of Burns:

> "My lov'd, my honour'd, much respected friend!
> No mercenary bard his homage pays:
> With honest pride, I scorn each selfish end;
> My dearest meed, a friend's esteem and praise."[38]

[36] Greg's *List of Plays,* p. 52.
[37] *Transcript of the Registers of the Stationers' Company,* Vol. IV, 254.
[38] *The Cotters Saturday Night,* ll. 1-4.

To these formal compliments to patrons Heywood has added short addresses of appeal "To the Reader," asking for support and favor similar to the kindly reception already tendered the stage performances. Equally candid is he in his avowal that he had never collected his plays for published volumes of "works." These letters mention also the title of the productions, "These Comedies bearing the title of The fair Maid of the West" and the names of the principal characters, "Spencer and his Western Besse."

Nothing definite is known of the exact source of this essentially wholesome comedy. As Miss Bates has shown, Heywood may have received inspiration from the ballad *"Mary Ambree,"* printed in the Percy *Collection,* for the romantic adventure undertaken by his heroine and the general lines of her heroic character; and he may have laid under contribution the popular accounts of one Long Meg of Westminster for his presentation of Bess Bridges as the model but shrewd inn hostess capable on occasion of donning men's clothes and using the sword with strength and agility. The same critic has also indicated the possibility of Heywood's indebtedness for the Morocco scenes to *"A . . . discourse of Muley Hamets rising to the three Kingdomes of Moruecos, Fes, and Sus—The Adventures of Sir A. S. . . . . in those countries,* by Ro. C., London, 1609" and the shorter account of the career of the same potentate as given in *"Purchas His Pilgrimes,* 1625."[39] If an early date for the play is accepted, any connection between the Morocco scenes and these sources would be impossible. The suggestion, however, of the Mary Ambree of the ballad and Long Meg of Westminster as prototypes for Heywood's "girle worth gold" is entirely tenable. Until, though, some other source has been discovered, to Heywood's invention must be laid the actual events portrayed in the play and the course of action. In the delineation of Besse Bridges, our

---

[39] *A Woman Killed with Kindness* and *The Fair Maid of the West.* Edited by Katherine Lee Bates, pp. 140-142.

poet has pictured most successfully a type dear to him, the attractive, wholesome English girl of the middle class. Bess Bridges is the vital center of the breezy, spirited action, but not a little of the charm of the appeal of the play lies in its lavish color of middle-class life and the pervading spirit of patriotism. This atmosphere is typical of Heywood. It is the distinguishing feature of the greater number of the Heywood plays, the indisputable characteristic of the poet's peculiar bent. As evidence of authorship the possible sources of *The Fair Maid of the West* are relatively unimportant. The essential elements of the appeal of the play—the vitality of the action, the delineation of the charming heroine, the local color—are striking indications of Heywood's hand, and, because of these happily blended features, *The Fair Maid of the West* may be considered an original creation.

Difference of opinion has existed as to the probable date of *The Fair Maid of the West*. Fleay surmises that the play was first produced about 1622. This guess rests upon internal evidence, the assumption that the lines

"Fair English Elizabeth, as well for vertue
As admired beautie,"

F. M. W. (II, p. 423)

refer to the Queen of Bohemia, a royal visitor in England in 1622.[40] Creizenach, following Fleay perhaps, alludes casually to the period of composition as "long after" the death of Queen Elizabeth.[41] An earlier date is suggested by Aronstein (before 1603),[42] and by Professor Schelling (1603 or 1604).[43] The reasons advanced for the earlier date are the intimate conversation upon the expedition of the

[40] *A Biographical Chronicle of the English Drama*, Vol. I, p. 296.
[41] *The English Drama in the Age of Shakespeare*, Wilhelm Creizenach, 1916, p. 130.
[42] "Thomas Heywood," Philipp Aronstein.
[43] *Elizabethan Drama, 1558-1642*, Felix E. Schelling, 1908, Vol. II. Appendix "List of Plays."

Earl of Essex which occurred in 1597, the panegyric upon Queen Elizabeth, and the looseness of structure of the play. Conjointly, these three reasons have weight, but, as has been noted, very little satisfaction as to the chronology of Heywood's plays can be derived from a consideration of structure alone.

A contribution to the question of the date has been made by Mr. Ross Jewell in a study of the sources and date of *The Fair Maid of the West.* He writes:

> There is in the play, however, one word which, rightly understood, solves the vexed question of date—*Mullisheg.* Our heroine's royal admirer is no other than Mulai Sheik, who after a period of civil strife following upon the death of his father was proclaimed King at Fez in 1604. There is not the slightest doubt that European interest in Moroccan affairs at this period was considerable, and the dramatist who had already brought the Virgin Queen upon the stage now introduces to London playgoers the temporarily triumphant Moroccan Prince whose enigmatical character and spectacular career make anything but dull reading at a distance of three centuries.[44]

Before leaving this question of the date of *The Fair Maid of the West,* we may quote a few passages from the play suggestive of certain lines of *Macbeth:*

> Oh, that we three so happily should meet.
>
> F. M. W. (II, p. 406)

> When shall we three meet again
> ....?
>
> Macbeth (I, 1, 1)

> Now shall I quite him home.
>
> F. M. W. (II, p. 414)

> That trusted home
> Might yet enkindle you unto the crowne,
> Besides the Thane of Cawdor.
>
> Macbeth (I, 3, 135-137)

[44] *Studies in English Drama.* Edited by Allison Gaw. *Heywood's Fair Maid of the West,* by Ross Jewell. *University of Pennsylvania Publications,* Vol. XIV, p. 67, 1917.

I am fast
Now is my task in labour, and is plung'd
In thousand throes of childebirth, dangerous it is
To deal where king's affaires are questioned,
Or may be parled.

F. M. W. (II, p. 360)

I am settled, and bend up
Each corporal agent to this terrible feat

Macbeth (I, 7, 93-94)

Too much importance should not be attached to mere verbalisms, or similarities in thought and expression. In this case, the instances suggesting the influence of one author upon another are too few to justify one's drawing a conclusion of any weight; and, granting the possibility of imitation, we can point to nothing indicating which poet was the imitator. Macbeth was written in 1605-06. The lines quoted serve merely to strengthen the theory advanced by Mr. Ross Jewell for a date for *The Fair Maid of the West* after 1604, perhaps about 1606 or 1607.

THE ENGLISH TRAVELLER

The announcement on the title page of the extant edition (1633) is that the play had been "Publikely acted at the Cock-Pit in Drury Lane: By her Majesties servants. Written by Thomas Heywood." The chosen motto is also used. The entry in the Stationers' Register under date of July 15, 1633, describes the play as a "Comedy called The Traveller by master Heywood."[45]

The English Traveller bears unmistakable signs of Heywood's authorship. That it was published with the poet's sanction is attested by the fully signed dedication to a patron and an epistle to the reader. These prefatory letters of *The English Traveller* do more, however, than help establish the authorship of the play. Writing in the spirit of unaffected

---

[45] *Transcript of the Registers of the Stationers' Company,* Vol. IV, 300.

appreciation for the friendship between his patron, "Sir Henry Appleton," and his uncle, "Master Edmund Heywood," Heywood left a clue to his family ties, strengthened by the discovery of the will of Edmund Heywood. Another significant point in the same letter is the language of Heywood's allusion to Prynne's attack upon stage plays. He says, "if they (stage plays) have been vilified of late by any Separisticall humorist, (as in the now questioned Histriomastix) I hope by the next Terme (Minerva assistente) to give such satisfaction to the world, by vindicating many particulars in that work maliciously exploded and condemned, as that no Gentleman of qualitie and judgement, but shall therein receive a reasonable satisfaction: . . . . ."[46] It is to be regretted that, if Heywood carried out this intention, the production has not come down to us. Another piece of dramatic criticism by the author of the *Apology for Actors,* written, though, in the later years of the poet's long stage career, would carry the weight of unquestioned authority and mature judgment. In the address "To the Reader," affixed to *The English Traveller,* is Heywood's much quoted confession of the remarkable number of plays of which he was entire or partial author. Aside from this reference to the enormous volume of work produced, this address is almost a replica of the one just noted from *The Fair Maid of the West,*—a reiteration of the poet's freedom from ambition to have his plays published, of his being driven to present authorized versions to protect himself against the piratical editions of unscrupulous booksellers, of his inability to secure many of his plays which either had been lost or were being held by companies. These writings, bearing intimate testimony of the poet's personal relations and his thoughts and feelings, do not suggest the slightest suspicion of fraud. Their greatest weakness—the insistent,

---

[46] *The Dramatic Works of Thomas Heywood,* Vol. IV. *The English Traveller,* Dedicatory Epistle.

nay almost monotonous, repetition of theme,—becomes for purposes of identification a positive merit.

We recall that *The English Traveller* according to its title page had been "Publikely acted at the Cock-pit in Drury-Lane by Her Majesties servants." In 1617 the Queen's men had come or were about to come to the Cockpit, then a new theatre. There they stayed until 1619, unless they returned to the Red Bull for a time while the Cockpit was under repairs.[47] This theatre was occupied apparently by Prince Charles' men from 1619-1622,[48] by the Lady Elizabeth's men from 1622 to 1625,[48] and by the Queen Henrietta's men from 1625 to 1636.[48] As the reference to "Her Majesties servants" would exclude Prince Charles' men and the Lady Elizabeth's men, the play must have been produced between 1617 and 1619 or between 1625 and 1633. Professor Schelling places the date as late as 1632.[49] Internal evidence suggests a date comparatively late in the poet's life. The following lines spoken by Reignald may or may not be a personal allusion to the poet's earlier years:

> *Ric.*   Grammercy Reignald,
> I love all those that wish it. You are the men
> Leade merry lives, Feast, Revell, and Carowse;
> You feele no tedious houres; Time playes with you,
> This is your golden age.
> *Reig.*   It was, but now Sir,
> That Gould is turned to worse than Alcamy,
> It will not stand the test; Those dayes are past,
> And now our nights come on.
>   E. T. (IV, 60)

Beyond doubt, significance should be attached to the striking similarity between the broad outlines of *The English Traveller* and *A Woman Killed with Kindness*. At first glance one wonders why an author should write two plays built upon

---

[47] *The Elizabethan Stage,* Vol. II, p. 240.
[48] *The Elizabethan Stage,* Vol. II, p. 302.
[49] *Elizabethan Drama,* by Felix E. Schelling, Vol. II, p. 562.

themes so closely related. Perhaps the popularity of *A
Woman Killed with Kindness* tempted our poet to try
another tune on the same string. Such a resolution, probably, came only after the lapse of many years, and at a
period in the poet's life when, invention lagging, he was
forced to repeat himself. Either time, from 1617 to 1619
and from 1625 to 1633, would be relatively late in Heywood's career. Then too, the words of the Prologue contain a suggestion as to the time, generally speaking, when
the play might have been produced:

> A Strange Play you are like to have, for know
> We use no Drum, nor Trumpet, nor Dumbe show;
> No Combate, Marriage, not so much to day
> As Song, Dance, Masque, to bumbaste out a Play;

> Will you the reason know? There have so many
> Beene in that kind, that Hee desires not any
> At this time in His Sceane, no helpe, no straine
> Or flash that's borrowed from anothers braine;

This protest against elaborate stage setting was doubtless
provoked by the popularity of the Stuart masques and the
effect they produced upon the presentation of regular plays.
Heywood voices not only his resentment against the lure of
the spectacular, to which so many dramatists of the late
Jacobean period had succumbed, but also his independence of
the trappings of the stage. As to his own atttude, this position was not new. None of Heywood's plays known to be
written after 1605 contained a chorus, and one only, *A
Maidenhead Well Lost,* a dumb show. Wanting positive
external evidence, I am inclined to place *The English
Traveller* as late as possible before its publication in 1633.

Heywood himself is authority for the suggestion that
the main plot of *The English Traveller* is based upon actual
occurrence. In a story narrated in *Gunaikeion,* the outlines
of *The English Traveller* are practically paralleled, except

that the suspicions of the father of Geraldine's prototype are aroused by rumor, not by the false disclosures of the betrayer, and the wife is confronted with her guilt through a letter.[50] Were it not for the positive assertion by the poet that he is retelling facts, one would be apt to surmise that the direct hints for the play came from the forty-third novel of Painter, to which *The English Traveller,* in the poet's conception of Mrs. Wincott, bears a close resemblance. The fact is, it is not Anne Frankford, but Mrs. Wincott, who in her intrigue displays the deliberate intention as well as the utter lack of remorse characterizing the guilty wives of mediaeval tales. In the production of the play the poet was doubtless guided by the "true story" of *Gunaikeion,* while he may have been influenced consciously or unconsciously by the forty-third novel of Painter.

Heywood's general indebtedness to Plautus in this as well as in others of his plays has been discussed by Professor Allan H. Gilbert.[51] It is the *Mostellaria*—the source, too, of Jonson's *Alchemist*—that furnishes the Lionel-Reignard action. As Professor Gilbert has noted, Heywood's adaptation of the plot is very close to the original: new names, with one exception, are bestowed upon the characters; a character from the main plot, the clown, discloses the true state of affairs to the hoodwinked father; and a new scene is added in the clown's description of the hallucinations of the drunken rioters. In using the clown as the agent who undeceives the elder Lionel, Heywood has strengthened the realism of the situation (the English valet would not so readily betray his master); and the characterization of the rioters becomes more vivid by the account of their carousing. Of course, it is clear that both of these changes are technical devices for joining the two plots. Most important of all, Heywood has Anglicized his characters and atmosphere.

[50] *Gunaikeion,* Thomas Heywood, 1624. Bk. V, p. 193.

[51] "Thomas Heywood's Debt to Plautus." Allan H. Gilbert in *Journal of English and Germanic Philology,* XII, pp. 593-611.

THE CAPTIVES

The Captives is the only one of Heywood's plays unrecorded as an early publication, its manuscript having been discovered in the British Museum by Mr. A. H. Bullen in 1885.

Strong external evidence exists for ascribing this play to Heywood. Sir Henry Herbert, Master of the Revels from 1623 to 1673, his duties of course being suspended during the Civil War and the Commonwealth, has recorded in his *Office-Book* an entry, which reads: "1624, September 3. For the Cockpit Company; A new Play, called The Captive, or The lost recovered; Written by Hayward."[52] As the theme of the play discovered by Mr. Bullen fits the title recorded in Sir Henry Herbert's accounts, no objection seems to have been raised to identifying this long hidden play as Heywood's *Captives*. Besides, as Mr. Bullen points out, there appear in the same volume with *The Captives* certain scenes from Heywood's *Golden Age* and *Silver Age* under the title *Calisto;* as distinguished from the other pieces in the volume, *Calisto* and *The Captives* are in the same very characteristic handwriting,[53] known to be Heywood's.

There is the possibility that when *The Captives* was licensed in 1624 for production, it might have been an old play of Heywood's that had been laid aside for some time. It is more likely that it had just been composed. The date of the entry in Sir Henry Herbert's register may denote the time of composition, for it accords well with the conclusions reached from a study of the metrical characteristics of the play.

[52] *The Dramatic Records of Sir Herbert,* Edited by Joseph Quincy Adams, Jr., p. 29.
[53] *The Captives or The Lost Recovered,* Edited by Alexander Corbin Judson, 1921. Introduction.

The source of the main plot is the *Rudens* of Plautus; of the secondary action, a novella by Masuccio di Salerno. Professor Judson in the Introduction to his edition of *The Captives* has made a detailed analysis of Heywood's indebtedness to the *Rudens*.[54] He notes that *The Captives* parallels closely the action and characterization of the Latin comedy and in many instances presents practically the words of the original, Heywood's independence showing itself in the addition of songs, in his interpolating scenes to connect the two plots, and in his rounding out the concluding events in such order that "the Elizabethan playgoer was enabled to learn how things turned out." In regard to the sub-plot, Professor Judson has also shown that Heywood has laid under contribution Masuccio's novel, Professor Koeppel's theory, rather than the old French fabliau *Le Prêtre Qu'on porte,* the source conjectured by Professor Kittredge and several other critics. If the novella were not in existence, one could easily see in the fabliau suggestions for the play. The events, viz., the monk's advances to the wife of a tailor, the ruse by which the woman lures her wooer to his death, the disposition of the monk's body, the deception of the abbot, and the final outcome, are not only the framework of the sub-action of the play, but in and of themselves could have inspired a dramatist of Heywood's imagination to write his play. A superficial reading of the novella, however, the gist of which is narrated by Professor Judson, discloses a close parallelism in minute details to be explained only in Heywood's use of the novella as source material. As Professor Judson has added, Heywood may have had access to a translation of Masuccio's story, a French version having been printed as early as 1555.[55]

In both plots of *The Captives,* Heywood, as in the case of *The English Traveller,* has used his originals in no sub-

[54] *Ibid.*
[55] *Ibid.*

servient fashion. Regardless of the fact that he has adhered closely to the borrowed threads of narrative, his play is more wholesome, withal more buoyant than its sources. The characters of the main plot have been Anglicized and the whole infused with Heywood's pervasive patriotism and kindliness.

A word or two of summary may be added. Although Heywood disclaimed the ambition of seeing his plays printed, the appearance of his name upon the title pages with the motto, recurring regularly after 1630, shows that these early editions were published with the author's sanction. More significant indications of authorship, however, are Heywood's signed dedications to patrons and prefatory addresses to readers. In their naïve candour, these prefatory addresses differ from the conventional epistle of questionable sincerity. The dates of printing of *The Four Prentices of London* and *If You Know Not Me You Know Nobody (1, 2)* force one to place these plays in the chronology of the poet's works before 1610; while Henslowe's entries for *A Woman Killed with Kindness* establish almost to a certainty the time of the writing of the latter play. The identification of *The Christmas play* of 1604 as *The Wise Woman of Hogsdon* places the latter play with the group of plays written before 1610. With almost the same certainty we can put *The Captives* and *The English Traveller* in the period extending from the middle of the third decade of the century to the middle of the fourth decade. The plays, then, from the point of view of date of composition, divide themselves into two groups: those written before 1610, those written after 1620. If it can be shown that the later plays disclose tendencies in thought and manner markedly different from the style of the earlier ones, it may be possible to strengthen our conclusion as to the date of the paradoxical *Fair Maid of the West*. Further, an estimate of Heywood's distinctive characteristics will not only help us to decide upon his share in the production of *Fortune by Land and Sea* and *The Late Lancashire Witches,* but will assist us to accept or reject for our poet the authorship of several other plays, which, at times, have been ascribed to Heywood.

CHAPTER III

HEYWOOD'S REALISM

The very first thing that arrests the casual reader, even, of Heywood is the pervasiveness of a picturesque background of Elizabethan life that colors brilliantly almost all of the plays. Vibrant in the richness of its varied hues, this setting of contemporary manners weaves itself inextricably into the context and brings to the foreground Heywood's theme as it, in turn, unfolds itself almost always as a phase of everyday life. In our preliminary survey, then, we shall examine the plays, not as tragedies or comedies, or as groups illustrating technical principles of style, but as studies divided according to the nature of the emphasis placed upon English life. In other words, it is our conviction that the plays present a largely objective world chosen deliberately as an expression of Heywood's attitude toward his environment.

"Romance" is the term used sometimes to describe the strange and marvelous, the "light that never was on land or sea," the world of ideals, as contrasted with "realism," the matter-of-fact incidents of humdrum existence presented in utter fidelity to known conditions of human life and character. Inasmuch as realism, from this point of view, is the portrayal of the actual or, at least, of the probable, it follows that the writer of realistic studies finds his material in the world about him, which furnishes him, as a point of departure, outline sketches, models, color for his created art. His men and women, individualized characters or stock types, do not rise above the human norm or sink beneath it; his situations do not transcend the experiences of life itself. In fact, so absorbed may the realist become in the externals of life as he views it, that he fails sometimes to interpret the inner meaning of the complexities of social conditions among classes, times, or places. It is in the varying possibilities of the treatment of his subject that the problem of the realist lies. His choice ranges from incidents depicting atmosphere alone, a shell without substance, to the studies of the thoughts and emotions of individuals representing familiar social groups, the revelations of the meaning of social conditions in terms of human reactions.

Among realistic plays—the "plays of everyday life"—the most important by far are those designated as "domestic drama," a rather inadequate expression for its more definite German counterpart "bürgerliches Schauspiel." Domestic drama comprises a wide range of plays, involving the common relations of family life: the problems of the erring wife, the faithless husband, the arbitrary parent, the prodigal son, and their more agreeable opposites. In the clashes among the recalcitrant members of the family circle emerge situations ending sometimes as comedy, sometimes as tragedy. That these conflicts of human will and emotion are portrayed among the middle class or the country gentry is explained according to Singer's theory in this way: As it is necessary for servants and guests in a family to be integral parts of the intimate action of the play, the family cannot be of a class restricted by the inflexible conventions of social decorum from permitting such informal relations in the household. Moreover, as the action is not developed about a violation of natural law but is at variance with customs, traditions built up in the development of human institutions, the background is found in the environment where respect for human institutions is greatest, namely in the middle class family, living in the country district.[1] Limitation to a particular class group, though, is an arbitrary restriction. A family of any rank might furnish characters and situations offering material for realistic treatment.

But the themes presented by the realist need not be centered

---

[1] *Das bürgerliche Trauerspiel in England bis zum Jahre 1800.* Hans Wolfgang Singer, 1891, p. 72.

in the joys and woes of the family. The plays of everyday life may be staged in the vast arena of the world at large presenting men at work and at play. A limitless range of situations growing out of the complexities of society is in the field of the realist. According to his mood he may see the life about him as a serious conflict among classes in a community or between individuals, as a serene picture of genre figures, or as a shifting canvas of guilt and folly provoking in turn our amusement and scorn. Often, too, the method of the poet varies. Plot becomes negligible as the lights are focused upon external incident, episodical situations of detached figures alone. Then it is that we miss the stress of emotion and will within the family or the wider world, the background of the admittedly disintegrated action looms out of all perspective, and the chief interest of the play becomes disconnected incident and character illustrative simply of the life of certain people at definite times. Finally, we must consider the plays that place characters exhibiting the manners and spirit of contemporary life in a series of events historically remote.

Having in mind these variations of realistic drama as types, we may classify accordingly the plays of Heywood selected for this study. As the grouping is not sharply defined there is much overlapping; and, although each play deserves a special discussion of its own with regard to its dominant characteristics, in all appears a background of English life, and in all may be recognized an underlying motive which is as unchangeable as it is persistent. It will be remembered that in the *Apology for Actors* Heywood declared that plays should be presented for the diversion and instruction of the playgoers. This instruction comprehends lessons in patriotism, virtue, and civil behavior; generally speaking, a sort of culture. Such is Heywood's theory of the purpose of the drama. If he was guided by this theory, his plays may be examined as pictures of certain phases of Elizabethan life and character presented deliberately to teach as well as to amuse the audience. A rough classification may follow some such grouping as this:

   I. Plays in which the action centers in emotional problems.

   II. Plays in which particular types of Elizabethan characters are presented to portray the virtues and follies of English life. In this class action is regarded as an expression of inner reality, but emotional complexities are absent.

In the two groups setting assumes an important part. The appeal, in large measure, grows out of the colorful atmosphere, the attractive pictures of Elizabethan manners.

Two of Heywood's plays, *A Woman Killed with Kindness* and *The English Traveller* present the problem of the erring wife. Of great interest to the student of Heywood are the real and apparent points of similarity between these two plays and the marked differences. In both plays the wronged husband, though aware of his own invaded rights, though making no compromise with wrongdoing, is at once both just and generous. This characterization is the cardinal point of the plays. In *The English Traveller* it is the wife's knightly admirer, Geraldine, who suffers rather than the aged husband, Mr. Wincott. These men have received the poet's most sympathetic interest. It is they who hold the reader in suspense; it is they, Master Frankford and Young Geraldine, who struggle to maintain faith in a cherished ideal against the direct reports of the disinterested servants Nicholas and Besse; it is they who overcome the sense of personal injury in attaining the higher plane where justice is entirely unmarked by selfishness and where the spirit of forgiveness eventually triumphs. Regardless, for the moment, of Heywood's conception of poetic justice, or of the dramatic effect of the maudlin ending of *A Woman Killed with Kindness,* one sees in Master Frankford and Young Geraldine the poet's ideal of the injured husband unselfish to the point of rising above personal injury keenly felt. That this conception of the course of action to be taken in dealing with infidelity was a deep conviction with Heywood is evidenced not solely because he has dwelt upon it in two of his known plays, but also because he has written in moments of serious reflection in a similar vein. Speaking of the attribute of modesty in women he says:

> . . . . for as there is nothing more divelish and deadly than a malitious and ill-disposed woman, so there is on the contrarie, nothing more wholesome and comfortable to man than one provident, gentle, and well addicted; for as she that is good and honest, will upon just necessitie lay downe her life for her husbands health and safetie, so the other will as willingly prostitute hers for his destruction and ruin.[2]
>
> . . . . Sufficient it is that we have laws to punish, and judges to examine and sentence all such transgressors. . . . . Neither is this discourse aimed to persuade men to too much remisnes in wincking at, and sleeping out the adulteries of their wives.[3]

Here is explanation for the forgiveness that does not condone, the resentment that does not demand the personal right of revenge.

Heywood has drawn these characters with undisguised sympathy. They are frank, loyal, upright, generously endowed natures unspoiled by petty faults. For the waywardness of the wives there is no excuse. Moreover, the supreme virtues of these ideal husbands are evidenced in the broader relations of the social contacts beyond the strict limits of the immediate family. Master Frankford, in the lavish display of true English hospitality, makes his home the center of modest entertainment offered without stint to his friends. Indeed, it is this spirit of genuine warmth of kindness and utter selflessness, which opened his house to the disloyal intruder and made relatively easy the path to dishonor. Notice the cordiality of Frankford's words:

> FRANK. Sir a word with you!
> I know you Sir to be a Gentleman

---

[2] *Gunaikeion.* Bk. III, p. 120.
[3] *Ibid.* Bk. LV, p. 179.

In all things; your possibilities but meene:
Please you to use my Table, and my purse,
They are yours.

WEND. O Lord sir, I shall never deserve it.

FRANK. O sir disparage not your worth too much,
You are full of quality, and faire desert;
Choose of my men which shall attend on you,
And he is yours. I will allow you sir,
Your man, your gelding and your table all
At my owne charge, be my companion.

WEND. M. Frankford, I have oft bin bound to you
By many favours: this exceeds them all,
That I shall never merit your least favour;
But when your last remembrance I forget,
Heaven at my soule exact that weighty debt.

FRANK. There needs no protestation: for I know you
Vertuous, and therefore gratefull. Prethee Nan
Use him with all thy lovingst curtesie.
W. K. K. (Vol. II, pp. 104-105)

Likewise, in *The English Traveller:*

WINC. Gentlemen, welcome, but what neede I use
A word so common, unto such to whom
My house was never private. I expect
You should not looke for such a needles phrase,
Especially you Master Geraldine,
Your Father is my neighbor, and I know you,
Even from the cradle, then I loved your Infancy
And since your riper growth better'd by travell;

———

I would have you
Thinke this your home, free as your Fathers house,
And to command it, as the Master on't;
Call bouldly heere, and entertaine your friends,
As in your owne possessions...............
E. T. (Vol. IV, p. 10)

When Wincott learns that Delavil is the friend of "the Noble
Master Geraldine," he includes in the freely offered hospitality the utterly unworthy newcomer. The fineness of

nature, which again manifests itself in an utter lack of suspicion of wrongdoing and in a high-principled reluctance to believe the evidence brought to each one by the trusted servants, is proof of the poet's clear intention: namely, to win the interest of the audience to a lofty nature castigated by suffering wholly undeserved. The answer to the question as to how far this interest is sustained involves the problem of Heywood's skill in characterization. What concerns us now is the type of man presented by Heywood as the model husband. In the strength of the conception is, however, its inherent weakness. As dramatic figures, Master Frankford and Young Geraldine are admirable foils to the inconstant wives; but, absolutely flawless, they are superhuman. Although Heywood's realism breaks down at this point, his purpose is sustained. In an English household he has pictured these fine natures attaining the supreme possibilities of unselfishness, loyalty, generosity, and spiritual strength. In idealizing his character, however, in overemphasizing the pathos of situations, in minimizing the element of responsibility for action, Heywood transcends reality, and to that extent these plays are tinged with sentimentalism.

In delineation of character Heywood succeeds better with his men than with his women. The men are more vital, more self-revealing. But the gain is of little moment. One is permitted to see the inner nature of the men, but, in the domestic dramas now under consideration, the men— Master Frankford and Young Geraldine,—are alike in kind. On the other hand, the women—Mrs. Frankford and Mrs. Wincott,—though barely sketched in unmotivated action, are sharply differentiated from one another. Mrs. Frankford and Mrs. Wincott, alike guilty of infidelity, are different personalities. Of the two Mrs. Frankford is less interesting; wholly ingenuous, she appears to fall into a chasm, whose yawning depths are perceived only after her foot is beyond the brink. Her immediate repentance, one feels, is sincere; but it affords only additional proof of a nature undeveloped, immature. Her utterance of feeble protest

> "What shall I say?
> My soule is wandring, and hath lost her way,
> O master Wendol, oh."
>
> W. K. K. (Vol. II, p. 112)

suggests the frightened cry of a helpless, bewildered child caught in a tangled maze from which her feeble efforts effect no escape. Miserable, she lacks the wit to initiate or even to imagine the possibility of a plan calculated to bring relief to her burdened soul; were an outlet offered her, she would lack the will to accept it. She is a pathetic creature, but never, however, insincere with herself. *The English Traveller,* usually compared with *A Woman Killed with Kindness,* resembles the latter play chiefly in the general lines of the plot, the background of English country-house life, and the characterization of the heroes. One does not forget, of course, the similarity between incidents, as, for instance, the rôle of Besse and Nicholas, and the soliloquies of Master Frankford and Young Geraldine as they hesitate to discover the undeniable evidences of guilt. Mrs. Wincott, however, in marked contrast to Mrs. Frankford, thinks for herself and takes the initiative in her own concerns. Restless under the yoke of marriage to a man much older than she, she welcomes the advent of Delavil, bespeaks his good graces to her husband, and, to throw suspicion from herself, pretends that she favors a match between the new guest and her sister Prudentilla. Note her words:

WINC.   Thous hast spoke
> That which not onely crownes his true desert,
> But now instates him in my better thoughts,
> Making his Worth unquestionable.

WIFE.   Hee pretends
> Love to my sister Prue. I have observ'd him,
> Single her out, to private conference.

WINC.   But I could rather, for her owne sake, wish
         Young Geraldine would fixe his thoughts that way,
         And shee towards him; In such Affinity,
         Trust mee, I would not use a sparing hand.

WIFE.   But Love in these kindes, should not be compel'd
         Forc'd, nor Perswaded; When it freely Springs,
         And of it selfe, takes voluntary Roote,
         It Growes, it Spreads, it Ripens, and brings foorth,
         Such an Usurious Crop of timely Fruit,
         As crownes a plentious Autume.

                                      E. T. (Vol. IV, p. 24)

That the play lacks action displaying the surrender of Mrs.
Wincott to Delavil or subsequent moments of remorse, is
due not so much to the poet's neglect or indifference to
demands of technique as to a conscious design in the portrayal of character. From the beginning she is the light
woman, unmoral. Sufficient to indicate her frail principles
are the lines above, expressing her intercession for Delavil,
and, in the next scene, her suggestions that are lost upon
the noble-minded Geraldine. And, even as she is utterly
devoid of all goodness, so she is contemptibly weak when she
is unmasked. Confronted by Geraldine with the evidence
of her guilt, she wavers a moment with a sorry feint at
bravado, and then, realizing the futility of further efforts to
maintain the deception, breaks down in fatal collapse.

In the third side of the triangle are the betrayers, Delavil
and Wendoll. They are foils to Heywood's pattern gentlemen, Master Frankford and Young Geraldine, but among
Heywood's group of genre characters they have no counterparts. Wendoll especially is a despicable person; there is
not one redeeming feature about him. The weak woman,
his victim, is the wife of the man who has befriended him
and has given him a home. Heywood's scapegraces, Jack
Gresham, Young Lionel—light-hearted, mischief-loving,
spendthrifts even—are never despicable. Wendoll's plans
for his future mark him as belonging in an entirely different
class:

WEND.................Ile over first to *France*
  And so to *Germany* and *Italy;*
  Where when I have recovered, and by travell
  Gotten those perfect tongues, and that these rumors
  May in their height abate, I will returne.
  And I divine (however now detected)
  My worth and parts by some great man praisd,
  At my returne I may in Court be raisd.

  W. K. K. (Vol. II, p. 152)

Aronstein feels that these words disclose Heywood's inability
to mete out to Wendoll his richly deserved punishment;
that a period of time having been devoted to expiation, the
culprit is to have another chance.[4] But the reference to the
possibility of Court favors seems to dispel the bright illusion.
In this case as generally with Heywood, Court life is synony-
mous with shallowness, glamour, intrigue. It connotes an
atmosphere wholly at variance with the wholesomeness portrayed in the daily life of the less exalted classes. What
Heywood intends, I think, is this: Wendoll, alike guilty of
disloyalty to friend and protector, will find employment for
his parts in a circle that does not idealize the simple virtues
of sincerity and open-handed action. Court life will offer
him his opportunity.

As to the problem of the erring wife, Heywood shows
usually one attitude. To him guilt, being abhorrent, must
be pictured as such; at the close of the action, therefore,
punishment awaits the transgressor. From the beginning
to the end of the plays, there is not a moment when there
is any doubt as to the side with which the poet sympathizes.
The offending wives are never pictured in an attractive light;
the deceived husbands are never the butts of ridicule. The
punishment of infidelity is inevitable, swift; the wronged
husbands are avenged not by steeping their own souls in
crime but by a higher power. With Heywood, the victory
in these cases is the moral one regardless of the possibilities
of intellectual appeal, in spite of the alluring attractiveness

[4] "Thomas Heywood," Philipp Aronstein, p. 234.

of the cleverness of deception emerging triumphant. In guiding the forward movement of action, Heywood fails sometimes to maintain an even balance between responsibility for guilt and the weight of punishment. Mrs. Frankford, as we have seen, becomes entangled in a net from which she cannot extricate herself; Sir Charles Mountford and his sister Susan are the victims of the plotting of Sir Francis Acton. The pathos of the situations and the artificial outcome of the action create sentimental drama: sentimental tragedy in the main plot of *A Woman Killed with Kindness,* sentimental comedy in the secondary action of the same play. Mrs. Wincott, in contrast, is no sentimental heroine. We have noted the cunning of her intrigue, her deception, her moral tone. In the figures of the injured husband, both plays have idealized the characters.

Another play of the period, *A Warning for Fair Women,* based upon a contemporary murder, is not dissimilar in spirit to Heywood's plays of the delinquent wife. Mrs. Sanders suggests Mrs. Frankford in that she readily falls into a trap laid for her undoing. The victim of the intrigues of others, she is guilty through sheer weakness, or at least, in the swiftness of the action, she is swept along in the current that overpowers her. What relates this play so closely to *A Woman Killed with Kindness* and *The English Traveller* is the identity of the ethical issues of the action of all three plays. Like Heywood, the author of *A Warning for Fair Women* has succeeded in sustaining the tone of the atmosphere and the incidents in direct harmony with the final moral judgment.

At the opposite end of the scale, not only in contrast to Heywood's specific solution of this domestic problem but in general attitude toward the moral issue involved, is the spirit of other Elizabethan plays on the subject of the delinquent wife, especially the plays of Middleton, Heywood's contemporary. A good case in point is the sub-plot of *The Roaring Girl,* unquestionably Middleton's work. Mr. Galli-

pot, the patient but stupid husband, is hoodwinked by his
adroit wife, the deception being presented as a laughable
episode. The extreme of Middleton's humor is reached
in two of the actions in *A Chaste Maid in Cheapside.* In
the one case, the fortunes of Lord and Lady Kex, sharpers
dupe the husband for whom no sympathy is evoked; in the
other, the Sir Walter Whorehound-Allwit action, the complacent husband winks at his shame, becomes even the inter-
mediary between his wife and Sir Walter to make the latter
his benefactor. But no moral principle is outraged where
none exists; the result is the outcome of a contest between
wit and dullness, the attitude toward family life foreshadowing the artificiality of Restoration comedy.

Another kind of domestic drama, opposed to the type just
considered in the marked absence of emotional intensity or
seriousness, is Heywood's adaptation of the prodigal son
motive. The term is used advisedly, because Heywood does
not present the conventional profligate, who, having sown
his wild oats and having suffered discomfort and degradation, returns in chastened mood to sue for forgiveness in his
father's home. Heywood has created his scapegraces under
the influence of Plautus. In an English setting he has placed
these wild youths, gamesters and spendthrifts chiefly; they
skate over the thin ice of bankruptcy and escape the consequences of their folly by a fortuitous turn of circumstances
or by sheer trickery. Young Lionel of *The English
Traveller,* Jack Gresham of *If You Know Not Me You
Know Nobody (2),* and Young Chartley of *The Wise
Woman of Hogsdon* are presented as types of the extremes
of frivolity evading the penalty by the superiority of its
wit. The exception here only proves the poet's rule, for,
although the inconstancy of Young Chartley motivates the
main plot of *The Wise Woman of Hogsdon,* in the other
two plays *If You Know Not Me You Know Nobody (2)*
and *The English Traveller,* the spendthrifts are in the subsidiary action.

The question of Heywood's indebtedness to the *Mostellaria* of Plautus for the sub-plot of *The English Traveller* has been worked out in detail.[5] Yet, as Mr. Gilbert, in speaking of Heywood's use of the *Rudens* as source for *The Captives,* has indicated: "Certain passages not affecting the plot which Heywood has added to the *Rudens* are the most striking examples to be found of his modification of the moral tone of his originals. Such alteration is perhaps necessary to fit a play of pagan Rome to the stage of Christian England, yet one reason for it surely is to be found in the character of Thomas Heywood . . ."[6]

This Elizabethan, nay rather Heywood's own coloring, permeates these plays under consideration. Rogues absolutely consistent Heywood is loath to picture. Even at the beginning of the action, Young Lionel thus analyzes his own situation:

> So it fares
> With us yong men; Wee are those houses made,
> Our Parents raise these Structures, the foundation
> Laid in our Infancy; and as wee grow
> In yeeres, they strive to build us by degrees,
> Story on story higher; up at height,
> They cover us with Councell, to defend us
> From stormes without; they polish us within
> With Learnings, Knowledge, Arts and Disciplines;
> All that is nought and vicious, they sweepe from us,
> Like Dust and Cobwebs, and our Roomes concealed,
> Hang with the costliest hangings; Bout the Walls,
> Emblems and beautious Symbols pictured round;
> But when the basic Tenant, Love, steps in,
> And in his Traine, brings Sloth and Negligence,
> Lust, Disobedience, and profuse Excesse;
> The Thrift with which our fathers tiled our Roofes,
> Submits to every storme and Winters blast.

[5] "Thomas Heywood's Debt to Plautus" by Allan H. Gilbert. *Journal of English and Germanic Philology* XII, 593-611.
[6] *Ibid.,* p. 599.

And yeelding place to every riotous sinne,
Gives way without, to ruine what's within;
Such is the state I stand in."

E. T. (Vol. IV, p. 18)

This speech is an excellent illustration not only of Heywood's way of adapting a Latin play to an English setting but of his conception of a young scapegrace. Indebted to Plautus for the imagery and in part for the language, our poet has transformed the empty rhetoric of Philolaches into reflections, which, expressive though they be of a fleeting mood, bear the stamp of sincerity. Young Lionel whirls in the vortex of rioting but connives at rather than initiates deception; he baffles his father but finally secures his own forgiveness. He is the picture of the weakness rather than the viciousness of youth. This in spite of the fact that it is in *The English Traveller* and not in the other two plays that the comic element is largely frivolity sinking at times into horseplay. Young Lionel appears with a wild group of revellers: abandoned women, gamblers, drunkards, carousing at the young master's expense. They are professional ne'er-do-wells, pleasure-seeking hangers-on, universal types of depravity, English simply because the setting is English. Jack Gresham and Young Chartley are stronger figures but of the same cult as young Lionel. Individualized by quickness of wit and dexterity in turning every impending disaster to their own advantage, they are far cleverer than young Lionel, for the quick-witted Reignald thinks and acts for Lionel. Young Chartley approaches more nearly the conventional prodigal son of the period. He is presented in an action of two themes: the problem of the prodigal son connected with that of the faithful, neglected wife. But here again Heywood has steered clear of extremes. Young Chartley has not really deserted a wife, but, fickle by nature, has run away from his betrothed to come to London; here he falls in love with a second maiden only to transfer his affections, after an incredibly short space of time, to a third.

Just as he is about to marry his third betrothed, his inconstancy is unmasked, chiefly through the wit of his first love assisted by the central figure of the play, the "Wise Woman." He is faithlessness incarnate; but he is not guilty of brutal, harsh, or ill-tempered conduct. The originality of Heywood's adaptation of the theme is marked. Master Arthur Lusam of *How a Man May Choose a Good Wife from a Bad* forces his wife not only to receive the courtesan as a guest but to relinquish her own seat of honor at the table in favor of the object of her husband's affections; he poisons his wife; he marries the courtesan, who, upon discovering the crime, promptly gives the offender into the hands of the law. When his fortunes are at the lowest ebb, his faithful wife, having escaped death because the "poison" was only a sleeping potion, not only forgives the deserter and would-be murderer, but with joy receives him into her home again. With slight variations of details this is the line of action of *The Fair Maide of Bristow*. Matthew Flowerdale, the hero of a third play, *The London Prodigal,* does not attempt to murder his wife, but the other elements of the action almost parallel those of *How a Man May Choose a Good Wife from a Bad.* Contrasted with the prodigal sons of the last three plays, young Chartley is a mild offender. To leave a betrothed is, naturally, a simpler problem than to unforge the bonds of marriage; Heywood, thus, creates a less complex situation, one easily solved by the wit of the first Luce and the tricks of a charlatan. The originality of his adaptation of the theme is marked.

Heywood's prodigal sons, moving in the center of comic action, afford much merriment. To the poet's realistic studies reflecting English manners, however, they make scant contribution. One cannot escape the feeling that they are placed arbitrarily in a class of English society, their escapades being the follies of any group and nationality. Humorous rogues, they capture our sympathy because their pranks are harmless diversions. At the end of the action the mock penitents are in high feather not only because of their intellectual triumph, but because they know that the audience is with them. In these instances the poet's judgment is based not upon the moral issue, but upon the artistic merits of the situation created in the conflict of slow-witted credulity pitted against clever knavery; and a comic effect is produced by the presentation of the incongruity between the punishment that is evaded and the undeserved reward that is achieved. The attitude of the poet toward his gay youths indicates a mood entirely dissimilar from that in which he customarily approaches his themes. But the change is not to be regretted. What is missed is the direct teaching of the other plays; this may be sacrificed for the aesthetic gain effected by the final issue undistorted to satisfy a code of poetic justice.

In *The Wise Woman of Hogsdon,* Heywood has conceived a character that is distinctively the conventional rogue. The central figure of the play, the "Wise Woman," is the sharper, the clever victimizer. Dramatically she is at once vital and entertaining; as a personality she is equally vital but entirely unmoral. Residing in Hogsdon (Hoxton), a suburb of London, she plies her unscrupulous trade, principally of fortune telling, among the credulous men and women of her neighborhood. But others of higher intelligence and standing come to her from far and near in every kind of questionable emergency. Truly, she is an unlovely creature, accosted by young Chartley in his derision as:

> "You Inchantress, Sorceresse, Shee-devill; you Madam *Hecate,* Lady *Proserpine,* you are too old, you Hagge now, for conjuring up Spirits your selfe; but you keepe prettie yong Witches under your roofe, that can doe that."

W. W. H. (Vol. V, p. 295)

As a matter of fact, she is an ignorant woman with a reputation for accomplishing wonders. These tricks she performs by sheer knavery and by the disclosures which she leads her unthinking patrons to make about their own affairs. She is strongly individualized among Heywood's men and women because she falls below them in her lack of moral tone. In the play she is the potent magnet of attraction for certain types of people; as such she illustrates a rather sordid element of London life. With masterly technique the poet brings this clever play to a close by presenting his comparatively inoffensive prodigal son in an entanglement of difficulties that are solved for him by the intrigues of the "Wise Woman."

The history play is an account of events forming a part of the life of a people, or an exposition of national ideals of life and character. Heywood, beginning to write in the last decade of the sixteenth century, the period of the highest development of the English chronicle play, and moved by his love for England, would, perforce, be attracted to this type of English drama, and he has used it in two ways: first, to present stories from the chronicles of England, and second, to portray ideals of English character. This brings us to the second group of Heywood's plays of contemporary life, "Plays presenting particular types of Elizabethan character selected to portray the virtues and follies of English life." In the group of English chronicle plays fall two of Heywood's known plays, the *First* and *Second Parts* of *If You Know Not Me You Know Nobody,* to which may be added the questioned *Edward the Fourth,* likewise a double play. In *Part One* of the former, the poet adheres closely to the simplest form of the chronicle play, that in which the events of history for a definite period or clustering around a certain personage are followed with slight or no deviation from the traditional stories of the chronicles. The troubles of the Princess Elizabeth are presented, not from "the cradle to the crown" as Heywood later describes them in his *England's Elizabeth,* but during the period of her struggle with her sister Mary. Into the scenes of this hastily written play Heywood has infused his patriotism. His loyalty to England has inspired him to picture the faithfulness and devotion of the attendants of Elizabeth—English Elizabeth winning her throne and triumphing over her enemies. The same loyalty to country has influenced him to represent the queen's adversaries in an entirely unsympathetic light.

Part Two of *If You Know Not Me You Know Nobody* departs from the earlier form of the chronicle play to approach the later biographical play. In lighter vein, Heywood has developed a faint plot around the characterization of Sir Thomas Gresham, the lordly London merchant of the sixteenth century. As in *Part One,* the chronicles furnish the source of the action, but from Stowe's bare statements recording Sir Thomas Gresham's benefaction, the gift of the Royal Exchange to the city of London, Heywood has conceived and presented his ideal of English tradesmen. The center of interest in this play is not so much the individual, Sir Thomas Gresham, as the personality representing a class, the English tradesmen, or typifying an idea, English loyalty. Heywood, as will be seen below, incorporated into many of his plays characters and situations clearly designed to impersonate a group, to vivify an idea. Here, however, he has found his model in the facts of history, but history has contributed, not a prevailing background for this setting, but a point of departure for the dominant idea of the play.

Sir Thomas Gresham is the princely merchant. He is characterized by wholesome pride in his business transactions, ambition to succeed in his ventures, alertness in bargaining, care in the details of routine, and constant integrity. As his agent puts it:

> Neither to flatter, nor detract from him.
> He is a Merchant of good estimate;
> Care how to get, and forecast to encrease,
> (If so they be accounted) be his faults.

> I. Y. K. N. M. II (Vol. I, p. 251)

These sound business principles of our merchant have amassed for him an enviable fortune, out of which he generously builds for the merchants of London the Royal Exchange. With the munificence of a fabled potentate he lays the first stone of the edifice with gold; later, when word reaches him that the costly marble statues intended for the house have been lost at sea, he scoffs at the misfortune, hears with indifference the reports of the failure of mercantile ventures, and finally crushes to atoms a pearl worth a king's ransom. "Gresham drinks this pearle unto his Queene and mistresse:" But lest he be misunderstood he adds:

> I doe not this as prodigall of my wealth;
> Rather to show how I esteem that losse
> Which cannot be regain'd. A *London* merchant
> Thus treads on a King's present.
>
> I. Y. K. N. M. II (Vol. I, p. 301)

But the lesson of public spirit becomes too plainly a lesson in a scene presenting Sir Thomas as he passes through the picture gallery of his friend, Doctor Norwell. The intention of building the Exchange has been announced, and now we must listen to a tedious rehearsal of names illustrious in the annals of London's benefactors: "Sir John Lilpot Mayor of London who levied for the city's defence an army of ten thousand soldiers;" "Sir Richard Whittington likewise a mayor but once a mercer's apprentice, who founded well known institutions in London;" and other worthies, men and women, numerous enough in all to enforce the sermon, but crowded into the action at the price of unpardonable dullness of stage business.

The charm of this play has been heightened by the introduction of some lively situations presenting colorful pictures of London shop life. In the warerooms of Hobson, whose trade differs from Sir Thomas' only because it is less pretentious, the apprentices are presented in the activity and bustle of the day's work. Hobson, the master of the shop, one of Heywood's rare "humor" characters, hectors his men, but always good naturedly:

Hob. Where be these varlets? Bones a me, at Tavern?
Knaves, villains, spend goods, foot! my customers
Must either serve themselves, or packe unserved.
Now they peepe like Italian pantelowns,
Behind an arras; but Ile start you, knaves,
I have a shooing-horn to draw on your liquor:
What say you to a peece of a salt-eele?
Come forth, you hang-dogs, Bones a me, the knaves
Fleere in my face, they know me too well.
I talk and prate, and lay't not on their jackes,
And the proud Jacks care not a fig for me;
But bones a me, Ile turne another leafe.

I. Y. K. N. M. II (Vol. I, p. 257)

But the apprentices are not dishonest at heart; they work under the master's eye only to slip out of the shop upon subterfuges when they are alone; master and apprentice are as one when, for instance, the interests of both are apparently threatened through a misunderstanding arising over a customer's bill. This customer leads us to a consideration of Heywood's third characterization of the English tradesman of this play, John Tawnycoat. John Tawnycoat, the gossipy peddler, belongs to the lowest rank of tradesman as Sir Thomas Gresham represents the highest class. Note how at heart both men are the same:

2. Pren. . . . . . How much ware would you have?
Taw. Five pounds worth in such commodities
As I bespoke last night.
1. Pren. They are ready sorted.
Taw. God bless you, Master *Hobson*.
Hob. Bones a me, Knave thou'rt welcome. What's the newes
At bawdy Barnewell, and at Sturbridge Faire?
What, have your London wenches any trading?

I. Y. K. N. M. II (Vol. I, p. 258)

And when the peddler returns to pay his reckoning:

Taw. . . . . . . Come, turn o're your books: I am come to pay
this same ten pound.
1. And we are ready to receive money. What might we call
your name?

Taw. Why, my name is *John Goodfellow.* I hope I am not ashamed of my name.

1. Your kinne are the more beholding unto you. Fellow *Crack,* turn o'er the kalender, and looke for *John Goodfellow.*

2. What comes it to?

Taw. Ten pound.

1. You will have no more wares with you, will you sir?

Taw. Nay, prethee not too fast: let's pay for the old, before we talke of any new.

2. *John Goodfellow?*—Fellow *Nimblechaps,* here's no such name in all our books.

———

Enter old Hobson

Taw. Good morrow to you, sir: have you any more stomacke to receive money than your men have this morning?

* * * * * *

Hob. How, knaves! thinke scorne to receive my money? Bones-a me, growne proud, proud knaves, proud?

1. I hope we know, sir, you do not use to bring up your servants to receive money unless it be due unto you.

Hob. No, bones-a me, knaves, not for a million.

I. Y. K. N. M. II (Vol. I, pp. 283-285)

In fact neither entreaty nor command is of avail until one sharp-eyed apprentice discovers that the peddler's name had been entered as John Tawnycoat not as John Good-fellow. As shrewd, honest merchants, Sir Thomas Gresham, Hobson, and John Tawnycoat are not unlike. Despite differences of wealth and rank naturally to be expected among three men engaged in business occupations varying so markedly in volume, the men themselves are characterized by the same sturdy business integrity, the same pride in their calling, and the same spirit of patriotism. Lingering the longest with us, though, is the bustling Hobson. As the center of his shop, he recalls, of course, Simon Eyre of *The Shoemaker's Holiday* and the Shoemaker of *A Shoemaker a Gentleman.* Heywood is unable to create the inimitable atmosphere of hearty fellowship permeating Dekker's play, or a vigorous tradesman like Rowley's Shoemaker, but Hobson in his scrupulous honesty, his bluster, his good-natured simplicity, is delightful. To the wholesome figures of Heywood's tradesmen we turn with relief from the realism of Middleton:

> Quo. Go make my coarse commodities look sleek;
> With subtle art beguile the honest eye.
> Be near to my trap-window, cunning Falselight.
> Michaelmas Term (I, 1, 86)
> Quo. Gentry is the chief fish we tradesmen catch.
> Michaelmas Term (I, 1, 137)

This treatment of types as exhibited in *If You Know Not Me You Know Nobody (2)* is an elaboration of what Heywood has done in greater or less degree, in all of his plays, that which is a distinctive feature of a number of the plays, dealing with contemporary life. Back of it must be a purpose, displaying itself in these type characters illustrating aspects of English life, and in a vivid coloring used as sympathetic background for these same figures. Although these type figures are inextricably a part of their atmosphere, the emphasis is sometimes directed toward the figures as in Millet's studies, at times upon the background, reminding us of Corot. As a rule, the poet confines the situations to the everyday world about him; once or twice, as in *The Four Prentices of London, The Fair Maid of The West (2),* and *Fortune by Land and Sea,* he goes afield, and in the remoteness of place yields to the opportunity of mingling romance and realism.

The preliminary sketches for Heywood's model tradesmen developed at large in *If You Know Not Me You Know Nobody (2),* appear in the four sons of Godfrey of Bouillon, the four prentices of London, in the play of that name. These youth, titled by birth, become London tradesmen because of exile and reverses in fortune. Heywood has not exhibited them in the humdrum of shop life, but as crusaders rising above the thraldom of their humble calling to display supreme valour upon the battle field. Bearing shields

embossed with the bearings of their trades, the mercers',
grocers', goldsmiths', and haberdashers' arms, they surmount
multifold dangers with courage. This courage, as they put
it, is the distinctive trait of London tradesmen. The
romance of thrilling escapes, fortuitous encounters after
fateful separations, marvelous triumphs against overwhelming odds, is another story. Through the glamour of the
picturesque and the improbable persist two ideals: the fineness of English democracy; the versatility and the prowess
of English tradesmen. Of course the poet's position is
weakened somewhat by the fact that his quasi-apprentices
are really of gentle blood, that they are by birth of the class
that would be expected to exhibit valour on the battlefield.
But in the presentation of these sons of Duke Godfrey of
Boulogne, as in the case of Crispianus of Rowley's play
A Shoemaker a Gentleman, the endowments of birth are
obliterated in the picture of the humble life elected by the
heroes. In the heat of battle, Guy wishes for the aid, not
of French noblemen, but of London apprentices. This idea
of democracy is personified in the conduct of the apprentices,
who, entirely undifferentiated, may be regarded as types. In
this exaltation of trade, Heywood's sincerity has been questioned, and the play has been called a satire. All doubt as
to Heywood's mood and intention are instantly dispelled by
the address "to the Honest and High-spirited Prentices, the
Readers," prefixed to 1615 edition of the play. The words
of commendation in this epistle for the practice of arms,
restored in the Artillery Garden but shortly before the time
of the poet's writing, and his reference to the share taken by
the apprentices in the renewal of a disused custom, indicate
his entire seriousness of mood, and the evident relation in
his mind between this incident and the motive of his play.
Satire could have had no place in his thoughts. Moreover,
he would hardly have dedicated a play in such unequivocal
earnestness to a group that he was holding up to derision.
The absurdity of the situations presented by Heywood in

The Four Prentices of London was satirized by Beaumont in *The Knight of the Burning Pestle.* But as Dr. Murch points out, the ultimate butt of Beaumont's shaft was the reading of mediaeval romances by the Elizabethan middle classes. What we are contending is not that Heywood was justified in ascribing such superlative virtues to his tradesmen and in creating situations bordering on the ridiculous, but that he was entirely serious in the development of an idea. In all probability his audiences at the Fortune and the Red Bull were highly delighted at this Utopian picture of English valour. Here too, as in his emotional dramas, the poet has idealized his characters.

A more artistic production than *The Four Prentices of London* is *The Fair Maid of the West.* This most charming play presents, too, a combination of realism and romanticism. In this instance, the central figure is a woman, a winsome English girl, though a barmaid. She is the personification of the poet's ideal of English girlhood, as she displays her essential soundness of character in a maze of adventures on land and sea. She is English shrewdness, English valour, and English loyalty and patriotism. Unlike *The Four Prentices of London, The Fair Maid of the West,* despite its loose connection between plots, is a spirited play bristling with humorous situations, not at all crude or tiresome. At the beginning of the action we are introduced to the "Fair Maid:"

CARR. . . . .
     Where shall we dine to-day?
2. CAPT. At the next Taverne by; there's the best wine.
1. CAPT. And the best wench, *Besse Bridges,* she's the flowre
     Of *Plimouth* held; the Castle needes no bush,
     Her beauty drawes to them more gallant Customers
     Then all the signes ith' towne else.
2. CAPT. A sweet Lasse
     If I have any judgement.
1. CAPT. Now in troth
     I thinke shee's honest.

CARR. Honest, and live there?
    What in a publike Taverne, where's such confluence
    Of lusty and brave Gallants? Honest said you?
2. CAPT. I vow she is for me.
1. CAPT. For all I think.
    I'm sure she's wondrous modest.
CARR. But withall
    Exceedingly affable
2. CAPT. An argument
    That shee's not proud.
CARR. No, were she proud, she'd fall.
1. CAPT. Well, shee's a most attractive Adamant.
    Her very beauty hath upheld that house,
    And gained her master much.

           F. M. W. I (Vol. II, p. 264)

As the plot develops Bess Bridges is by turns the capable but modest barmaid, the independent mistress of her own inn at Foy, the benefactress of her native town, the owner of a ship that conquers England's enemies upon the seas; withal she is faithful to her beloved Spencer, for is it not in devotion to his memory—she has received word of the supposed death of her lover—that she starts on her romantic voyage? Wholesome English life, hearts loyal and undaunted are fused into the action of this double play captivating the reader from beginning to end. Amidst the whirl of romantic adventure and the matter-of-factness of everyday life the poet has interspersed a scene or two introducing pathos. The news of Spencer's supposed death stuns Bess:

BESSE. Why, as I take it, you told me he was well,
    And shall I not rejoyce?
1. Sail. Hee's well in heaven. For Mistrisse, he is dead.
BESS. Hah, dead! was't so you said? Th'ast given me, friend
    But one wound yet, speake but that word againe,
    And kill me out-right.
2. Sail. He lives not.
BESS. And shall I? Wilt thou breake heart?
    Are these my ribs wrought out of brasse or steele?
    Thou canst not craze their barres?

BESSE. That it should be my fate. Poore, poore sweet-hart
I doe but thinke how thou becomst thy grave,
In which would I lay by thee: what's my wealth
To injoy't without my *Spencer*. I will now
Study to die, that I may live with him.

BESSE. It cannot sure be true
That he is dead, Death could not be so envious
To snatch him in his prime. . . . .

BESSE. To dye, and not vouchsafe some few commends
Before his death, was most unkindly done.

F. M. W. I (Vol. II, pp. 299-302)

But as soon as she learns of Spencer's constancy she is
inspirited to action, "To be a patterne to all Maides."

Besse Bridges and the second Luce of *The Wise Woman
of Hogsdon* possess a charm of their own. The essential
characteristics of Heywood's treatment of the prodigal son
motive have been mentioned. Even as his prodigal sons are
unconventional, so is the second Luce differently conceived.
Faithful she is, but no "patient wife" according to the
pattern. Taking the initiative she follows the errant scapegrace, motivates his unmasking, and though she forgives
him, she lets fall a gentle hint as to what she expects of
him!

2. LUCE. Then I dare confidently undertake to helpe you to a
wife who desires to have an honest man or none,
looke on mee well, simple though I stand heere I
am your wife, blush not at your folly man.

W. W. H. (Vol. V, p. 352)

As dramatic figures Besse Bridges and the second Luce
are superbly vital, but they share with the other heroines,—
Susan Mountford of the sub-plot of *The Woman Killed
with Kindness,* Bella Franca of *The Four Prentices of
London,* and the first Luce of *The Wise Woman of Hogsdon*—the qualities that typify Heywood's charming English
girls. Contrasted with the erring wives, they represent a

finer type of womanhood, preserving their innate modesty in the trying vicissitudes of tavern life and the atmosphere of busy shops. They fit harmoniously into Heywood's pictured world, for of their essential soundness of character the poet never leaves us for a moment in doubt. As counterparts of the upright men, these women, too, are idealized, that is, again the motive of the poet instinctively exalts his characters. Not at all significant is the fact that Bess Bridges, the strongest of the group, is a tavern maid. In the less favored walks of life appears the poet's ideal of English womanhood. This attractive characterization of an humble girl may be considered also an expression of the purpose behind the plays.

These figures showing several sides of middle class life are presented, as a rule, in their own environment. If we except the romantic atmosphere of the mediaeval feats of *The Four Prentices of London,* and the wholly extravagant enterprise which led Bess Bridges into a fantastic world remote from the sober reality of her inn at Foy, Heywood keeps close to England and his own time. As an actor, he appreciated the importance of setting too keenly to neglect the opportunity of using the material at hand. With a minuteness of detail, one of Heywood's distinctive qualities, he has made his plays fairly live in the unstinted coloring of his chosen background. To generalize gives no idea of what is really presented. One must read the plays to appreciate the pervasiveness of this local color: English recreations—card playing, hare hunting, dancing, songs, feasting—and other customs of town and country. At times there seems to be no ulterior purpose beyond the mere desire to furnish adequate setting for the situations; at times again there is plainly evident the intention of awakening interest in class consciousness. Most brilliant in coloring are the type figures making up the background of realistic Elizabethan life. First in importance, because of their occurrence in practically all of the plays, are the household servants and the employees of inns and taverns. The former are invariably presented as faithful loyal servitors, grumbling harmlessly, perhaps, at the hardships of menial work or at the uncertainty of the dispositions of their masters. Blessed with a saving sense of humor, they are never bitter:

> JENKIN .... My Master hath given me a coate here, but he takes paines himselfe to brush it once or twice a day with a holly-wand.
>
> W. K. K. (Vol. II, p. 106)

In the effort, however, to adjust this native humor to the demands of loyalty, Heywood's servants find themselves, on occasions, in difficult but amusing situations. They have the wit always to make hairbreadth escapes into the harbor of safety, furnishing thereby distinctive contributions to the comedy of the plays. One notes also the fullness of treatment given to these lesser characters. The household servants do not pass and repass over the stage as lay figures uninteresting in themselves. Subordinate they certainly are, but they are never completely out of the action. Of highest importance dramatically are the watchful Nicholas of *A Woman Killed with Kindness* and the equally alert Besse of *The English Traveller,* the servants braving chastisement to preserve the honor of their masters. Reignald of the latter play, like his Plautine prototype and his descendant Scapin, is the ubiquitous master of intrigue, but his pranks to deceive the elder Lionel are wholly devoted to the service of the young master of the house. The employees of inns and taverns, the drawers who represent a part of the atmosphere of inns and tavern life, serve rather as elements of a picturesque background than as figures displaying national virtues or vices. Insignificant as social studies, they are presented particularly as a dramatic device. At the same time, they are on and off the stage in such frequent recurrence that one can never forget their presence and, incidentally, their bustle and activity and infectious humor.

Pictures of tavern life include, of necessity, the habitués

of the resorts, the blades of the period enjoying pleasure as
the breath of life. Heywood's idle youths, Carrol of *The
Fair Maid of the West,* Sencer and Harringfield of *The
Wise Woman of Hogsdon,* are also type figures, embryonic
studies they might be called, for Heywood's prodigal sons.
Indeed, it is by the intention of the poet that they are not
vitalized into the active personalities of the former group.
As the prodigal sons do not sink into the utter depths of
degradation, so these fainter patterns do not drain to the
dregs the cup of pleasure. Carrol of *The Fair Maid of the
West,* under the influence of drink, precipitates a quarrel
that leads to bloodshed. In his rash behavior, the grave
consequences of the folly of drink and gambling are depicted.
Similarly, the fray between Sir Charles Mountford and Sir
Frances Acton in *A Woman Killed with Kindness,* though
not a tavern brawl, is the outcome of a quarrel at sport and
is fraught with disaster. (Sir Francis, of course, furnishes
more than atmosphere in his play.) In both instances, the
unfortunate issue assumes its peculiar character by virtue
of the force of social distinctions in rank and the influence
of wealth upon poverty. In both instances the immediate
occasion is the spark of ungovernable temper, unpremeditated
anger fired, as it were, by the touch and go of a sport.
These extreme cases, however, do not represent Heywood's
prevailing mood. The young men scattered through the
plays do not cause suffering or come to grief. Under less
exciting conditions, they exhibit the harmless nature of
frivolity consciously or unconsciously held in bounds.
Withal one gets excellent pictures of one side of Elizabethan
recreations: drinking, gaming, and whiling the time away
in tavern, in the hospitality of friendly home circles, or in
chance meeting places in and about London. Heywood has
created but one bully, one ruffian upon English soil, Roughman, the "miles gloriosus" of *The Fair Maid of the West
(1),* and he, upon being proved the arrant coward of his
type, faces right about and becomes not only the loyal pro-

tector of his intended victim, but lives to show that he really
possesses his boasted courage. At his worst, Roughman
was more bluster than anything else.

A few quotations will best illustrate Heywood's coloring:

BESSE. Your olde Master that dwelt here before my comming,
hath turn'd over your yeares to me.
CLEM. Right forsooth: before he was a Vintner hee was a
shoo-maker, and left two or three turneovers more besides
myselfe.
BESSE. How long has thou to serve.
CLEM. But eleven yeares next grasse, and then I am in hope of
my freedom. For by that time I shall be at ful age.
BESSE. How old art thou now?
CLEM. Forsooth newly come into my Teenes. I have scrap'd
trenchers this two yeares, and the next Vintage I hope to
be a Barre-boy.

F. M. W. I (Vol. II, p. 276)

TAWNYCOAT. Faith, sir our Country Girls are akinne to your
London Courtiers; every month sicke of a new fashion.
The horning busk and silken bridelaces are in good request
with the parsons wife: your huge poking sticke, and French
periwig, with chamber maids and waiting gentlewomen.
Now your Puritans poker is not so huge, but somewhat
longer; a long slender poking sticke is the all with your
Suffolke Puritane. Your silk-band half farthingales, and
changeable fore-parts are common; not a wench of thirteene
but weares a changeable fore-part.

Besides, sir, many of our young married men, have tane an
order to weare yellow garters, points, and shootyings; and
tis thought yellow will grow a custome.
HOBSON. 'Tas been us'de long at London.

I. Y. K. N. M. II (Vol. I, pp. 258-259)

JENKIN. No quarrelling for Gods sake: truly if you doe, I
shall set a knave betweene ye.
SLIME. I come to dance, not to quarrell: come, what shall it
be? *Rogero?*
JEN. Rogero, no; we will dance the beginning of the world.
SISLY. I love no Dance so well, as *John come kisse mee now*.

NIC.   I that have ere now deserv'd a cushion, call for the
        cushion dance.

ROGER.   For my part I like nothing so wel as *Tom Tyler.*

JENK.   No wee'l have the hunting of the Fox.

SLIME.   The Hay, the hay, there's nothing like the hay.

NICK.   I have saide, I do say, and I will say againe.

JEN.   Every man agree to have it as Nicke sayes.

ALL.   Content.

NICK.   It hath bene, it now is, and it shall be.

SISLY.   What Master Nichlas, what?

NIC.   Put on your smocke a Monday.

JEN.   So the dance will come cleanly off: come, for Gods
        sake agree of something; if you like not that, put it to the
        Musitians, or let me speake for all, and wee'l have Sellengers
        round.

ALL.   That, that, that.

                              W. K. K. (Vol. II, pp. 97-98)

WISEWOMAN.   Fie, fie, what a toyle and a moyle it is,
        For a woman to bee wiser than all her neighbors?
        I pray good people, presse not too fast upon me;
        Though I have two eares, I can heare but one at once.

        Ey I warrant you, I thinke I can see as farre into a
Mill-stone as another: you have heard of Mother *Notting-*
ham, who for her time, was prettily well skill'd in casting
of Waters; and after her, Mother *Bombye;* and then there
is one *Hatfield* in Pepper Alley, hee doth prettie well for a
thing that's lost. There's another in *Coleharbour,* that's
skill'd in the Planets. Mother *Suttron* in *Goulden-lane* is
for Forespeaking. Mother *Phillips* of the *Banke-side* for
the weaknesse of the backe: and then there's a very reverent
Matron on *Clerkenwell Green,* good at many things: Mistris
Mary on the *Banke-side* is for recting a Figure: and one
(what doe you call her) in *Westminster,* that practiseth the
Books and the Key, and the Sive and the Sheares: and all
doe well, according to their talent. For myselfe, let the
world speake: harke you my friend, you shall take—(shee
whispers)   ------------

WISEWOM. You are welcome Gentlewoman.—

WOM.   I would not have it known to my Neighbors that I
        come to a Wise-woman for anything, by my truly.

WISEWOM. For should your Husband come and find you here.
WOM.   My Husband woman, I am a Widdow.
WISEWOM. Where are my brains? tis true, you are a Widdow;
    and you dwell, let me see, I can never remember that place.
WOM.   In *Kentstreet.*
WISEWOM. Kentstreet, Kentstreet! and I can tell you wherfore
    you come. . . . .
                        W. W. H. (Vol. V, pp. 291-293)

Other striking instances of Heywood's use of realistic
setting are the popular hawking scene and the card game
in *A Woman Killed with Kindness,* Delavil's discourse of
markets in *The English Traveller* and the dialogue between
Robin and Reignald in the same play, the gossip of court
life in *The Royal King and Loyal Subject* and *A Challenge
for Beauty,* the inn scenes in *The Fair Maid of the West*
and *The Wise Woman of Hogsdon,* not to mention shorter
passages of a line or two occurring on almost every page of
the plays. The poet's treatment of contemporary incident
ranges from the infrequently occurring topical allusions
in his purely romantic plays—note the patches of color in
A Maidenhead Well Lost, A Challenge for Beauty, and *The
Royal King and Loyal Subject*—to the constant background
of pictures of Elizabethan manners forming the warp and
woof of the realistic plays. From references to places and
the forcing in of superficial incidents, it becomes a portrayal
of customs of social conditions revealing the very soul of
life itself. Because of Heywood's faith in the virtues of
Englishmen, he does not see the cony catchers, the sharpers,
the unscrupulous Londoners that delighted Middleton;
wholly direct by nature and not possessed of the imagination
of a great poet, he lacks the contagious humor and scintil-
lating wit of Ben Jonson; spread over such a huge canvas
his coloring seems pale beside Dekker's brilliancy. What
satisfies the lover of Heywood, though, is the fact that the
poet, living for so many years in an environment made up
of all types of humanity, could deliberately, consistently, and
continuously write, in the main, of the better side of life.

This consecration to an ideal becomes the more strongly apparent as one contrasts Heywood's work with what was being produced about him. Omitting Shakespeare—and Lamb had in mind Shakespeare's attitude toward life rather than the achievement of his dramatic art when he compared Heywood to the Master[7]—no other dramatist, writing in the first part of the seventeenth century seemed to dwell as far above the ugly spots of life. If Heywood's pictures are distorted, the slant leans in the direction of virtue, his idealizations turning his realism into sentimentalism.

In his sympathy, Heywood is nearest Dekker, but we miss the charm of Dekker's spontaneous humor and innate liveliness. From Dekker, Middleton, Chapman, and Jonson, he is different in that he seems more absorbed in class consciousness. Note in the plays Heywood's direct complaints about social conditions, especially those involving injustice as the result of the spirit of caste. The fray at the hunting party in *A Woman Killed with Kindness* arises over a dispute in regard to hawks. Sir Francis in the eyes of all is the aggressor; however, Sir Charles is aware of the grave consequences he will have to bear in that, as his sister Susan says:

"Sir *Francis* hath great friends,"

W. K. K. (Vol. II, p. 101)

This expression of feeling against social injustice seems the result of conscious reflection. It is the poet's attitude toward one of the problems of his time. In these instances the dramatic situation is the result of a social complexity which differs from the others that come under observation not alone in the intensity of the suffering in its wake, but in that the responsibility for this suffering is in a system and not in the error of the individual.

From Heywood's selection of subjects and his attitude

[7] *The Dramatic Essays of Charles Lamb.* Edited with an introduction and notes by Brander Matthews, 1891, p. 208.

toward the representation of certain phases of Elizabethan
life, we see that his was a broadly sympathetic nature. But,
in spite of the trend of his sympathies and the fact that the
imagination of the poet colors all, it is borne in upon us that
the plays as social studies in lighter vein are evolved from an
idea, a conviction expressive of Heywood's theory of life.
In the main we must be content to gather this theory from
the general principle upon which, we believe, Heywood
worked as he wrote. The most careful study of the plays,
though, does not bring to light such depth of speculative
thought as one finds in Hamlet's soliloquies or the medita-
tions of Jacques. From a poet of Heywood's rank that
is scarcely to be expected. Nevertheless, scattered here and
there throughout the plays are lines reflecting a credo that
is wholly unambiguous. How far this philosophy represents
original thinking would be difficult to prove; what we do
know is that the expressed thoughts recurring again and
again were evidently the poet's accepted beliefs. As crisp
sententious utterances, they might easily pass into the saws
of the language, but they are woven firmly into the context
and impress us always as the spontaneous words of sincere
conviction. In general the tone is that of one, who, in facing
the perplexities of life, seeks to preserve a carefully adjusted
balance. We are spared the extremes of morose, bitter
cynicism on the one hand, and the fatuity of complete satisfaction with men and things on the other. But if Heywood
is not gloomy, he is inclined to dwell upon the darker rather
than the brighter side of the picture. Optimism is not banished from his kingdom. As he puts it:

> "At the lowest ebbe
> The tides still flow; besides being on the ground,
> Lower we cannot fall."
>
> F. M. W. II (Vol. II, p. 388)

Note however the tinge of stoicism at the end. Against
this rarely expressed hopefulness, there is the more usual
insistence upon the untoward conditions that confront even

though they may not overwhelm us. First, there is the calm acceptance of worldly selfishness: "This is no world in which to pity men." W. K. K. (Vol. II, p. 125.) "Each man for himself." W. K. K. (Vol. II, p. 126.) "Rich flyethe poore as good men shun the devill." "When the rough hand of want Hath cast us downe, it loads us with mishaps." I. Y. K. N. M. II (Vol. I, p. 303.) But the responsibility for the suffering, meted out to the poor and less favored, is not placed at the hands of the world alone. Heywood bows to a fate which predestines and governs all—"Some men are borne to mirth, and some to sorrow." W. K. K. (Vol. II, p. 125.) And in his contemplation of this controlling power he sees its fullest force in the swift and sure approach of death. We might say that his consciousness of the final end awaiting us is never asleep. He is not, however, oppressed by the fear of death, for "Death doth not fear the good man but the ill." I. Y. K. N. M. II (Vol. I, p. 292.) It is, first, the inevitableness of death and then death as the solace. Naturally, he likes to muse upon the transiency of this world:

> "Indeed, the end of all things must end
> Honour and riches all must have an end;
> And he that thinks, he doth the most prevaile,
> His head once laid, there resteth but a tale."
>
> E. F. II (Vol. I, p. 55)

"Death is the end of all calamity." W. K. K. (Vol. II, p. 128), "All things that have beginnings have their ends." I. Y. K. N. M. II (Vol. I, p. 266.) In this vein, he contemplates the end of man's finite existence. In this thought, too, he finds comfort, for although there is little said about life beyond the grave, the end that is heralded is the finality of suffering, disappointment, pain.

To Heywood the theme of *The Royal King and the Loyal Subject* must have been especially attractive. This fidelity to a beloved master is the mainspring of the important rôles of Nicholas in *A Woman Killed with Kindness*, and

Besse in *The English Traveller.* As for the loyalty of friendship, the sheer joy of friendship itself, nothing in life he
finds more comforting. "Time's now not lost that's spent
to make men friends." I. Y. K. N. M. II (Vol. I, p. 263),
"Friendship can more with me than rude constraint," F. P.
L. (Vol. II, p. 188), are more than empty words with Heywood. While no one of the plays is an apotheosis of friendship, there is no one play but contains Heywood's tribute to
the virtue underlying the ties that bind men together in
happiness. But the faithfulness that makes friendship possible is only another expression of the supreme human
virtue—truth. Recalling the *Apology for Actors,* and the
Hierarchie, one likes to remember that love of truth is the
basic principle of Heywood's ethical teaching. So also in the
plays it is the deviation from truth, the false action that fires
the train of suffering. Even in his lightest, his most frivolous mood, Heywood cannot utterly divest himself of
this accustomed way of thinking. As Gratiana says, "A
smooth and square behavior likes mee most." W. W. H.
(Vol. V, p. 301.)   And again "Either speake true or do not
speake at all." F. P. L. (Vol. II, p. 180), "Honor scornes
to lye." F. P. L. (Vol. II, p. 178.)

> "Truth's à word
> That should in every language relish well,
> Nor have I that exceeded."
>   E. T. (Vol. IV, pp. 10-11)

These words, short passages at most, taken separately would
be insignificant, perhaps mere platitudes. As part of the
context they are convincing of the entire sincerity of the
poet in his exaltation of truth.

We have said that Heywood's reflections constitute no
elaborate system of thought. His philosophy, as far as the
term can be applied to the expressed thought of the plays,
is confined to the simple, straightforward, unambiguous
utterances upon the questions underlying man's relation to
man and the immediate problems of existence. For these

problems there is but one solution: unfaltering truth, entire sincerity, and reliance in self. He sees the selfishness of the world which he cannot absolutely reject, but though he voices little faith in the disinterestedness of men, he is rarely bitter. Undoubtedly he lacks breadth of vision, the broadly comprehensive view of life, but he sees the complexity of life's problems and the many-sidedness of humanity; then too, the very brevity of his words—mere conclusions as it were—causes the hearer to feel that he has missed something. The poet does not carry us with him as he works out his theories. We are robbed of the processes of thinking, of everything except the bare statement of the conclusion. This meagerness as to detail, this absence of so much that contributes to the richness of thought, is accounted for, perhaps, in the nature of his themes and in his conception of the play as the embodiment of action.

Considering, then, Heywood's realism, one may summarize as follows: A certain group of his plays may be described, from the point of view of theme, as representations of the life of the times, studies of emotional problems and pictures of social customs and habits. The characters are drawn from the London trading class and the English country gentry, principally from the middle class, which he respected and in which many of his associations were made. In his graver mood, he has presented the erring wife and the arbitrary parent. These men and women, endowed with natures that are stirred by the same influences affecting people of greater wealth and more exalted rank, resent the lash of injustice and they suffer the pangs of remorse. The best of them are distinctively fine in their innate goodness and strength; the worst are never incorrigibly vicious. In general, they are types, not individuals, but they reveal the emotions of human nature rather than artificial passions arbitrarily assigned to a class. In another mood, Heywood exhibits the lighter, almost frivolous side of life; at these times emotional depth or intensity, "high seriousness," is replaced by the spirit of mischief, wantonness, shallow sport, harmless play. Between the extremes, appear other figures, evidently from their perennial recurrence in Heywood's plays the characters he loved most to draw. Less interesting dramatically than either of the other types—the men and women whose feelings are harassed under the strain of domestic problems and those who create merriment by their frivolity or mischief—this group seems to be closer to reality. Here are the Englishmen of everyday life presented in normal occupations under highly favorable though not artificial conditions. It will be conceded that lights and shadows are thrown at will upon these figures passing and repassing over Heywood's stage: the London apprentice and the master merchant, the inn drawer and the tavern maid, the peasant and the soldier of fortune. Because perspective, however, seems true, caricature, as a consequence, is lacking. Indeed, it is Heywood's sympathetic attitude toward the life he portrays, in other words his almost entire freedom from satire, that accounts for the attractive pictures that he has left us. And the prevalence of this attitude suggests its source in a fixed design: namely, our poet's desire to reveal his faith in man's better nature. This conclusion is naturally strengthened by what is inferred of Heywood's own life and personality as mirrored in his more serious writings. The insistent emphasis upon nobler ideals proves of itself the staunch belief in the sturdy virtues of man. In Heywood's case it must be interpreted as faith in Englishmen. In the plays presenting English types in an English setting, the poet, as it were, lets himself go in the exaltation of English ideals, English virtues, and England itself. In this patriotism on the one hand and his expressed theory as to the purpose of the drama, on the other—Heywood reveals clearly his position. He exhibits contemporary manners not to promote the teaching of ethics in its restricted sense, but to awaken interest in the life of the middle class and to arouse, incidentally, the virtue of human sympathy.

Under varying conditions, in different types of plot and character, he has presented the life of his time; but he is always influenced, consciously or unconsciously, by his double motive. This becomes increasingly obvious as one studies the plays more closely. The balance in this double intention, however, is so completely preserved, that one rarely suspects cudgelling; nevertheless, it is evident that the poet's portrayal of Elizabethan life is so constant as to suggest this ulterior motive. In actual practice, then, the instruction transcends a narrowed ethical purpose to embrace the broader social aim.

The satire of *The Wise Woman of Hogsdon* constitutes a notable exception to Heywood's directness of method. In this play, the butt of ridicule is the credulity and superstition of simple-minded folk, the consistent humor of the situations being maintained as an intellectual triumph for the imposter. The continued prosperity of the "wisemen" and "wisewomen" in and about London offered an opportunity of irresistible appeal. In the last analysis, Heywood's selection of this theme proves his entire fairness and preserves a sane balance in his realism.

Among his contemporaries, who were alike absorbed in portraying the life about them, Heywood is distinctive for the genuine kindliness of his attitude, a tendency falling often into the error of idealizing unto exaggeration the virtues of a class. It is this frank simplicity of mood, regardless of differences in poetic reach or power of dramatic technique, which makes it impossible to mistake the intention of Heywood for that of Chapman, Middleton, or Ben Jonson. Heywood's realism is a sympathetic portrayal of the life he presents; where he assumes judgment, the decision is, in the main, based upon a moral issue. When this sympathy leads him into idealization of his characters, as is frequently the case, his plays become tinged with sentimentalism. Between Dekker and Heywood the distinction is less striking; but though the volatile Dekker is the greater

dramatic genius, Heywood, influenced by his underlying
purpose, brings to his writings an ingenuous appeal, at times
humorous, at times pathetic. The supreme merit of his
charm is its pervasive sincerity. This virtue, disarming
criticism, becomes a quality of enduring force.

CHAPTER IV

HEYWOOD'S TECHNIQUE

Heywood's "men and women," his "Elizabethan life," may be illuminating indications of his breadth of vision and his simple faith in humanity, or they may be true reflections of the passing show of the times, but a complete appreciation of the poet's dramatic art involves a study of his formal technique as well as an analysis of his themes. This other half of our discussion seems rather pertinent because we are forced to admit that in spite of the attractive wholesomeness of Heywood's own personality and the nature of his subjects, his plays are not widely read. An inquiry, then, into the elements of the poet's style may reveal peculiarities accounting for this lack of general appeal, which Heywood's most enthusiastic admirers cannot deny.

In bare outlines of structure, Heywood's plots may be classified roughly in two principal groups: (1) Epical. The action in these plots is made up loosely of detached episodes connected, internally, by a character or characters appearing in two or more episodes, and, externally, by a chorus. (2) More regularly dramatic. The action consists of (a) a single main plot supported by subsidiary plot or enlivened by episodes, or (b) double plots connected only superficially. In the latter subdivision the greater number of the plays falls. As extremes of consistent looseness of structure in the connection of simple, unrelated elements into a continued action are the *Ages* and *The Four Prentices of London*. Considering *The Four Prentices of London*, we find that the action is a series of episodes diverging from a common motivation presented in the opening scene of the play. This initial impulse is Godfrey's intention to go to the Holy Land. Following this, a "presenter" forecasts the trend of events:

PRE. Thus have you seene these brothers shipt to Sea,
Bound on their voyage to the holy Land,
All bent to try their fortunes in one Barke.

. . . . .

Imagine now yee see the aire made thicke
With stormy tempests, that disturbe the Maine,
And the foure windes at warre among themselves.
And the weake Barkes wherein the brothers saile,
Split on strange rockes, and they enforc't to swim:
To save their desperate lives: when what befell them
Disperst to severall corners of the world,
We will make bold to explaine it in dumbe Show:
For from their fortunes all our Scene must grow.

F. P. L. (Vol. II, pp. 175-176)

According to promise the dumb show does reveal the separation of the heroes. Then the play ambles along, as each brother is in turn the center of vicissitudes remarkable for improbability but barely distinguishable one from another. Toward the close of the action, the divided elements are joined by miraculous meetings, after which mutual recognitions and feats of prowess mark the successful end of the adventure. Plot as such is entirely lacking, the appeal lying in the liveliness of movement within the scene and the presentation of familiar figures of London life in the alluring halo of mediaeval romance.

A step further in the development of this kind of structure is *Part Two* of *If You Know Not Me You Know Nobody.* (*Part One,* though a unified whole, is a crude draft, a rough sketch of scenes following faithfully the chronicles and connected by interposed dumb shows.) In *Part Two* the main episode, supported by minor episodes, is centered in the exaltation of the character of Sir Thomas Gresham, the princely merchant, but the plot as such is concluded at the end of the fourth act. After the gap is bridged between Acts IV and V by a chorus, matter entirely unrelated in spirit to the earlier action is added. An attempt to effect an integral connection between the two elements of the action

is produced in the closing scenes of Act IV by the appearance
of the Queen to christen Sir Thomas' gift to the city.
What marks the advance in technique of *If You Know Not
Me You Know Nobody (2)* over *The Four Prentices of
London* is the single line of development in the Gresham
action and the dependence of the minor episodes upon this
central theme. It is true that these minor episodes, as
episodes, develop their own interest, principally the events
surrounding Jack Gresham's escapades in Paris and Hobson's ridiculous journey across the channel; nevertheless
their subordinate relation is consistently maintained. In
contrast to this method of grouping of incidents the earlier
play presents the adventures of the four brothers as of
parallel importance. As yet, however, there is no evidence
of complication, nor of the rise of action to a climax followed by a fall. Moreover, the appended fifth act is simply
an isolated fragment.

Part Two of *The Fair Maid of the West* illustrates the
highest point of development in Heywood's epical plots. It
is divided into a play (Acts I, II, and III) and an episode
(Acts IV and V). In the first action, the principal characters Besse and Spencer pass through harassing experiences
while guests at the Court of Mullisheg of Morocco and his
wife Tota. Here the plot involves the frustrated attempts
of the rulers, each ignorant of the scheme of the other, to
destroy the happiness of the young strangers. In detail, the
events are: the presentation of the two schemes; the devised
counterplot to be undertaken by Goodlack and Roughman,
the faithful attendants of the strangers; the success of the
first steps in the counterplot; the unlucky accident introducing the complication which sustains suspense in the falling action; and the catastrophe. Condensed into three acts
are all the elements of a complete play, except the introduction, naturally supplied in *Part One;* the exciting forces,
namely the desires of the king and queen, put into action
the unwilling agents, Goodlack and Roughman; when the

two agents compare notes, motivation for the counterplot is furnished; this in turn effects the climax of the main action; in Spencer's apprehension by Joffer, complication enters and the arrested falling action is held in suspense over almost all of the third act; the reappearance of the strangers at court, however, averts the king's wrath and the play ends in the happiness of all, but in the complete defeat of the initial action. To eke out the conventional length of the play, Heywood interposes the Chorus to narrate further adventures befalling the lovers before they undergo their final trials on their way to England, and then he adds the episode. In point of dramatic appeal Acts IV and V are far below Acts I, II, III. Interest is maintained at the expense of probability and some humor is produced by the clown, but in the conception of the fundamental plan there is a distinct falling off in power. The only integral connection between these two elements of the play are one group of principal characters and their attendants and the harmonious tone of the course of events. Different are the scenes of action, the characters that form the opposition, and the structure. The superiority of Acts I, II, III over Acts IV, V is, however, more than a relative matter between the two parts of one play. It places the play as a whole far in advance of *The Four Prentices of London,* and *If You Know Not Me You Know Nobody,* and indicates Heywood's mastery of the fundamental essentials of the technique of the single plot. What one regrets here is the poet's inability or disinclination to sustain in Acts IV and V the constructive skill exhibited in Acts I, II, and III or to develop the whole into a unified plot.

As we have seen, the plays in which Heywood has used the Chorus are *The Four Prentices of London, If You Know Not Me You Know Nobody, The Golden Age, The Silver Age, The Brazen Age* and *The Fair Maid of the West.* The early dates of *The Four Prentices of London* and *If You Know Not Me You Know Nobody* have been considered. The *Ages* were written in part, perhaps, before 1600.[1] Notwithstanding Heywood's consistent indifference to the demands of plot construction, he did discard the chorus, at least, after these early plays.

The preference for the technically unrelated double plots appears in practically all of Heywood's plays. *A Woman Killed with Kindness, The English Traveller, The Captives, A Challenge for Beauty,* and *The Royal King and the Loyal Subject* are characteristic of Heywood's method; while *The Fair Maid of the West (1), Love's Mistress, The Rape of Lucrece, The Wise Woman of Hogsdon,* and *A Maidenhead Well Lost* are modifications of the general plan. The essential difference between the epical plots and the plots of the plays just mentioned is that in the former group the action of the play is composed of a number of successive units, each being completed before another is added; in the latter group there are two distinct plots, principal and subordinate, running as a rule in alternate scenes throughout the play. These two plots connect superficially in one or two scenes at the beginning and at the end of the double action, thus:

Each of the two plots of *A Woman Killed with Kindness* develops independently of the other except for one or two points of superficial contact: all of the characters except Wendoll appear in the ensembles at the beginning and the

[1] *Supra,* p. 14.
   *   — — — Main plot.   — — — Sub-plot.

end of the play; the news of the disaster at the hunting match, the first stage of the action of the sub-plot, is brought to the principals of the main plot; and Anne Frankford is sister to Sir Francis Acton. The first connection of the two plots of *The English Traveller* occurs in Act II, Sc. I. by the Clown's bringing word to the Wincott home of the revelling in the Lionel home, but barring this wholly irrelevant link, the two plots do not touch until the end of the play. In tone Heywood's main plots are usually more serious than the sub-plots. This contrast is, however, not always strongly marked; despite its happy conclusion, the sub-plot of *A Woman Killed with Kindness* is close to tragedy. The essential completeness of each plot in itself indicates nothing so clearly as this, that the defect of the structure as a whole lies in the absence of integral connections between principal and secondary actions rather than in an inherent inability upon the part of the dramatist to appreciate the interrelation of the elements of the simple plot. *The Fair Maid of the West (1), The Wise Woman of Hogsdon, The Rape of Lucrece, Love's Mistress,* and *A Maidenhead Well Lost* from the point of view of structure may not be grouped with the plays characterized by epical plots or with those presenting the technically unrelated double plots. These five plays, representing a minority of the twenty-four, do not all display the uniformly excellent plot construction of *The Wise Woman of Hogsdon*. The harmony of *The Rape of Lucrece* is jarred by the incongruous tone of the interspersed songs and low comedy, and the extraneous elements do not, of themselves, make a sub-plot. The dialogue of Midas and Apuleius in *Love's Mistress* constitutes a superfluous Chorus, there being no wide gaps between the elements of action. In this play Heywood has introduced the Chorus, thinking perhaps to add to a play based upon a mythological theme an element of classical drama. Heywood's supreme reach in plot construction is attained in *The Wise Woman of Hogsdon,* a comedy of intrigue. The strongly motivated situations, at times completely involved, are brought to a focus in the last act by the central figure, the pivot of the action throughout the play. By the wit of one personality the threads of action are twisted into what looks like a hopeless maze, and then by the same force they are set straight again. At moments the unity is threatened, as in the Sir Boniface-Sencer scenes, but these elements are made to function integrally in the whole. Most of all, the sustained harmony of tone, the persistent humor, and the recurring appearance of the centralizing force, produce an unquestioned unity of effect.

Unfortunately such masterful skill is not Heywood's consistent practice. In this matter of technique our poet falls below his fellow dramatists who were attracted to the presentation of contemporary life. Leaving out of consideration the technique of Jonson and Middleton, one sees in the minor playwrights nothing exactly in Heywood's manner. Dekker atones for his looseness of structure, first, by the harmonious atmosphere of the play and, then, by the vigor of his characterization and the charm of his poetry. In *The Shoemaker a Gentleman* Rowley throws into juxtaposition a saint's legend of early Britain, the romance of a king's son in the disguise of a shoemaker wooing a princess, and the realism of the everyday life of busy tradesmen, but the disparate elements join more compactly than the actions of Heywood's best plays. By way of exception Chapman, as Professor Parrott shows,[2] displays in *Monsieur d'Olive* a mechanical connection only between the romantic main plot and the comic sub-plot of that play.

In the rapid development of Heywood's plots, there is little complication; what there is appears, as a rule, in the fortuitous intervention of external events; rarely is it caused by the clash of contending emotions or will. As would be

[2] *Chapman's All Fools and Gentleman Usher.* Belles-Lettres ed., 1907, p. XXV.

expected, the dramas of domestic problems tend to present complication arising out of subjective struggle; the other plays of contemporary realism exhibit action arrested by accidental circumstances. In neither case, however, is complication a strong element. Similarly, motivation with Heywood is slight. As a result, the effect is surprise; often, however, explanations follow. Shafton's first words in *A Woman Killed with Kindness* are

> Sir Charles, a hand, a hand, at liberty:
> Now by the faith I owe I am glad to see it.
> What want you? Wherein may I pleasure you?
>
> . . . .
>
> To rid you from these contemplations,
> Three hundred pounds you shall receive of me:
> Nay five for faile: Come sir, the sight of Golde
> Is the most sweet receit for melancholy,
> And will revive your spirits.
>
> W. K. K. (Vol. II, p. 107)

His aside a few moments later accounts in part for the unexpected generosity but hardly justifies the vindictiveness of the scheme he has in mind. Heywood's disregard of the technical principles governing the motivation of action has caused him in one or two instances to be indifferent to the natural course of human events. Not to mention the improbabilities of *The Four Prentices of London* and *The Fair Maid of the West,* pardonable, perhaps, as the extravagances of the purely romantic background, Heywood's realism is distorted by the strained effects forced into the atmosphere of everyday life. The convenient deaths of Mrs. Wincott and Mrs. Frankford, the absurd relation between Geraldine and Mrs. Wincott, and the straits in which Tawnycoat found himself toward the end of *If You Know Not Me You Know Nobody* are instances in point.

Despite these limitations in the structure of the whole and in some of the minor details of development, Heywood's plays evidently played well. Being of the theatre for such a long and uninterrupted period, our poet, writing evidently for the moment, stressed that which could be made most effective at a minimum expenditure of time and effort. Consequently Heywood excels in the structure of scenes, situations, episodes. This perfection, relatively speaking, of the single element may explain the power enabling the poet to produce a play of two plots complete and well-balanced in themselves but devoid of logical coherence. Be that as it may, the situations are vigorous, compelling in interest, marked by variety of charm, and enlivened with stage business. The frequency of the entrances and exits of characters in the shifting changes of grouping produces an activity approaching bustle and thus avoids tedium. Classified as to composition there is the conventional majority of dialogue scenes except in *The Four Prentices of London,* a play presenting a heavy proportion of ensembles, soliloquies, and, occasionally, an aside.

Heywood's soliloquies, ranging from couplets to the longer speeches of thirty and forty lines, are rarely the expression of subjective struggle or the voice of pent up emotions. The exceptions are the notable lines spoken by Master Frankford and young Geraldine, the significant examples of Heywood's highest achievement in characterization and expression of emotion. Essentially inferior in every way is the soliloquy of Wendoll, the revelation of his brief struggle just before he induces Mrs. Frankford to her fatal guilt. The usual course, however, with Heywood is the shorter situation soliloquy, the few lines spoken at the beginning or the end of a scene forecasting or concluding in summary a course of action, commenting upon situation or character, explaining personal feelings, or philosophizing upon human affairs. As often as not the speeches are in buoyant mood, employed mainly as a diverting Chorus, with this distinction that the speakers are selected at will from the characters. Heywood does not use Ben Jonson's differentiated "demon-

strator,"[3] the spectator commenting objectively upon the
passing show, but taking no active participation in the sweep
of movement.   In Act I of *The English Traveller* the Clown
delivers a short monologue, which, in its humorous philosophy, echoes the dominant strain of the scene just concluded. Further functioning is lacking. In the next scene
of the same act young Lionel delivers the exceedingly long
moral discourse upon the downward path of youth. Serving,
however, as an index of Lionel's character and as an introduction to the action of the sub-plot, this monologue, though
tedious, is a compact part of the movement. So also is
Reignald's first monologue, the exposition of his determined
course of action for the assistance of the young master of
the house:

> And yet something prompts me,
> Ile stand it at all dangers; and to recompence
> The many wrongs unto the yong man done:
> Now, if I can doubly delude the old,
> My braine, about it then; All's husht within,
> The noise that shall be, I must make without;
> And he that part for gaine, and part for wit,
> So farre hath travell'd, strive to foole at home:
> Which to effect, Art must with Knavery joyne,
> And smooth Dissembling meet with Impudence;
> Ile doe my best, and howsoere it proove,
> My praise or shame, 'tis but a servants love.
>
> E. T. (Vol. IV, p. 37)

This not only states purpose but gives more than a hint of
the devious path of escape to be followed by the culprits.
Later in the same play, when young Geraldine has learned
from the faithful Besse the unwelcome news of Mrs. Wincott's frailty, he falls into a soliloquy revealing his mental
uncertainty at the moment and the triumph of his belief
in the loyalty of his idol. The transitory nature of the

---

[3] *Studies in Jonson's Comedies.* By Elisabeth Woodbridge, 1898,
p. 32.

mental struggle barely differentiates this soliloquy in type
from the preceding ones; it forms a step in the approach
to Geraldine's master soliloquies in the fourth act: the debate
with himself as to whether or not he will heed Wincott's
note summoning him to an interview; and his struggle as
to his course of action after he discovers the undeniable
evidence of Mrs. Wincott's guilt.   The other soliloquies in
The English Traveller, and there are a good half dozen more,
revert to the type appearing in the first half of the play,
undramatic in development, mere confidences with the
spectator as to what has already been presented in action,
or what will be shortly seen.   In the pure comedies there is
practically no deviation at all from this type of soliloquy.

In contrast to the soliloquy are, of course, the dialogue
groups and the ensembles.   The ensemble is used by Heywood with marked frequency.   In the serious plays it is
more persistent in the sub-plot than in the main plot, where,
used as relief, it furnishes much local color.   In the pure
comedies, the method varies.   Mass scenes will alternate
more or less regularly with two- or three-part dialogues
throughout the play.   In *If You Know Not Me You Know
Nobody (2)* this plan has been followed, consciously or not
on the part of the poet.   In *The Fair Maid of the West (2),*
the first three acts are two- and three-part dialogues with an
occasional ensemble or soliloquy, while the fourth act is
practically all ensemble, and the fifth act more than half
ensemble.   In *The Four Prentices of London,* the court
scenes in *The Fair Maid of the West,* the last act of *If You
Know Not Me You Know Nobody (2)* and in the other
plays infrequently, there is massing for the background while
the dialogue is maintained by two or three individuals in
the center of interest.   As the utmost reach in mass scenes
is the grouping of huge numbers in *The Four Prentices of
London.*   Here, the incidents of the formless action, the
adventures of bandits and the encounters of battle, demand
ensembles in order that a faint semblance of reality may be

produced. So too, in the other plays, Heywood is influenced more by the actual exigencies of the plot than by the lure of spectacular background chosen for its own sake. The life pictured in these plays is ever near "the busy hum of men"; in tradesman's shops, inns and taverns, and manor houses; in a bustling suburb like Hoxton and the meeting places resorted to by merchants and young gallants, where there would naturally be the intercourse of men in great numbers. Accordingly the mass scenes are not forced. On the other hand Heywood has not been blind to the dramatic possibilities of his selected material. To present the atmosphere of English middle class life, or rather to portray typical scenes from middle class life, numbers of characters have been necessary; then, the activity and bustle of the concourse of people have contributed to the vitality of the scene, to the effectiveness of the presentation. Just as, in the use of soliloquy, Heywood is found to show preference for the soliloquy which simply records, as it were, the progress of action or announces predetermined plan, so the dialogue scenes also are almost regularly situation dialogues, designed for the play alone. The spirit of the words of the prologue to *The English Traveller* protesting against the inflation of plays by the interpolation of song, dance, dumb shows and the trappings of combats and masque would seem to exclude everything that the bare necessity of the plot does not demand. The sub-plot of this same play, adhering closely to the original of Plautus, is a succession of superlatively lively incidents, but every scene functions in the whole. It is in the more serious parts of the plays, however, that Heywood's mastery of the related situation is apparent. The card scene in *A Woman Killed with Kindness,* the final court scene in *The Fair Maid of the West (2),* situations forming a part of the warp and woof of the action, reveal the poet's indisputable skill in craftsmanship; the scene in *A Woman Killed with Kindness,* in which Mrs. Frankford is confronted with her guilt, as well as the parallel scene in *The English Traveller,* shows also strength and fineness of feeling. In the latter instances Heywood has attained a high dramatic reach, although it must be confessed that the familiarity of a repeated scene robs the situation of the charm of freshness and betrays the playwright's proneness to incorporate into late plays popular parts of the earlier plays. Such scenes, unfortunately, which display opposing forces in interaction leading to a climax and fall marked by the triumph of one side over the other, are only too few. With rare exceptions, there is the sudden capitulation, the absolute surrender before the spectator has a chance to enjoy the exhibition of the play and counterplay of opposing forces. This does not mean that Heywood's dialogue scenes are without animation or charm. Complication is not entirely lacking, only tension is rarely at the straining point. The appeal is in the novelty, the pathos, the humor. The unit is presented with simplicity and directness; even when there is an entangled knot of threads, the effect is never blurred. In mood, the range is from boisterous merriment to utter seriousness. Alive scenes they are, bespeaking Heywood's mastery of the vital situation and one other thing, his versatility; he displays the power to use any one of the devices of stagecraft in creating an inherently interesting incident and he appreciates the dramatic appeal of the commonplace factors of contemporary life.

In spite of this noticeable ability to conceive and present situations revealing imagination, feeling, and dramatic sense, this ideal of attainment is by no means Heywood's uniform achievement. The greater number of the situations function in the development of the action of the plot, but it must be admitted that our poet could be and was tempted to employ the intrinsically diverting episode that could be sacrificed without marring the effect of the whole. Examples of the amusing but incidental scene are the cook's beating a soldier and the clown's outwitting Benningfield in *If You Know Not Me You Know Nobody (1),* Jack Gresham's courtship

of the Widow Ramsey in *If You Know Not Me You Know
Nobody (2)*, and the choosing of the country dance in *A
Woman Killed with Kindness.* What has furnished grounds
for the charge that Heywood was careless as to the relevancy
of so much of the matter in his plots is the fact that the
episodes introduced into the admittedly loose structures are
in themselves highly entertaining. Because of the inherent
virility of Heywood's episodes, one may enjoy them apart
from the context, in an isolated presentation, or in random
reading. Here and there, the plays are spoiled by the absolute dullness of unmotivated scenes, leading episodes devoid
wholly of appeal. The picture gallery scene in *If You
Know Not Me You Know Nobody (2)*, while clearly a
dramatic device to give Quick time to reach Gresham, is in
its dialogue a clumsy, uninspired patch quoted from the
chronicles. It is not without merit as a bit of moralizing,
but it is very stupid stage business. Likewise, there is the
artificiality and straining of the forced issue in the meeting
between Besse and Spencer at the Court of the Duke of
Florence in *The Fair Maid of the West (2)* and the situation centered in Spencer's keeping to the strict letter of his
oath in the same play. After all, however, these uninteresting scenes are the exception rather than the rule. Though
he was tempted at times to present the detached episode, there
is not much straying from the path.

Examples are not lacking of the variety of use to which
situations are put. Dramatic foreshadowing is evidenced
in the unwillingness of the servants to wait upon Wendoll
in *A Woman Killed with Kindness*, in Mrs. Wincott's excuse
for Delavil's presence, and in her plea for freedom for the
lovers in *The English Traveller*. In the first instance our
poet uses a group of characters utterly unrelated to the
principals and utterly unconscious as to the implied drift of
their dialogue. The scene is entirely humorous; it could
easily be the grumbling of servants resenting the generic
visitor whose advent into a household increases their labors;

it serves, however, to prepare the reader for Wendoll's offense. The incident in *The English Traveller* illustrates another method. In this instance the words of Mrs. Wincott are born of a plan to hoodwink her husband, and thus she becomes a conscious agent of the author's purpose. Again, there is the spectacular motivation of the shower in *If You Know Not Me You Know Nobody (2)* and the appearance of Nicholas upon the scene just after the moment of Anne's surrender in *The Woman Killed with Kindness*. It is the spark put to the tinder that kindles the disaster. On the other hand the combination of two situations, Tota's mastery of Roughman, and Mullisheg's control of Goodlack *(The Fair Maid of the West 2)*, is brought into play to initiate the counterplot.

As would be expected, the plays abound in situations of character portrayal. In Heywood there is little action in character but much presentation of character through action. Regardless of his device of introducing his principal characters in a few lines of description in the first scene of the play—note the information given about Bess Bridges, Mrs. Frankford, Sir Thomas Gresham, and the "Wise Woman" before they enter into the action—nevertheless the characters become known to us through their actions, the well-chosen situations enabling us to know and remember so distinctly Heywood's men and women. As studies of Elizabethan life these characters have already been considered. We have seen that they are figures presented with a view to depicting the complexities of Elizabethan middle class ideals. Although they are vital elements of the play, they are, however, subordinated to the author's conscious or unconscious purpose. Consequently they appeal less as individual personalities than as types adjusted to external action, created to satisfy the author's patriotism and to appeal to the sentiment of the spectators.

In the two distinct types of plays in our group—the domestic drama on the one hand, and the comedy of external incident on the other—there would be, as a matter of course, different treatment of the main characters. But the difference is not strikingly marked. In the domestic dramas there is little presentation of inner life, especially among the women, and in the other plays, as would be expected, none at all. Then too, what of inner nature there is exhibited undergoes little change in the course of action. The brief struggle of Wendoll to conquer an ignoble desire barely rouses our curiosity, much less our sympathy, for Wendoll has not been presented in a light to draw forth the interest or admiration of the spectator. Until he appears in meditative mood, weighing the temptation in the balance, one has hardly been aware that he is a part of the action and, almost as soon as one learns that there is an offender at war with himself, the fateful decision has been made. Thus it is with the other characters in the serious plot. Frankford and Young Geraldine and Generous are stunned when they learn that they may have been deceived. The revelations of guilt bring unspeakable anguish to them, but their reactions—the unselfish decisions of Frankford and Young Geraldine, the justice of Generous—are almost instantaneous. Nothing in Heywood is finer than his portrayal of the grief of his wronged husbands. What is equally clear is that these heroes are patterns of righteousness and that, consequently, there is but one course of action open to them. Frankford indeed withdraws for a moment to his study before announcing to his already penitent wife her doom. But in this failure to utilize a situation of the highest dramatic possibility for the presentation of character, Heywood betrays his inability to rise to the occasion. Before Frankford returns to the stage, even when he withdraws, one knows the tenor if not the details of the outcome. These characters are but half drawn; one is shown noble natures in moments of poignant grief in their sensibility to pain. In this respect they are human. The poet, too, carries his point, for the moments of soliloquy, the hurried bits of scenes of rapid action, are long enough to afford us glimpses beyond the surface. We must admit that these fitful flashes of light are upon developed personalities. Where one would hope for action in character, in one stride the gap is spanned; where there is a little delay, the decision was unambiguous from the first. There is no display of natural human weakness; if the characters are not gods, they are at least perfect men. Heywood's other characters, the genre figures of his sub-plots and comedies, in which there is little emotional complexity and the chief interest is focussed in the externals of contemporary manners, need scant discussion. They are, however, lively creatures forwarding the action of situations and distinguishable as types by striking traits portraying a group rather than an individual. In no sense are they "humor" characters distinguished by one overpowering trait, but rather the embodiment of common virtues and vices heightened to enable them to stand out in relative vitality. Out of the action, though, these type characters of Heywood would be tame, spiritless, colorless, perhaps. This lack of individualizing traits in his characters has brought upon Heywood a not altogether unmerited criticism: "Heywood could write a spirited and entertaining play, but his people are nearly always wooden, arousing interest merely from the rôle they play in a lively series of events . . . . I picture the prolific Heywood moving his people like chessmen, ... I cannot escape the feeling that to Heywood his people were counters in a narrative . . . . ."[4] The part of this estimate to which exception must be taken is the reference to Heywood's attitude toward his characters. Heywood's men and women are indeed firmly embedded in the context of the plays just because our poet is picturing certain phases of the life of his times. This life he represents by the action into which the individual personalities fit. But that he was indifferent to his creations is difficult to believe.

[4] *William Rowley* by Charles Wharton Stork, 1910, p. 28.

They are so indissolubly woven into the life he loved that one cannot be considered without the other.

Professor Schelling, in his discussion of Heywood's authorship of *Edward the Fourth,* has noted especially Heywood's treatment of child life as it is evinced in the poet's presentation of the princes. In *Edward the Fourth* as well as in *A Woman Killed with Kindness,* and *If You Know Not Me You Know Nobody (1),* there are pictures of children displaying not only an intimate knowledge of child life but a wonderfully sympathetic, kind, tender nature. Professor Schelling has pointed out, "There is a simple pathos in this short scene between the motherless little princes which exhibits Heywood at his best . . . . . Nowhere else in Elizabethan drama, except perhaps in the scene between Lady Macduff and her son, have the simple faith and sheer weakness of childhood been brought closer to our ears."[5]

In an utterly different spirit, but born too of a love for children, is the hearty appreciation for the sportive mischievousness of the small boy in *If You Know Not Me You Know Nobody (1).* We can almost hear the poet's chuckle when the youngster plays a prank upon the tyrannic constable:

CONST.   Stay him, stay him!—Oh have I caught you, sir?
         Where have you been?
BOY.   To carry my young lady some more flowers.
HOW.   Alas, my lord! a child. Pray, let him go.
CONST.   A crafty knave, my lords.—Search him for letters.
SUSS.   Letters, my lord! It is impossible.
CONST.   Come, tell me what letters thou carryedst her?
         Ile give thee figs and sugar-plums.
BOY.   Will you, indeed? Well Ile take your word,
         For you looke like an honest man.
CONST.   Now, tell what letters thou deliveredst?
BOY.   Faith, gaffer, I know no letters but great A, B, and
         C: I am not come to K yet.
         Now, gaffer, will you give me my sugar-plums?

                         I. Y. K. N. M. I (Vol. I, pp. 219-220)

The English Chronicle Play by Felix E. Schelling, pp. 147-148.

Whether or not the absence of children in the later plays is due to any changes in Heywood's own personal life is a matter of pure conjecture. Be that as it may, we would not forego Heywood's contribution to the child in literature, for his children have the charm of entire naturalness.

Heywood has much humor in his lighter scenes. This humor is seen, chiefly, (a) in the surprising turn of events,—note the clean triumph of wit in the contrast between what a character has expected to happen and what transpires, as in the humiliation of Roughman in *The Fair Maid of the West (2)*—or in Jack Gresham's turning the tables upon Hobson in *If You Know Not Me You Know Nobody (2);* (b) in satire, as in the dialogues of the pedants in *The Wise Woman of Hogsdon;* (c) in comic misunderstandings, as when Roughman makes love to Tota in *The Fair Maid of the West (2);* (d) in intrigue and dissembling, as in the intrigues of Reignald in *The English Traveller.* As would be expected of one writing plays for audiences of the Red Bull and the Cockpit, the humor is entirely frank and spontaneous, there are no subtleties, but horseplay is not common, and, even in the light of modern standards, there is little that is essentially coarse.

A further source of appeal lies in the adaptability of the themes to the tastes of the audience. There is the portrayal of the familiar in the oft-repeated tavern scenes, the games, the well-known songs and dances. Likewise the choice of incidents depicts the nobler elements of English character: bravery, honor, integrity, sympathy, sense of justice and love of fair play strike an echo of sympathy in hearts fired by the patriotism characteristic of Elizabethan England. Regardless of the exaggerations in the astounding feats of courage shown in *The Four Prentices of London* and *The Fair Maid of the West,* the ideal is sound fundamentally, and as such was sure of its appeal.

In the construction of scenes and plot, Heywood betrays changes in manner not to be attributed arbitrarily to different stages in the development of the poet's art. *The Four Prentices of London,* a very early play by the most convincing of external evidence, exhibits the looseness of structure that one would expect in a workshop product. Turning to *A Woman Killed with Kindness* (1603), we are forced to reach the conclusion that he reached the zenith of his dramatic power before 1605 and that from structure alone one cannot decide upon the strict chronological order of the later plays. The explanation for this unevenness in method may lie in the vagaries of the poet; it is probable that, writing hastily for the moment, he was indifferent to every issue except that which contributed to the success of the moment. At all events, recognizing the artificiality of extraneous and showy devices, he soon discarded the dumb show; but there is no steady growth in the fundamental quality of dramatic power after the early success of *A Woman Killed with Kindness* and *The Wise Woman of Hogsdon.* The construction of plot may be viewed more or less as a conscious process, predetermined by the author's attitude toward his sources and the effect he wishes to produce. In the ordering, then, of the framework of the play, he sets out to select and arrange the parts according to a preconceived plan. Consequently it happens, as the case of Heywood illustrates, that an author may produce, during one stage of his development, plots betraying varying degrees of dramatic power.

In the matter of versification, however, the case is relatively different. At this point, we are leaving out of consideration the poet's use of prose and verse in a play, for his choice in this matter is an arbitrary one influenced chiefly by the nature of incidents and the rôles of characters. In the writing of verse itself, the poet develops skill and mannerisms characteristic of his essential style, his spontaneous expression. This would not be noted so much in his preference for rhyme or blank verse as in the construction of the verse line. If the poet has once acquired the power of spontaneous line flow, the mastery of the run-on line,

Table I

Plays	Total Lines	Prose	Verse	Un-rhymed	Rhymed	Adjacent Rhymes	Alternate Rhymes
1. The Four Prentices of London	2608	106[1] / .04	2502[1] / .96	1568[2] / .63	934[2] / .37	901[2] / .35	34[2] / .013
2. If You Know Not Me You Know Nobody (I)	1454	147 / .101	1307 / .899	987 / .76	320 / .24	314 / .24	6 / .004
3. If You Know Not Me You Know Nobody (II)	2031	660 / .225	2271 / .775	1943 / .96	328 / .14	298 / .131	30 / .013
4. A Woman Killed with Kindness	2018	339 / .167	1679 / .833	1305 / .78	374 / .22	366 / .218	8 / .004
5. The Wise Woman of Hogsdon	2338	1278 / .546	1060 / .454	934 / .881	126 / .119	120 / .113	6 / .005
6. The Fair Maid of the West (I)	1856	281 / .151	1575 / .849	1496 / .949	79 / .051	69 / .043	10 / .006
7. The Fair Maid of the West (II)	2543	303 / .119	2240 / .881	2060 / .92	180 / .08	166 / .074	14 / .006
8. Fortune by Land and Sea	2393	778 / .325	1615 / .675	1354 / .839	261 / .161	255 / .158	6 / .003
9. The Late Lancashire Witches	2974	1921 / .646	1053 / .354	845 / .802	208 / .198	198 / .188	10 / .009
10. The Captives	2713	282 / .103	2431 / .89	2253 / .927	178 / .073	160 / .066	18 / .007
11. The English Traveller	2615	252 / .096	2363 / .904	2283 / .97	80 / .03	66 / .028	14 / .005

[1] Percentages based on total lines of play.

[2] Percentages based on number of verse lines.

TABLE 2

	Verse Lines	Feminine Endings	Extra Syllables Slurred	Short	Alexandrine	End Stopped	Run-on	Reversed Accent
1. The Four Prentices of London	2502	192 / .076	74[1] / .029	48[1] / .019	6[1] / .002	150[3] / .75	50[2] / .25	194[1] / .077
2. If You Know Not Me You Know Nobody (I)	1307	223 / .17	111 / .084	186 / .142	31 / .024	162 / .81	38 / .19	143 / .109
3. If You Know Not Me You Know Nobody (II)	2271	395 / .173	264 / .116	212 / .093	70 / .031	127 / .635	73 / .375	232 / .102
4. The Wise Woman of Hogsdon	1060	98 / .092	62 / .058	153 / .144	15 / .014	140 / .70	60 / .30	67 / .063
5. A Woman Killed with Kindness	1679	300 / .178	79 / .047	80 / .047	15 / .009	130 / .65	70 / .35	101 / .06
6. The Fair Maid of the West (I)	1575	326 / .207	68 / .043	202 / .128	35 / .022	148 / .74	52 / .26	78 / .049
7. The Fair Maid of the West (II)	2240	505 / .225	187 / .083	329 / .146	96 / .043	142 / .71	68 / .34	223 / .099
8. Fortune by Land and Sea	1615	303 / .187	72 / .044	109 / .067	15 / .009	153 / .765	47 / .235	174 / .107
9. The Late Lancashire Witches	1053	202 / .191	64 / .06	295 / .28	40 / .038	127 / .635	73 / .375	82 / .077
10. The Captives	2431	502 / .206	143 / .058	249 / .102	61 / .025	105 / .525	95 / .475	289 / .118
11. The English Traveller	2363	441 / .186	166 / .07	197 / .083	46 / .019	120 / .60	80 / .40	148 / .062

[1] Percentages based upon verse lines of play.　　　　[2] Percentages based upon 200 lines of play.

in other words, if his verse has become a flexible instrument controlled by thought and feeling rather than by the demand of rhythmic laws, he is not apt to revert, in any measure, to the restrictions of the end-stopped line and the regularly recurring masculine endings. Unconsciously, he will write in the freer way when once it has become a habit. To do otherwise would be as though one who had once developed technical skill in the mastery of a manual art would revert to the crude performances of apprentice days. On the other hand, since the possible variations of form in blank verse are not unlimited, the characteristic line of a poet is rarely unique. A study of the versification of Heywood does reveal the trend of one phase of the poet's development and it does assist us to place the plays in a relatively chronological order; it is of little value in determining his authorship of certain plays.

The figures in the preceding tables are based upon the plays chosen for this study. At the outset difficulty was met in counting the total lines of the play because one could not be sure whether certain lines were to be counted as short lines or part lines. The method used was to count as part lines two or more successive lines not aggregating more than ten syllables. Some deviation from this rule may have occurred, but I do not believe that the exceptions have affected materially the final conclusions. The figures upon end-stopped and run-on lines are based upon 200 lines in each play; the lines have been selected not arbitrarily from the same acts and scenes in the respective plays but where opportunity was afforded to read as large a unit as possible of continuous verses. It is obvious that verses used in a dialogue composed of one- and two-line speeches are inadequate as a test of the poet's use of the end-stopped or run-on line, the ultimate mechanical test of the poet's command of blank verse.

In Heywood's use of verse and prose there is nothing extraordinary. As a rule, prose is spoken by the characters bearing the humbler rôles: the servants, the clowns, the apprentices. It is chosen generally for farce and light comedy. The practice, however, is not an invariable one. A character speaking verse may suddenly fall into prose and vice versa. But prose becomes an earmark of the prevailing tone of the play or of particular parts of the play. Thus, we cannot state with decisiveness that the proportion of prose and verse bespeaks a stage in the development of the poet's art. Yet, we cannot escape a suspicion that Heywood's method as to the use of prose and verse gradually changed during the years of his experience. From the character of the two plays, *The Late Lancashire Witches* and *The Wise Woman of Hogsdon,* one is not at all surprised to discover in these plays the heaviest proportion of prose. If we accept Professor Martin's assignment of the Seely story and the Lawrence-Parnell story in *The Late Lancashire Witches* to Brome,[6] Heywood's contribution to the prose of this play is seen to be very slight. In this consideration, then, *The Late Lancashire Witches* need not be considered. But there remain other plays, *If You Know Not Me You Know Nobody (2),* and the humorous episodes of *A Woman Killed with Kindness,* in which the method, as far as the use of prose is concerned, approaches that of *The Wise Woman of Hogsdon.* Yet *The English Traveller* with its sub-plot of boisterous mirth shows only 9.6 per cent prose as against 54.6 per cent of *The Wise Woman of Hogsdon.* If the lines in the sub-plot are considered separately, the percentage of prose is even lower. Likewise the comedies *The Fair Maid of the West (1, 2)* contain 15.1 and 11.9 per cent respectively. What would cause such disparity in method between two groups of plays relatively similar in mood? While this fact alone establishes nothing conclusive, it suggests that the plays were hardly composed during the same period of time. Taken in consideration with other internal evidence, the percentage of prose points toward a compara-

---

[6] "Is The Late Lancashire Witches a Revision?" Robert Grant Martin. *Modern Philology* XIII, September 1915, pp. 253-265.

tively late date for *The English Traveller*. But the proportion of prose in *A Challenge for Beauty*, generally accepted
as a late play, scatters to the wind any theory as to Heywood's systematic development in his use of prose and verse.
All we can say is that he shows a tendency, more or less
elastic, toward a diminishing use of prose.

One reaches a similar conclusion in regard to the poet's
attitude toward rhyme. Basing the percentages upon the
number of verse lines, we find that while the larger percentage of rhymed verses are found among the plays entirely
serious or among these with serious main plots, there are
plays in the same serious mood, as *A Woman Killed with
Kindness* and the main plot of *The English Traveller*,
between which there is the widest variance in the use of
rhyme. As all the later plays, *The Royal King and the
Loyal Subject* (1618), *A Challenge for Beauty* (1633),
Love's Mistress (1634), *A Maidenhead Well Lost* (1633)
contain little rhyme in contrast to plays known to be earlier
in time of composition, this difference between *A Woman
Killed with Kindness* and *The English Traveller* may be
attributed to the later date of *The English Traveller*. But
If You Know Not Me You Know Nobody (2), *The Wise
Woman of Hogsdon*, on the one hand, *If You Know Not Me
You Know Nobody (1)*, and *A Woman Killed with Kindness* on the other, all four written probably within a few
years of one another, may be grouped in pairs because of the
peculiar variation in the proportion of rhymed to unrhymed
lines. Can it be that the poet was influenced by the difference in the tone of the plays—the sustained gaiety of the
first two plays causing him to use fewer rhymes? This
conclusion is far from satisfying. The only thing that
seems clear upon this whole question of rhyme is that the
plays, known to have been written relatively late, tend to
show fewer rhymed lines proportionately than the plays of
the earlier dates.

With the exception of *The Four Prentices of London* and

If You Know Not Me You Know Nobody (2), the plays display little variation in the relative number of alternate or scattered rhymes to the entire number of verse lines. Some peculiarities of Heywood here should be noted. On account of the large proportion of identical words in rhymes and of the tendency to repeat in one play, frequently in the same dialogue, the same rhymes, the tone coloring becomes monotonous and pale. Note the repetitions of sound in the following lines:

EUST.   Halfe of al's mine, I claime it as my due:
        In which bright Virgin, I except not you.
TAN.   I do containe my love with much ado:
        For her (methinkes) I could turne Out-law too.
TANC.   . . . .
        You claime her as your right.   *To Charles*
CHAR.   Tis true I do.
TANC.   And Captaine, you say she belongs to you?
        . . . .
CHAR.   So say I too, and Out-law life adiew.
TAN.   And welcome love, which must keepe for you.
                        F. P. L. (Vol. II, pp. 194-195)

                  (Within 38 lines.)

And again:

GODF.   What art thou with thy browe confrontest me?
GUY.   One that thinkes scorne to give least place to thee.
        . . . .
GUY.   Wee are no babe: or if wee were, yet know
        Thy proud face cannot like a Bug-beare show.
GODF.   . . . .
        That we will yeeld the upper hand to thee?
        I let thee know thou hast dishonoured mee.
GUY.   I let thee, know thou hast done as much by me;
        Think'st thou, thou canst outface me? proud man, no.
        Know I esteeme thee as too weake a foe.
        . . . .
GUY.   Thy armes want strength, thou canst not tosse me so.
GODF.   No, can they not? By heaven I'le try a throw.
                        F. P. L. (Vol. II, pp. 196-197)

                  (Within 24 lines.)

LADY.   He will have none to truss his poynts but me.
         At boord to waite upon his cup but me:
         To beare his Target in the field, but me.

                          F. P. L. (Vol. II, p. 205)

GUY.   I am all hers,
ROB.   That Lady seemes to me
         The fairest creature ever eye did see.
BELL. *Tancred,* of all, thy face best pleaseth me:

                          F. P. L. (Vol. II, p. 215)

GUY.   Hold me so still: where ere I next shall meete thee,
         This sword, like thunder, on thy crest shall greet thee.

                          F. P. L. (Vol. II, p. 215)

BELL. Why though he do; tis vertue in a woman,
         If she can beare his imperfections.
FREN. Upon my life they are made sure already,
         Shee's pleas'd with any imperfections.

                          F. P. L. (Vol. II, p. 217)

SOP.   . . . .
         What say you Lords?
LORDS.   Then let us issue out.
ALL.   Set ope the gates, and let us issue out.

                          F. P. L. (Vol. II, p. 235)

ROB.   . . . .
         And in the steed thereof hung up his shield.
EUST. Witnesse this royall Crowne upon my head
         I seiz'd the Ensigne, I hung up that shield.

                          F. P. L. (Vol. II, p. 235)

Although this comparative absence of shading might be expected in an early play like *The Four Prentices of London,* the later plays betray Heywood's lack of appreciation apparently for variety of tone effects and his inability to acquire a flexible vocabulary. Never once do the repetitions of words and lines suggest an artificial device or a conscious effort as the exaggerations of the recurring word or phrase in *How a Man May Choose a Good Wife from a Bad* affect us. As Heywood was using less and less rhyme, the aggregate number of repetitions diminishes, but if there is any rhyme at all, the proportion of lines rhyming with identical words remains just as great in the later plays as in the earlier. Professor Adams has referred to the "frequent patches of rhyme"[7] found in Heywood, groups of rhymed lines of varying number thrown arbitrarily into scenes written mainly in blank verse.

His facility in writing blank verse marks itself in a change from the inflexible norm to measures varying in verse length, position of accent, and phrasing. In a word, the development is from the restricted five-foot iambic, a stiff instrument for dialogue, to smoothly flowing lines adjusted naturally to the expression of thought and feeling. Although the proportion of run-on lines does not vary materially, a steadily increasing number of feminine endings lightens the pause at the end of the line. As the figures in Table II are but slight hints of the actual effect of the change in rhythm, a few examples illustrative of Heywood's line may be cited. The lines from *The Four Prentices of London* are wholly in the formal manner:

> *Bel.* He that best loves me, pierce me with his sword.
> Lest I become your generall overthrow:
> I do conjure you by the love you beare me,
> Either to banish this hostility,
> Or all at once to act my Tragedy.
> A blow is death proclaim'd by Parliament:
> Can ye make lawes, and be the first that break them?
> Knew I that this my beauty bred this strife,
> With some black poyson I would staine my cheeks,
> Till I lookt fouler than an *Aethiop.*
> Still do ye brandish your contentious swords?
> This night shall end my beauty, and tomorrow
> Looke to behold my Christall eyes scratcht out,
> My visage marty'rd, and my haire torne off;

[7] "The Authorship of A Warning for Fair Women." By Joseph Quincy Adams, Jr. *Publications of the Modern Language Association of America,* Vol. XXVIII, No. 4, pp. 594-620.

Hee that best loves it, ransome it with peace
I will preserve it, if your fury cease;
But if ye still persist, the heavens I call
As my vowes witnesse, I will hate ye all.

F. P. L. (Vol. II, p. 210)

The shifting of the caesura cannot redeem the monotony caused by the regularly recurring masculine endings and end-stopped lines. This is, of course, an extreme case, but the average of one run-on line out of every four does not raise the general level much higher.

In contrast note these lines, the first group from *The English Traveller,* the second from *The Fair Maid of the West:*

Y. Ger. In the height of their Carowsing, all their braines,
Warm'd with the heat of wine; Discourse was offer'd
Of Ships, and Stormes at Sea; when suddenly,
Out of his giddy wildnesse, one conceives
The Roome wherein they quafft, to be a Pinnace,
Mooving and Floating; and the confused Noise,
To be the murmuring Windes, Gusts, Marriners
That their unstedfast Footing, did proceed
From rocking of the Vessell: This conceiv'd,
Each one begins to apprehend the danger,
And to looke out for safety, flie saith one
Up to the Maine-top, and discover; Hee
Climbes by the bedpost, to the Teaster, there
Reports a Turbulent Sea and Tempest towards;
And wills them if they'le save their Ship and lives,
To cast their Lading over-board; At this
All fall to Worke, and Hoyste into the Street,
As to the Sea, What next come to their hand,
Stooles, Tables, Tressels, Trenchers, Bed-steds, Cups,
Pots, Plate, and Glasses:..............

E. T. (Vol. IV, p. 28)

Besse. Oh thou the perfect semblance of my Love,
And all that's left of him, take one sweet kisse,
As my last farewell. Thou resemblest him
For whose sweet safety I was every morning
Downe on my knees, and with the Larkes sweet tunes
I did begin my prayers; and when sad sleepe

Had charm'd all eyes, when none save the bright starres
Were up and waking, I remembred thee,
For all, all to no purpose. F. M. W. (Vol. II, p. 304)

In spite of the irregularities occasioned by interposed
trochees, extra syllables, and incomplete feet, Heywood's
lines are easily scanned; rarely is one baffled by verses,
which, like Rowley's, refuse to be measured by any scheme.
Before leaving the mechanics of Heywood's verse, we
should consider one other feature: namely, the relation of
speech endings to verse endings. In *The Four Prentices of
London* and in both parts of *If You Know Not Me You
Know Nobody*, speech endings coincide in large measure
with the end of the five-foot line, that is, the proportion in
these plays ranges from 93 to 84 per cent. This represents
the comparison between the number of speeches ending regularly with the line and the entire number of speeches written in verse. In the other plays the proportion becomes
less, diminishing to 55 per cent in *The English Traveller*.
As we have seen, a similar gradation in proportion is true
of Heywood's use of frequent rhymes, regularly recurring
accents and measures, and end-stopped lines. Certain plays
were composed in stricter conformity to the letter of the
laws governing the mechanics of verse structure than others,
while at times our poet wrote in a comparatively free,
unshackled manner. Knowing that the mastery of the
technique of versification falls naturally in the later stages
of a poet's development, we are forced to conclude that, all
things being equal, plays characterized by the more formally
written verses are earlier productions. In the case of Heywood, the rule holds: *The Four Prentices of London, If
You Know Not Me You Know Nobody (1, 2)* and *A Woman
Killed with Kindness*, plays bearing strong marks of the
cruder technique, are known to have been written before
1610. We must remember, however, that the data involving
this question of metrics are of value only when taken into
consideration with the larger elements of dramatic style.

The predominant note of Heywood's dialogue is his extreme simplicity of utterance and unfailing directness. Free from involved constructions his language offers no subtle problems of interpretation. This entire clarity of diction is due largely to conditions inherent in the particular themes of the plays and in the poet's own temperament. The dramas of contemporary incident portraying external manners do not demand lengthy passages of introspection or subjective struggle. Practically all is external action; so the dialogue would be crisp, pointed, and unequivocal. But even in the longer speeches of the more serious plays, the same clearness of phrasing is maintained. For greater exactness, Heywood has recourse to an extreme minuteness of detail. This love of detail is one of Heywood's earmarks, and when the simplicity of a situation rejects analysis, the poet satisfies his fondness for particulars by the lavish use of detail:

Y. GER.   A villaine were hee, to deceive such trust,
        Or (were there one) a much worse Carracter.
WIFE.   And she no lesse, whom either Beauty, Youth,
        Time, Place, or opportunity could tempt,
        To injure such a Husband.

                        E. T. (Vol. IV, p. 31)

FRAN.   To part you it were sin.
        Now gallants, while the Towne Musitians
        Finger their frets within: and the mad lads
        And the countrey lasses, every mothers childe,
        With Nose-gaies and Bridelaces in their hats,
        Dance all their country measures, rounds, and Jigges,
        What shall we do? Harke, they are all on the hoigh,
        They toile like Mill-horses, and turne as round;
        Marry, not on the toe: I, and they caper,
        But without cutting: you shall see tomorrow
        The hall floure peckt and dinted like a Mill-stone.
        Made with their high shooes; though their skill be small,
        Yet they treade heavy where their Hob-nailes fall.

                      W. K. K. (Vol. II, p. 95)

LADY.   I do beleeve you; faire Knight do you love?
GUY.   To ride a horse as well as any man;
          To make him mount, curvet, to leape, and spring;
          To chide the bit, to gallop, trot the ring.

                              F. P. L. (Vol. II, p. 179)

                    . . . .

          To march, to plant a battle, lead an Hoast,
          To bee a souldier and to goe to Warre,
          To talke of Flankes, of Wings, of skonces, holds,
          To see a sally, or to give a Charge,
          To leade a Vaward, Rereward, or maine Hoast;
          By heaven I love it as mine owne deere life.

                          F. P. L. (Vol. II, pp. 179-180)

GOODL.   'twas compos'd
          Of Dragons poyson and the gall of Aspes
          Of Serpents venome, or of Vipers stings,
          .Had a parliament
          Of fiends and furies in a synod sat
          And devis'd, plotted, parlied, and contriv'd,
          They scarce could second this.

                          2 F. M. W. (Vol. II, p. 350)

As an Elizabethan Heywood did not escape the weakness of Euphuism. Consequently his distinctive frankness is occasionally marred by the artificiality of the balanced construction and a strained affected diction. Fortunately, however, the antithetical expression is rarely a prolonged comparison or contrast involving a chain of intricate rhetorical phrases. More usually it is a word, as:

     SUSAN. Unhappy jest that in such earnest ends.

                              W. K. K. (Vol. II, p. 100)

At most it is a brief phrase that fits the thought so naturally that one discovers it only when on the conscious search for it. Then it is, and only then, that one really appreciates what Heywood's Euphuism is.

In the expression of finer emotions Heywood's reaches are uneven, his diction in spots being pathetically inadequate to the occasion. Note, that while we are not untouched by

the pathos of the situation, we fail to respond to Mrs. Frankford's own presentation of her case. The over insistence
upon the word of appeal for forgiveness has a blighting
effect:

> FRAN.   This hand once held my heart in faster bonds,
> Then now 'tis grip'd by me. God pardon them
> That made us first breake hold.
> ANNE.   Amen, amen.
> Out of my zeale to heaven, whether I'me now bound,
> I was so impudent to wish you heere;
> And once more begge your pardon. Oh (good man)
> And father to my children, pardon me.
> Pardon, O pardon me: my fault so heynous is,
> That if you in this world forgive it not,
> Heaven will not cleere it in the world to come.
> Faintnesse hath so usurp'd upon my knees
> That kneele I cannot: But on my hearts knees
> My prostrate soule lies throwne downe at your feet
> To beg your gracious pardon; Pardon, O pardon me.

W. K. K. (Vol. II, p. 155)

In sharp contrast to this is the restrained language of
Young Geraldine in *The English Traveller*. Similarly,
strength of feeling is felt in the simplicity of Spencer's farewell from Besse:

> SPENC.   Thou art faire,
> Joyne to thy beauty vertue. Many suiters
> I know will tempt thee: beauty's a shrewd baite,
> But unto that if thou add'st chastitie,
> Thou shalt ore-come all scandall. Time cals hence,
> We now must part.
> BESSE.   Oh that I had the power to make Time lame,
> To stay the starres, or make the Moone stand still,
> That future day might never haste thy flight.
> I could dwell here for ever in thine armes,
> And wish it alwayes night.
> SPENC.   We trifle howers. Farewell.
> BESSE.   First take this Ring:
> Twas the first token of my constant love
> That past betwixt us. When I see this next,

And not my *Spencer,* I shall thinke thee dead :
For till death part thy body from thy soule
I know thou wilt not part with it.

F. M. W. (Vol. II, pp. 273-274)

It must be admitted that passages of such emotional intensity as the ones last quoted are the exception rather than the rule with Heywood. They are illustrations of the poet's utmost power of attainment. What one finds ordinarily is, as Professor Adams expresses it, "the same general level of excellence, the same easy-flowing, though rarely inspired, blank verse, the same lack of rich or violent imagery, or of attempts at the Marlovian 'mighty line.' "[8] As has been noted, though, the occasion for deep or fiery utterance is usually lacking. The play of contemporary incident, the portrayal of manners among every-day people rather than of intense feeling rarely evokes a dialogue that rises above the mean. Heywood's verse is bright if not resplendent in color ; the infrequency of passages of impassioned diction expressive of sustained depth or intensity of feeling is due largely to the poet's chosen themes.

A word or two in regard to Heywood's imagery. Its range is extremely narrow, and it rarely suggests subtle relations or fresh comparisons. In the first place, one looks in vain for pictures of the quieter aspects of external nature as reflected in woods, streams, skies, flowers. Heywood draws his similes from showers, gusts, and storms, rocking winds and turbulent seas ; and there are frequent allusions to the rough blasts of winter, thunder and lightning, ice and snow, to brass, flint, and iron, to the owl, the eagle, the lion and the serpent. It is in his delineations of human character that he has recourse to those unpleasant if not distinctively repellent sides of nature. Especially prominent is the serpent. Of course there are the conventional references to the sun, the lark, morning dew, and (once or twice) to

[8] *Ibid.,* p. 598.

roses. His definite and repeated allusions to the sun are
in contrast to the usual vagueness of his generalizations of
the brighter aspects of the world of out-of-doors. As a
rule, when Heywood's imagery is specific, he is thinking of
nature's sterner moods. Inasmuch as this attribute is consistently maintained, it cannot but be regarded as significant.
It does not suggest merely a lack of acquaintance with
country life and a long sojourn in London. These facts
would account for vagueness of reference if it were impartial.
Heywood's predilection for this one-sided imagery seems the
result of limited imaginative power, in the first place, and in
the second of a seriousness of temperament forcing him to
dwell upon the sober pictures of external life. Without
being either gloomy or morose, he was serious in his con-
templations, and, not being gifted with the imaginative range
that marks the genius of a great poet, he was led perforce
toward the sights and sounds that had arrested him, those
that fitted his constant mood. Only too conscious of the
middle class life about him, he constrained his vista; his
imagery loses in richness; he strikes, however, no inhar-
monious notes.

A few remaining peculiarities distinctive of Heywood
remain for mention. These minor elements of style, involving the poet's diction, are expressions of the same habits of
thought and feeling, of the same powers which account
for Heywood's themes and the general structure of his
plays. Characteristic of his attitude toward his subjects is
the supreme quality of directness; Heywood is nothing if
not straightforward. In tune with this mood is the simplicity
of his vocabulary. Writing of and for everyday men, he
employs a language composed of words of common usage.
Yet he is not commonplace or flat; rather has he employed
an unsophisticated diction, at once adequate and transparently
clear.

The casual reader will observe Heywood's predilection
for allusions: Shakespearean, classical, Biblical. His knowl-

edge of the Bible asserts itself in direct quotation, specific or vague allusion, and display of Biblical lore. In the early play, *If You Know Not Me You Know Nobody* *(1)*, the concluding lines are an apostrophe to the Bible. In deeply reverential spirit the Queen pays a tribute to the book that has been her guide and solace, the "true food for rich men and for poore," "the fountaine, cleare, immaculate." From the naïveté of these words, one might suspect the poet of leanings toward Puritanism, were it not for the derisive picture he has painted of the Puritan hypocrite Timothy in the *Part 2* of the same play. Of course, this single occurrence of satire of the sect proves very little, especially when the laughter is directed against insincerity. Heywood would be expected to do just this sort of thing. Timothy is a comic incident, serving paradoxically to round out the tone of the religious coloring given to the plays by the profuse use of Biblical allusions. Heywood, however, quotes from the Bible for two purposes. As a rule, the words are used in the entirely serious vein of their original implication, but occasionally they become the poet's expressions of humor:

GAGE.	This did she bid me say—*tanquam Ovis,*
	Farewell, I must away. *Exit Gage.*
1.	*Tanqus ouris?* Pray, what's *tanqus ouris* neighbor.
2.	If the priest were here, he'd smell it out straight.
COOK.	Myself have been a scholar, and

I understand what *tanquam Ovis* meanes.
We sent to know how her Grace did fare:
She *tanquam ovis* said: even like a sheep
That's to the slaughter led.

1.	*Tanquam ovrus:* that I should live to see *tanquam ovris.*
2.	I shall ne'er love *tanquam ovris* again, for this tricke.

I. Y. K. N. M. I (Vol. I, p. 223)

Thus we see that no source is too sacred for Heywood's indulgence in his fondness for playing with words, juggling with sound and sense. On these verbal gymnastics, the poet relies for one kind of his humor. His vagaries range from the meaningless jargon of words assembled because of likeness of sound with little or no relation in sense, through the unpardonably long list of puns uttered for their own sake, to the sharp thrusts of Frankford's double entendre in the notable card game of the play. The mood of the card game scene is not in Heywood's usual vein. Rarely is his humor marred by the slightest suspicion of bitterness or gloom. The absence of these unpleasant features is due perhaps to the fact that the scant touches of satire in the plays are directed toward external conditions of living, manners rather than deeply seated springs of emotions. What we find is gay sport, practical jokes, harmless trickery capturing the sympathy of the spectator for the victimizer because the victory is an ethical as well as an intellectual one. Subtleties of wit are infrequent. Heywood's is the surface jest, immediately apparent, devoid of sparkle and brilliancy, but essentially wholesome and spontaneous. Withal it is relatively free from much that made up the broad farces of the Elizabethan Age.

Heywood was deeply steeped in classic lore. The influence of this kind of learning is immediately apparent not only in the chosen themes of several plays, the *Ages, Love's Mistress,* the *Drammas and Dialogues* and in his reluctance to relinquish the Greek Chorus, but also in flavor given to the dialogue by the lavish use of classical allusions. These allusions range from single words—the name, perhaps, of a Greek or Roman deity—to apt quotations and countless references to classical legend. So pervasively insistent is Heywood's classicism that one would be justified in regarding with incredulity a play attributed to Heywood that showed no mark of classical influence.

Miss Hibbard, in discussing the authorship of *The Fayre Mayde of the Exchange,*[9] has alluded to the number of

---

[9] "The Authorship and Date of The Fayre Mayde of the Exchange" by Laura A. Hibbard. *Modern Philology,* Vol. VII, No. 3, Jan. 1910, pp. 383-394.

expressions in Heywood suggestive of the influence of Shakespeare. It may be added that Heywood seems particularly well-versed in the sentiment of *Macbeth,* doubtless one of his favorite plays. Note the hints of *Macbeth* in *The English Traveller:*

> Nor ever was I studied in that Art,
> To judge of Mens affection by the face.
>
> E. T. (Vol. IV, p. 24)

> There's no art
> To find the mind's construction in the face:
>
> Macbeth I, IV, 12-13

> You have made mee
> To hate my very countrey, because heere bred
> Neere two such monsters. First, Ile leave this House
> And then my Fathers; Next Ile take my leave
> Both of this Clime and Nation, Travell till
> Age snow upon this Head!
>
> E. T. (Vol. IV, p. 70)

> Farewell ever
> Tis thou, and onely thou hast Banisht mee
> Both from my Friends and Countrey.
>
> E. T. (Vol. IV, p. 91)

> Fare thee well!
> These evils thou repeat'st upon thyself
> Have banish'd me from Scotland.
>
> Macbeth IV, III, 111-113

When the "Wise Woman" gives satisfactory promises to Boyster, Senser, and Luce (*The Wise Woman of Hogsdon,* Vol. IV, p. 334), she recalls the similar scene (As You Like It, V, II, 188-131) in which Rosalind raises the hopes of Phoebe, Orlando, and Silvius. Minor allusions of a word or two are frequent, the words that have passed into the idioms of the language. The conclusion in such cases is of course that the lesser poet imitated the greater. A passage in *A Woman Killed with Kindness* compared with certain lines in Macbeth suggests the reverse process.

FRAN. Soft, soft; wee have tied our geldings to a tree two flight
shoot off, lest by their thundering hoofes they blab our
comming back. Hearst thou no noise?
NIC. Heare, I heare nothing but the Owle and you.
W. K. K. (Vol. II, p. 136)
MACBETH. I have done the deed. Didst thou not heare a noise?
LADY MACBETH. I heard the owl scream and the cricket cry.
Macbeth II, 14-15

Common proverbs and old saws fit easily and naturally into
Heywood's dialogue. The greatest number are to be found
in the earliest comedies. "Cold comfort for me"; "Will
these wild oates never be sowne?" "A catt may looke at a
King." "Wool-gathering already," "You shall find us at
sixe and at seven," "between two stools" (*The Wise Woman
of Hogsdon,* Vol. IV, pp. 290, 295, 302, 313, 341, 350):
"Care not a fig for Me," "Ile turne another leafe." "Mind
your manners," "To take me napping," "Up with the sun"
(*If You Know Not Me You Know Nobody 2,* Vol. I, pp.
257, 257, 257, 312, 325). Significant of the later date of
The English Traveller with its boisterously merry sub-plot
is the fact that it contains no such array of proverbial
expressions.

As would be expected of one having to his credit such a
tremendous output of writings, Heywood has fallen into the
habit of repeating himself, repeating themes, situations,
sentences, phrases, words. In the evaluation of evidence
of authorship too much weight should not be given to this
recurrence of mere verbalisms unless it can be shown that
the words in mind are used almost exclusively by Heywood.
As Miss Hibbard remarks, "Heywood's vocabulary was not
distinctive; the over used words are as a rule the common-
places of English diction." Two or three expressions, like
"the grave" and some others, as pointed out by Professor
Adams,[10] are repeated with such constant frequency that
they may be considered Heywood's own.

[10] "The Authorship of A Warning for Fair Women" by Joseph
Quincy Adams, Jr. *Loc. cit.,* p. 610.

In five plays, Heywood speaks of death as one's going to
the grave.

> We'le make the sea their graves.
>
> > I. Y. K. N. M. I (Vol. I, p. 336)
>
> They are providing for me all things, all things
> I even my grave
>
> > I. Y. K. N. M. I (Vol. I, p. 205)
>
> Alas my love sleepes with him in his grave.
>
> > F. M. W. I (Vol. II, p. 305)
>
> Wee by this
> Had made the carkasse of your ship your graves.
>
> > F. M. W. I (Vol. II, p. 307)
>
> 'T shall with me to my grave.
>
> > Ch. for B. (Vol. V, p. 22)
>
> —he meets a living grave.
>
> > Ch. for B. (Vol. V, p. 25)
>
> I should have gone contented to my grave.
>
> > E. T. (Vol. IV, p. 13)
>
> On which trusting
> I thus abortively, before my time,
> Fall headlong to my Grave
>
> > E. T. (Vol. IV, p. 48)
>
> I the like
> Suffer'd when I my Wife brought into her grave.
>
> > E. T. (Vol. IV, p. 93)
>
> .... but let me go
> Perfect and undeformed to my Tombe.
>
> > W. K. K. (Vol. II, p. 139)

What a study of the structure of Heywood's plays seems
to afford is this: Although Heywood grasped the essentials
of plot construction to the extent of producing at least one
unified play, *The Wise Woman of Hogsdon,* and although
the single parts of his double plots cohere as single elements,
his plays are characterized by a superficial and loose connection between the main and the subordinate actions. This

defect in structure may be traced, probably, to the hurried
labor of preparing the large number of plays of which he
claimed entire or collaborative authorship. His strength
lies in his mastery of the basic element of the play—the
scene. His scenes are striking in appeal because of the
vivacity of movement, the ensemble of characters, and the
contrast of opposing forces. The characterization is technically weak, there being little action in character. Heywood's
men and women are not deep, strong, emotional natures
presented in the complexities of human struggle. By way
of exception there are the men of noble impulses whose
perfection in strength and patience and firmness render them
flawless as models of human behavior but one-sided as dramatic conceptions. The other characters—the type characters of genre figures—move in and out of the plays as
pictures of various aspects of Elizabethan life. In the minor
details of style may be noticed the flexibility of his "rarely
inspired blank verse," the monotony of tone color, the
"patches" of prose and verse interspersed at will, and the
remarkable simplicity of his language. His clear, direct
phraseology is pleasing and of a certain force; being unpretentious it is not marred by the poet's occasional use of
balanced sentence structure, inversions, and repetitions. His
range of imagery is limited, his allusions are direct. The
distinctive charm of his technique is its lucidity.

Heywood lacked a vigorous dramatic genius, a higher
poetic reach. His medium was inadequate for his lofty
ideals, his wholesome, tolerant, kindly nature, his staunch
faith in humanity. Gifted with the thought and feeling of
a great poet, he lacked the imagination and technical skill
which would have enabled him to have produced works of
enduring appeal. The pathos of his position is not lessened
by his continuous output, a succession of plays, extending
over a period of well-nigh forty-years, marked by little
development in the mastery of dramatic art. The greatest
successes came almost at the beginning of the poet's career;

he was content to write in a relatively uninspired vein, achieving greater flexibility in versification, but acquiring little else that differentiated the productions of his later years from the plays of his workshop period.

Measured by the principles of dramatic structure, poetic diction and the supreme reaches of thought and feeling, the plays of Heywood are light in the scale. What is lost in technique and inspired genius is offset by the wholesomeness of his types of character, the liveliness of the situation, and the magnetism of his good will.

CHAPTER V

Edward the Fourth

This double play was printed in 1600, the title page of the edition reading:

> "The First and Second Parts of King Edward the Fourth, Containing His mery pastime with the Tanner of Tamworth, as also his love to faire mistresse Shoare her great promotion, fall and miserie and lastly the lamentable death of both her and her husband. Likewise the besieging of London, by the Bastard Falconbridge, and the valiant defence of the same by the Lord Maior and the Cittizens. As it hath divers times beene publikely played by the Right Honorable the Earle of Derbie his servants."[1]

On August 28, 1599 the play was entered in the Stationers' Register as: "Twoo playes beinge the ffirst and Second parte of Edward the IIIIth and the Tanner of Tamworth with the history of the life and deathe of master Shore and Jane Shore his Wyfe as yt was lately acted by the Right honorable the E(a)rle of Derbye his servants."[2] An entry for February 23, 1600 attests the transfer of rights in the play from "John Busby" to "Humphrey Townes."[3] On December 26, 1594, the Admiral's and the Chamberlain's men, as we note from Henslowe, presented at the Rose a play described as "the sege of London." Following this date, which, it has been presumed, marked the first performance of the play, there are entries for eleven other performances—January 14, 22, February 3, 13, March 3, 14, 1594; August 30, September 20, January 13, 1595; June 14, July 6, 1596.[4] The name

---

[1] *A List of English Plays*, Greg, p. 48.

[2] *A Transcript of the Registers of the Stationers' Company*, III, 147.

[3] *Ibid.*, III, 156.

[4] *Henslowe's Diary*, F 11, p. 21; F 11[v], p. 22; F 12[v], p. 24; F 13, p. 25; F 14, p. 27; F 21[v], p. 42.

given to this play is not only appropriate for the first episode in *Edward the Fourth* but is repeated almost verbatim in a portion of the detailed phrasing of the inclusive title of the edition of 1600. Turning again to the *Diary*, we note Henslowe's entry of a sum of money lent to Chettle and John Day at the instance of Heywood and John Duke for the "plays wherein shores wiffe is writen" for the Worcester's company.[5] As this play was "newly to be written" in 1602,[6] and as there is no doubt as to the appearance of *Edward the Fourth* two years before this date, Fleay concludes that the "shores wiffe" was an abridgement by Chettle and Day of the *Edward the Fourth*, which, in turn, was an elaboration of the "sege of London" of 1594.[7]

Edward the Fourth is a combination of different types of the history play. Its plots are superficially connected. The Falconbridge rebellion of *Part One* and Edward the Fourth's campaign in France of *Part Two* are illustrations of the type of history play, in which the action follows with fidelity the narratives of the chronicles. In this case the sources are Holinshed and Stow. The character of Shore, however, as Professor Schelling observes, is substituted for Basset, and Spicing and Jocelyn are given greater prominence.[8] Further liberty is taken with the chronicles. Heywood, because of a feeling of patriotism, perhaps, forbears to mention the proposed marriage between the daughter of Edward the Fourth and Charles the Dauphin and transfers to the English king the honor of unmasking the Duke of Burgundy, an incident ascribed by Holinshed to the cleverness of the King of France.[9] The Hobs episode, a charming picture of English peasant life in its attractive wholesomeness, is drawn from a

---

[5] *Ibid.*, F 121, p. 190.
[6] *Ibid.*, F 100ᵛ, p. 160.
[7] *A Biographical Chronicle of the English Drama.* Vol. I, p. 288.
[8] *The English Chronicle Play*, Felix E. Schelling, 1903, pp. 144-146.
[9] *Holinshed's Chronicles of England, Scotland, and Ireland.* London, 1807. Vol. III, pp. 330-340.

familiar ballad, recounting a romantic adventure of Edward the Fourth.[10] For minor details—the incognito of the king, the exchange of horses, Drayton Basset as the scene of action, the tanner's suspicion of the honesty of the king, and the name of the tanner's mare—the ballad is laid under contribution, but the tanner's daughter and the events of the evening spent in the tanner's house as well as the characterization of the tanner himself are original. Hobs of the play is more than the shrewd, humorous peasant; he is the incarnation of homely virtues, withal, an ideal of English patriotism. The strongest appeal, however, of *Edward the Fourth* is not in the historical events or even in the sage humor and homely philosophy of a genre figure but in the Shore action. Leaving Holinshed, whose meager account of Jane Shore confines itself to the penance and miserable condition of the quondam royal favorite,[11] the poet again has recourse to a ballad,[12] one of the many popular accounts of a theme of perennial appeal. To this source he is indebted for the figures of the ungrateful Mrs. Blague and the faithful Ayre and a few incidents of the action: Jane's charities, Matthew Shore's leaving England, and the death of Jane; he himself is responsible for the scenes in which the king woos Jane in the goldsmith's shop, the interviews between Jane and the wronged queen, and likewise the interview between Matthew Shore and Richard the Third. Most of all he has developed the story as a problem of domestic relations. Matthew Shore is the wronged husband; he is torn between the sense of personal injury, on the one hand, and sympathy for his suffering wife, on the other; he yields finally to his nobler impulses. Matthew Shore is not to be judged by the

---

[10] *The English and Scottish Popular Ballads,* edited by Francis James Child. Vol. V, pp. 67-87.

[11] *Holinshed's Chronicles of England, Scotland, and Ireland.* Vol. III, pp. 386-7.

[12] *Reliques of Ancient English Poetry.* . . . . By Thomas Percy. Vol. II, pp. 268-280.

figure he presents in the effusively sentimental scene at the close of the fifth act of *Edward the Fourth (2)*. He is remembered as the sturdy Englishman, faithful, sympathetic, and strong, a bourgeois counterpart of Master Frankford, Young Geraldine, and Mr. Generous. Out of the thin figure hovering in the background of the popular ballad and the chronicle, Heywood has constructed his middle class hero whose domestic life is wrecked by the royal profligate and a vain, weak wife. Of finer nature than Mrs. Wincott, Jane Shore is another Mrs. Frankford in her spirit of contrition, for it is the remorse immediately following in the wake of her guilt that gives her a dignity of character missed in the early scenes of the plot. In the characterization of Jane Shore and her husband, in the course of action, is presented a sympathetic study of the erring wife and wronged husband. The final judgment is based upon the ethics of the conflicting elements.

Although Heywood's name does not appear opposite "Edward the 4th. 1st. part. C., Edward the 4th. 2d. part C." in Kirkman's list of plays (1661),[13] the later booksellers, the historians, and the critics, with the single exception of Fleay, concur in assigning this play to our poet. Fleay's argument rests upon the fact that this play, as attested by the entry in the Stationers' Register was written for the "E(a)rle of Derbye his servants," at a time (1599) when Heywood was bound to Henslowe. Moreover, he finds his doubts as to Heywood's authorship strengthened because there is no clown and because Hobs talks in doggerel mixed with prose.[14] While no external evidence has been discovered which indicates that Heywood wrote the "sege of London," the *Edward the Fourth* of 1599 for the Earl of Derby's company, or the "Shore's wife" for the Earl of

---

[13] *A True, Perfect, and exact Catalogue of all the Comedies, etc.* Francis Kirkman, 1661: *Tom Tyler and his Wife.* Tudor Facsimile Texts, 1912.

[14] *A Biographical Chronicle of the English Drama.* Vol. I, p. 288.

Worcester's men, three plays fundamentally one and the
same, perhaps, there is nothing in the facts that points away
from Heywood's hand. As Dr. Greg has noted, Heywood's
contract with Henslowe prohibited the subscriber's acting not
writing for others.[15] Equally weak is the justification for
the conclusion Fleay reaches from internal evidence. The
absence of a clown—the basis of Fleay's first contention—
proves nothing. There is no clown in *A Woman Killed
with Kindness*. Moreover, *Edward the Fourth* loses none
of Heywood's humor because the conventional clown has not
been included in the play. In *Part One* merriment is sustained by means of the wordy battles of Falconbridge and
Spicing, the humours of Jocelyn; and the characterization
of Hobs and Jockie of *Part Two* furnishes a slight bit of
comic relief. Again, Fleay finds that the doggerel in
Edward the Fourth suggests a hand other than Heywood's.
It is entirely true that *Edward the Fourth (1)* contains more
doggerel (24 lines) than any other of Heywood's known
plays, barring the two written in collaboration; yet the count
for the other plays shows these figures: *If You Know Not
Me You Know Nobody (2)* (19 lines), *The Wise Woman
of Hogsdon* (12 lines), *The English Traveller, Edward IV
(2)*, and *The Woman Killed with Kindness* (each 6 lines),
The Four Prentices of London (4 lines), and *If You Know
Not Me You Know Nobody (1)* (3 lines). This seems to
indicate that the inclusion of doggerel among his verses was
the rule rather than the exception with Heywood. Opinion
upon the authorship of *Edward the Fourth* is now virtually
unanimous. This agreement in the concession of the play
to Heywood is based upon the very sound grounds that the
play bears all the marks both of theme and style that are
associated with Heywood's name. As a history play *Edward
the Fourth* recounts events in the history of England, events
exhibiting English loyalty and valor, calculated, too, to

[15] *Henslowe's Diary.* Part II, p. 173.

appeal to the patriotism of the playgoers. In the characterization of Hobs and of Matthew Shore the sturdy virtues of
the English peasant and tradesman are exalted. The theme
of the main plot presents the problem of the erring wife, a
problem treated by Heywood in *A Woman Killed with Kindness* and *The English Traveller* in a way paralleling the
plan of *Edward the Fourth*. The well-known historical
figures are admirably suited to Heywood's adaptation of this
species of domestic drama. To convert the Jane Shore of
the chronicle to the easily-tempted Goldsmith's wife and
Matthew Shore to the patient yet resentful husband was no
difficult task; a monarch, however, cannot be presented as
an inmate of the fated household. To create the semblance
of disloyalty where the bonds of friendship do not exist, the
dramatist has depicted the royal betrayer as indifferent to
the obligation due a subject who has helped to put down a
treasonable uprising. The three elements of *Edward the
Fourth* thus fused—the unfaithful wife motive, the genre
figures idealizing homely Englishmen, and the chronicle narratives—are the subjects of Heywood's realism. His genial
nature and sound morality are discovered in the play's wholesome humor and lofty ethical tone.

The structure of *Edward the Fourth* is the epical plot, the
technique of the plays of Heywood written before 1605.
In *Part One* the Falconbridge action is completed, the Hobs
episode intervenes, the Shore action is introduced, and the
play closes with an added scene presenting Hobs again.
Edward the Fourth's campaign with France occupies the first
third of *Part Two*: after this the threads of the Shore action
are gathered together again and developed into a tragic plot.
This kind of structure is paralleled in the *Fair Maid of the
West (2)*. The figure of the king is the link that connects,
though superficially, the elements of both plays, elements
intrinsically disparate. Heywood's ability to create and
sustain situations of strong appeal is his greatest dramatic
gift. The effective scenes of this play are illustrations of

Heywood's various methods of scene composition. So inherently diverting are the Hobs episodes that they have been edited and published independently as a playlet.[16] Hobs is the manly, wholesome, shrewd peasant attracting the disguised king and captivating the audience by the sound philosophy under his spontaneous wit. Notice his political satire:

KING. I'll give thee a noble, if I like her pace. [They are discussing bartering horses.] Lay thy cowhides on my saddle, and let's jog towards *Drayton*.

HOBS. 'Tis out of my way; but I begin to like thee well.

KING. Thou wilt like me better before we do part. I prithee tell me, what say they of the King?

HOBS. Of the Kings, thou meanest. Art thou no blabbe, if I tell thee?

KING. If the King know't not now, he shall never knowe it for me.

HOBS. Mass, they say King *Harrie's* a very advowtry man.

KING. A devout man? And what's King *Edward?*

HOBS. He's a frank franion, a merry companion, and loves a wench well. They say he has married a poor widow, because shes faire.

KING. Dost thou like him the worse for that?

HOBS. No; by my feckins, but the better; for though I be a plain Tanner, I love a faire lasse myself.

KING. Prithee, tell me, how love they king *Edward?*

HOBS. Faith, as poor folks love holidays, glad to have them now and then; but to have them come too often will undoe them. So, to see the King now and then 'tis comfort; but every day would begger us; and I may say to thee, we feare we shall be troubled to lend him money; for we doubt hees but needy.

KING. Woudst thou lend him no money, if hee should neede?

HOBS. By my halidome, yes. He shall have half my store; and Ile sell sole leather to helpe him to more.

KING. Faith, whether lovest thou better *Harry* or *Edward?*

HOBS. Nay, thats counsel, and two may keepe it, if one be away.

[16] *The King in the Country. A Dramatic Piece in Two Acts.* Acted at the Theatres Royal, at Richmond and Windsor, 1788.

KING. Shall I say my conscience? I think *Harry* is the true king.

HOBS. Art advised of that? *Harrys* of the old house of *Lancaster;* and that progeny do I love.

KING. And thou doest not hate the house of *York?*

HOBS. Why, no; for I am just akin to *Sutton Windmill;* I can grind which way soe're the winde blow. If it be *Harry,* I can say, well fare *Lancaster.* If it be *Edward,* I can sing, *Yorke, Yorke,* for my money.

KING. Thou art of my mind; but I say *Harry* is the lawful king. *Edward* is but an usurper, and a fool, and a coward.

HOBS. Nay, there thou liest. He has wit inough and courage inough. Dost thou not speake treason?

E. F. I (Vol. I, pp. 44-45)

. . . .

HOBS. And I like thee so well, *Ned,* that, hadst thou an occupation (for service is no heritage; a young courtier, an old beggar), I could find in my heart to cast her away upon thee; and if thou wilt forsake the court and turn tanner, or bind thyselfe to a shoomaker in *Liechfield,* ile give thee twenty nobles ready money with my *Nell,* and trust thee with a dicker of leather to set up thy trade.

E. F. I (Vol. I, p. 50)

Other scenes pointing to Heywood's hand are the King's first meeting with Matthew Shore, the pathetic dialogue of the princes in the Tower (quoted by Professor Schelling), Matthew Shore's repudiation of Jane, and the King's courting Jane in the goldsmith's shop. Heywood's method of characterization is seen in the rebels' description of Jane and in the monologues: the Lord Maior's long monologue in *Part One,* the King's debate with himself before he courts Jane, and Matthew Shore's recital of Jane's guilt and his own future course of action. The last-named recalls monologues used similarly in *The English Traveller, The Fair Maid of the West, A Woman Killed with Kindness,* and *The Wise Woman of Hogsdon.*

Of the minor details of Heywood's style, the play affords

abundant evidence. Marked by simplicity and clearness of phraseology, the flexible blank verse shows a proportion of feminine endings and run-on lines (.084, .102) characteristic of Heywood's versification at the early period of his career. There is a generous sprinkling of familiar proverbs, Biblical and classical allusions, and topical references. Nor should we forget the short, pithy sayings, Heywood's way of expressing his philosophy of life.

> And for this life, this paltry brittle life,
> This blast of winde, which you have labour'd so,
> By juries, sessions, and I know not what,
> To robbe me of, is of so vile repute,
> That, to obtaine that I might live mine age,
> I would not give the value of a point.
>
> E. F. I (Vol. I, p. 54)

> Indeed, the end of all kingdoms must end;
> Honour and riches all must have an end;
> And he that thinks he doth the most prevaile,
> His head once laid, there resteth but a tale.
>
> E. F. I (Vol. I, p. 55)

> True fame survives, when death the flesh hath slaine.
>
> E. F. I (Vol. I, p. 24)

> Trust me, true friends bide touch in time of neede.
>
> E. F. II (Vol. I, p. 150)

We note the triteness of imagery, the predilection for details, and the repetitions of sounds producing a monotony of tone color. Finally, we recognize the oft-used expressions, many of which are cited by Professor Adams: "coile," "mirror of her kind" ("mirror of perfection"), "millions," "somewhat" "for want of a better" ("for fault of a better"), "grave," etc.

Taken conjointly, these points indicating the poet's larger conceptions of theme and art and the minuter details of style, though insignificant when considered separately, mark *Edward the Fourth* as distinctively Heywood's. The play was written in all probability between 1594 and 1599.

The Fair Maid of the Exchange

Like *Edward the Fourth, The Fair Maid of the Exchange: With the pleasant Humours of the Cripple of Fanchurch*,[17] an anonymous play of 1607, lacks Heywood's formal introductions—dedicatory epistle, address to reader, complimentary verses from friends. Equally non-committal is the entry in the Stationers' Register of April 24, 1607.[18]

As yet no external evidence has been discovered for settling the vexed question of the authorship of *The Fair Maid of the Exchange*. Miss Laura Hibbard makes out a strong case for Heywood's authorship.[19] She cites the twenty-one authorities by whom the play is ascribed to Heywood as opposed to the six others who fail to see his hand in the play. Although three of the latter, Ward, Dr. Greg, and Professor Schelling, are writers whose judgments may usually be accepted as final, in this case, as Miss Hibbard contends, their decision appears to be opinion founded upon "overhasty personal impression" rather than upon conclusions drawn from a minute analysis of the style of the play as compared with certain unique characteristics of Heywood. Fleay's objections, though more specific and detailed, are shown to be so weak that they may be put aside. In answer to Miss Hibbard's article, Philipp Aronstein challenges Heywood's authorship.[20] Following Fleay, Aronstein reads literally the line, "the tender pamping twig," as the words of a novice referring to his youth instead of accepting Miss

[17] *A List of English Plays*, Greg, p. 50.
[18] *A Transcript of the Registers of the Stationers' Company*, III, 347.
[19] "The Authorship and Date of The Fayre Mayde of the Exchange," Laura A. Hibbard. *Modern Philology*, Vol. VII, pp. 383-94.
[20] "Die Verfasserschaft des Dramas, The Fair Maid of the Exchange," Philipp Aronstein. *Englische Studien*. XLV-XLVI, 45-60.

Hibbard's sounder interpretation of the phrase as a characteristic note of Heywood's modesty, a note sounded frequently in his writings. According to Aronstein, the immaturity of the writer is confirmed by the stilted, florid dialogue and by the crude imitations of Shakespeare and Ben Jonson. He feels that the exquisite lyric of the play, "Ye little birds that sit and sing," is artificial, quite the opposite of Heywood's directness and sincerity. More convincing, however, is this critic's discussion of the characterization. It is quite true that the "humor" characters betray the unquestioned influence of Ben Jonson. But there is no evidence that the author of Heywood's acknowledged plays had ever sat at the feet of Ben. The case is quite the opposite. Then too, as Aronstein says, Phillis is not to be compared, as Miss Hibbard suggests, to the erring wives, Mrs. Frankford, Jane Shore, and Mrs. Wincott. In contrast she is a buoyant, merry hearted, capricious, upright young girl. Her sudden change of sentiment at the close of the action is regretted, not because she is inconsistent with herself but because the author could not free himself from the shackles of a dramatic convention demanding that the fair heroine wed a handsome gallant. Phillis is simply no match for the superior wit of Frank Golding and the Cripple. In a word, Aronstein rejects the play on the ground that it is not written in Heywood's manner.

Practically all that Miss Hibbard has said of our poet's characteristics is true. But whether *The Fair Maid of the Exchange* illustrates these distinctive qualities as to treatment of scene, character, plot, language and versification is another question. Admitting Miss Hibbard's contention that the references to London, though few, are "the words of one sure of his local color," one cannot but note the strong contrast in number between the nine specific local allusions in this play and the fourteen in *The Royal King and the Loyal Subject,* the twenty-one in the *Wise Woman of Hogsdon,* the thirty-four in *If You Know Not Me You Know Nobody*

(2) and the fifty in *Edward the Fourth (1)*, plays of London life. Although *The Royal King and the Loyal Subject* has a London background, its immediate atmosphere is the Court; this accounts, probably, for the comparatively few allusions to the haunts of the city. No play ascribed to Heywood is centered more exclusively in the life of the London tradesman than *The Fair Maid of the Exchange;* but, in spite of the fact that the London setting of this play is clearly indicated, local color is not applied as Heywood was wont to apply it in his plays of London life. Topical allusions alone do not satisfy his notion of pictures of external life. The tavern scenes, the intimate revelations of shop life, the songs, games, and sports of men of different classes, Elizabethan hospitality, dress, feasting have all been noted as the external features of Heywood's atmosphere; on the other hand, he is wont to reveal, just as concretely, the inner meaning, the realities of the social aspects of his background. With the exception of the sparse allusions, one here, one there, to the work of the shop—"the lawns, cambrics, ruffs." "Italian cutwork," there is little in the way of description of environment or dialogue embracing the jargon of shops or trade. The play is staged in the Exchange, principally in the shop of the Cripple. It follows the fortunes of a group of characters ostensibly of the upper middle class, but there is little or no allusion to middle-class life, as Heywood is given to picture it in the setting for his characters. The dialogue is confined to the business of the plots, but the action could happen anywhere in any age. Reference has already been made to Miss Hibbard's interpretation of the character of Phillis. Too much significance, moreover, should not be attached to the fact that Phillis like Jane Shore and the first Luce is courted in the shop. In *The Shoe-maker's Holiday,* Jane, the wife of the absent journeyman Ralph, is approached by Master Hammon as she keeps her shop. Both Dekker and the author of *The Fair Maid of the Exchange* have used a device of stagecraft, an adapta-

tion of the familiar street scene of Latin comedy, which appears again in the commonly featured setting of the Exchange in Restoration drama. The observations made by Miss Hibbard upon the other characters in the play, as well as her analysis of plot and language and her references to parallelisms in details, are pointed. But minor elements of technique are relatively light in the scale when weighed with the larger problems of a poet's philosophy and general attitude toward his art. With Heywood, the major interest is in the themes of his plays. We may develop further Aronstein's main contention, viz., that the prevalent tone of the play is not indicative of Heywood. *The Fair Maid of the Exchange* is a comedy made up of several actions each of which concludes with a victory for the wits. When Bowdler says "By heavens Franke I do commend thy wit" (p. 86), he strikes the dominant note of the play. Regardless of the moral issues, it is sheer cleverness, shrewdness, that carries off the palm. Frank Golding with the help of the Cripple outwits his brothers, Anthony and Ferdinand; the Cripple, to get his revenge upon Bowdler, deludes Moll into believing she loves Barnard instead of Bowdler, at the same time outwitting Master Berry; Frank also outwits Mr. and Mrs. Flower; Mrs. Flower outwits her husband. Now, this attitude is entirely foreign to Heywood's accustomed method of concluding action. In each of his plays, leaving out of consideration plays based upon classical themes, the judgment is a moral one, or if it records the triumph of wit, the schemers, Reignald, Young Lionel, Young Chartley, Jack Gresham confess the errors of their way, pledge a reform, and make their bow as penitents, even though they may be hypocritical sinners. Thus only could Heywood square with his conscience an unrighteous victory. Is it possible that in *The Fair Maid of the Exchange* his position is entirely reversed?

The utmost, it seems, that can be conceded to Heywood is the outline of the plots, sketches of some situations, and indications of the leading lines of characterization. In view of the fact that the consistently sophisticated tone of the play is in such utter contrast to Heywood's simplicity, that there is a marked absence of the graphic pictures of Elizabethan life and manners chosen by Heywood generally to vivify his background, and that the play lacks Heywood's wholesome charm of frankness and simplicity, it is quite unlikely that he is entirely responsible for the play in its present form. Written before 1607, it must have appeared during the years of Heywood's busiest recorded activity; this fact decreases the likelihood of Heywood's sole authorship of the play.

Fortune by Land and Sea

This play, the last to be printed of the early editions of Heywood, did not appear until 1655, some years after the poet's death. Its title-page bears Heywood's name with that of his collaborator, William Rowley, and the familiar statement that the play "was acted with great applause by the Queen's servants."[21] The entry in the Stationers' Register of June 20, 1655, is in the interest of "Master John Sweeting" for "a booke entituled Fortune by Land and Sea, a tragi-comedie, written by Tho. Heywood & Wm. Rowley."[22]

The external evidence, for ascribing the play in part to Heywood, exists in the entry in the Stationers' Register, in the appearance of Heywood's name upon the title-page of the edition of 1655, and in the mention of the name of an actors' company, the "Queen's Servants." This was probably not the later company of Queen Henrietta Maria, but Queen Anne's, with which Heywood was affiliated for a number of years after 1603. As Rowley is believed to have acted with this company for a time,[23] it is easy to account for the collaborated authorship of *Fortune by Land and Sea.*

---

[21] *List of Plays,* Greg, p. 54.
[22] *A Transcript of the Registers of the Stationers' Company,* p. 486.
[23] *A Chronicle History of the London Stage,* p. 188.

Mr. Stork, in his "Life of Rowley" prefixed to the edition of Rowley's *All's Lost by Lust* and *A Shoemaker, A Gentleman,* follows Fleay in placing the date of composition of *Fortune by Land and Sea* at 1609. Fleay bases this conclusion upon the circumstance of Heywood and Rowley's being members of the Queen's company during the years 1607-1609, and upon the further fact that the public was excited by pirates in 1609.[24] The earlier date, between 1600 and the Queen's death, advanced by Barron Field and indorsed by Collier, rests mainly upon the slight internal evidence found in the language of the proclamation forming a part of one of the scenes of the play. In 1602-3 Heywood was busily engaged in writing plays and in other activities for the Earl of Worcester's company, soon to be re-named Queen Anne's, but the record of his tremendous output of plays for those years challenges any suggestion as to further work during that time. Of course we are uncertain as to Heywood's whereabouts or employment between 1600 and 1602; Rowley's age at the time presents another complication. If the birthdate of 1585 is accepted for Rowley, his youth would preclude the notion of any serious work by him around 1600. Again, certain words of Purser suggest that the play was written after the coronation of James I:

> Oh the naval triumphe thou and I have seen,
> Nay ourselves made, when on the seas at once
> Have been as many bonefires as in Towns,
> Kindled upon a night of Jubilee,
> As many Ordnance thundring in the Clouds
> As at Kings Coronations, and dead bodies
> Heav'd from the hatches, and cast over-board
> As fast and thick as in some common Pest
> When the Plague sweeps Cities.
>
> F. L. S. (Vol. V, p. 428)

Finally, as has been suggested, Rowley's membership in the Queen's company between 1607 and 1609 points to the likeli-

---

[24] *A Biographical Chronicle of the English Drama,* I, 294.

hood of the play's having been produced between those years.

No source for the plot of *Fortune by Land and Sea* has as yet been noted. In the theme of the play, though, is a world-old motive, the story of true love not running smoothly because of parental opposition. The arbitrary parent, who by reason of pride of wealth or place or because of family feud interposes his authority to thwart the happiness of young lovers, sets in motion a train of events offering infinite possibilities of treatment. Among Elizabethan plays there is a long list upon this subject. As extremes of variation are *Romeo and Juliet* and *The Merry Devil of Edmonton*. In utter contrast as to final outcome—the difference between failure and success for youthful lovers—in the initial motivation the tragedy and the comedy were characterized by similar impulses. Further than this, from the events developed as far as the climax, *Romeo and Juliet* might have been concluded as a comedy, *The Merry Devil of Edmonton* as a tragedy. The distinctiveness of these plays, presenting the arbitrary-parent motive, rests in the solution of the complex situations engendered by the initial problem. Up to a certain point the steps in the action of *Fortune by Land and Sea* are conventional: the eldest son of the family, Philip Harding, marries Susan Forrest in defiance of his father's will, the father's hostility being due to the poverty of the Forrest family. What gives the plot distinction is the father's unnatural retaliation and the apparent meekness of his son: the newly married pair are condemned to live as menials in the parental home, serving not only the father and the young stepmother, who alone is the ally of the offenders, but also the two unsympathetic younger sons. Because of the marvelous good luck achieved by Susan's brother in adventures at sea, the fortunes of the Forrest family are retrieved just as the sudden death of Harding senior leaves the despised Philip sole heir to the estate. By one turn of the wheel, Philip and Susan conclude their degrading existence, and the two younger brothers atone for their unnatural conduct.

It is entirely possible that some direct source for the plot of this play may be discovered, but the menial position of Philip and Susan in the family household is a conscious or unconscious adaptation of the Cinderella story in all its main features—the humiliating service, the arrogance of the two fortunate brothers, the kindness of the stepmother—a veritable fairy godmother—the munificent good-fortune of those who had suffered, and the punishment of the haughty brothers. In the sub-plot there is nothing unique. It is the story of the fortunate youth, who, sailing the seas as an outcast, achieves fortune and honor through miraculous adventures with luck always on his side. A suggestion has been made as to the prototypes of the two pirates of the play. Barron Field, in the edition of *Fortune by Land and Sea* edited for the Shakespeare Society, calls attention to a tract in the Bodleian Library containing the signed confessions of three pirates about to be executed. Two of these documents could furnish suggestions for the delineation of the pirates in the play. He concludes from the type and other circumstances that the tract must have appeared long before 1600. This date of the tract would not, of course, alter our decision as to 1607-1609 as to the date of the production of the play.

The outlines both of plot and sub-plot of *Fortune by Land and Sea* have been developed in an Elizabethan setting presenting the clash of class distinctions and at the same time picturing humorous details of contemporary life. Ward has characterized *Fortune by Land and Sea* as one of Heywood's loosely constructed double plots.[25] It seems to me that this play is rather more compactly built than the typical Heywood plot. It is admitted that there are the two actions; the events growing out of the arbitrary parent motive, the "fortune by land"; and the lucky adventures following Young Forrest, the "fortune by sea." Moreover, each

[25] *A History of English Dramatic Literature,* Adolphus William Ward, 1899.

develops to an extent independently; but there is interlacing at crucial points. When Young Forrest is cornered in his desperate efforts to escape the relentless clutches of a one-sided justice, he not only appeals to Anne Harding, but his escape is made possible through the efforts of Anne and his sister Susan, both figures in the main plot. The news of Harding Senior's losses at sea causes the latter's death and thus removes the immediate source of unhappiness in the Harding household; and Young Forrest's rescue of the cargoes, which at first had fallen into the hands of pirates, brings about the complete solution of the domestic complication. This appears a closer relationship between the two parts of the play than the mere presence of the principals of the two plots at a banquet or a death-bed scene *(A Woman Killed with Kindness)*, or the endorsement of a bond not mentioned subsequently in the play *(The Late Lancashire Witches)*, or a servant's bringing to the characters in the main action the news of rioting in the subordinate action *(The English Traveller)*.

Rowley's share in this play is relatively slight. Mr. Stork considers the play "altogether in Heywood's vein," limiting the other collaborator's part to "at most but an occasional short scene or touch."[26] The touches of Rowley, Mr. Stork finds in the dialogue of the pirates' farewell, in the more spirited parts of the Harding rôle, and in the characterization of the clown.

I think that this division of authorship is, in the main, sound. The general tone of the realism, a sympathetic attitude toward misfortune with the final outcome satisfying an ethical judgment, is of course like Heywood's usual vein, as are also details of situation and characterization. We note the slightly motivated cause of initial action in the quarrel between Frank Forrest and Raynsforth recalling forthwith the fatal termination of the hunting party of *A*

[26] *William Rowley*, Charles Wharton Stork, 1910, pp. 60-61.

Woman Killed with Kindness and the spark and tinder parley of Carrol and Spencer in *The Fair Maid of the West.* The instant remorse of young Forrest

> Had I but known the terrour of this deed,
> I would have left it done imperfectly.
> Rather then in this guilt of conscience
> Laboured so far. . . . .

                              F. L. S. (Vol. VI, p. 386)

parallels not only the mood of Sir Charles Mountford and Spencer but that of Mrs. Frankford as well. Foster, Goodwin, and Raynsforth are replicas of the "wild youths" of *The English Traveller, The Wise Woman of Hogsdon,* and *The Fair Maid of the West,* while the women, Susan and Anne, are endowed with the wholesome virtues of Heywood's typical English girls. Again, we recognize our poet's characteristic humor in the exposé of the time-serving Foster and Goodwin, in the verbiage of the clown, the perennial fun maker. Mr. Stork thinks that the clown of *Fortune by Land and Sea* is of the same type as Rowley's clown, particularly Jaques of *All's Lost by Lust.* Yet the clown of *Fortune by Land and Sea* is of a piece with all of Heywood's clowns, who enliven the action with wit a trifle less subtle than that of their more sophisticated counterparts in Rowley's plays. Finally, *Fortune by Land and Sea,* in its main action, presents a train of incidents almost identical with the romantic adventures of Spencer in *The Fair Maid of the West (1).* Nothing in the characterization suggests Rowley, for the vigor of his dramatic figures is entirely lacking. The ranting of the pirates (Mr. Stork ascribes the farewell dialogue of the pirates to Rowley) reminds one of Rowley's language, but we know that Heywood, at times, falls into sheer bombast, especially in his earlier plays. (Cf. the quarrels of Spicing and Falconbridge in *Edward the Fourth.*) Inasmuch as *Fortune by Land and Sea* was printed after Heywood's death, it is possible that Rowley alone prepared the edition as we have it. Several superfluous repetitions, such as the merchant's announcing the news of his intended voyage, news previously detailed in the dialogue, point to a different hand writing hurriedly, perhaps, the last part of the play. The pervading atmosphere, then, the principal incidents, the characterization, and the versification, being all in Heywood's manner, suggest that he was responsible for the early stage version. Rowley, I think, furnished the main outlines of technique—hence the closely knitted plot—and, in the final revision of the play, interpolated lines here and there or rewrote lines—the farewell dialogue of the pirates already referred to as cited by Mr. Stork and the halting blank verse of the first two scenes of Act IV.

The case of the arbitrary parent, as here treated, does not approach, in the gravity of the issues involved, Heywood's presentation of the problem of the erring wife. The consequences of the defiant marriage though humiliating and exasperating were at most transient, and they sink into insignificance when contrasted with the enduring spiritual suffering left in the wake of the erring wife. The play does not present characters in deep emotional crises; it serves rather to exhibit the unhappy situations resulting from attendant poverty and class distinctions, and the immediate happiness following a mere turn in fortune. It does not exalt the disrespectful, disobedient, undutiful child, but it does expose to ridicule the extreme length to which the illogical demands of tyrannic parents may lead. The sympathy of the poet is entirely with the youthful pair, not because he would picture filial disobedience in an attractive light, but because he recognizes the distinction between parental power rightfully exercised and despotism. Similarly he resents the restrictions imposed by caste and wealth.

> Forr. Hee's gone, the Law is past, your life is cleared,
> For none of all our kindred laid against
> You evidence to hang you; y'are a Gentleman,
> And pitty 'twere a man of your discent
> Sould dye a Felons death;
>
> F. L. S. (Vol. VI, p. 377)

OLD HARD. I had smal leisure to importune that,
            Onely this much I learnt, the man that's dead
            Was great in fault, and he that now survives,
            Subject unto the danger of this search,
            Bare himself fairly, and his fortune being
            To kill a mann Ally'd to Noble men,
            And greatly friended: is much pittyed.

                                    F. L. S. (Vol. VI, p. 391)

                        . . . .
OLD FORR. Tis no disparagement unto your birth,
            That you converse with me, if I mistake not,
            Sure, sure, I am as wel born.
OLD HARD. And yet sure, sure,
            Tis ten to one I shall be better buried.
OLD FOR.   I am as honest,
OLD HARD. Nay there you are a ground
            I am honester by twenty thousand pound.
OLD FOR.   Are all such honest then that riches have?
OLD HARD. Yes, rich and good, a poor man and a knave.

                                    F. L. S. (Vol. VI, p. 401)

The main issue is not shifted, but the relatively narrow domestic problem is the outcome of the social problem created by wealth. Here again, as in the plays depicting the unfaithful wife, Heywood aligns himself on the side of right. In the romance of the play, the despised lovers are restored to their rightful place. Indeed, so completely is the case carried, that realism gives place to romance, and the tedium of the English home is replaced by the adventures of the high seas where the marvelous feats of heroism and sheer good luck reap the spoils that bring the play to its happy conclusion. On the other hand, the realistic setting of the play, especially in the earlier scenes, was evidently close to Heywood's heart. It furnishes the romance and is the mainspring of the action. The final outcome is success. The tables are turned and virtue, shackled by poverty and inferiority in rank, emerges triumphant in the gifts of fortune.

The popularity of the arbitrary-parent motive attests itself in the long line of Elizabethan plays upon this theme, a consequence of the romantic possibilities afforded by the subject. Many of these plays present the plot developed in a realistic setting. Grouped into the conventional divisions of drama, the comedies are those in which youth triumphs over age, and the tragedies those in which the success of the parent's will sets moving a trend of events ending in death or disaster. As *Fortune by Land and Sea* is a tragi-comedy, some plays of the first group may be noted: *Wily Beguiled, The Merry Devil of Edmonton,* the main plots of *The Roaring Girl,* and *A Chaste Maid in Cheapside.* In each one of the four comedies, the triumph of youth is effected through the direct plotting of the principal characters sometimes assisted by fortuitous circumstances. Regardless of setting, character, or incident, the ultimate victory is an intellectual judgment. That this intellectual judgment coincides with the moral issue, thus satisfying the ethical sense and the natural bent of human interest and sympathy, is a happy accident. In Heywood's tragi-comedy, on the contrary, the youthful pair submit to the humiliating punishment imposed by arbitrary authority in a mood strangely at odds with the defiance that led them at first to take the bit between their teeth. The turn of events that banishes their sorrows and brings in its wake a cornucopia of blessings is brought about, on the one hand, by the successful adventures of another character, and, on the other, by fate itself. But this paradox in characterization justifies itself in the probable intention of the author, who, having conceived an extraordinary situation, needs extraordinary figures to support it. The main plot of *Fortune by Land and Sea*—course of action and character—recalls, faintly perhaps, Heywood's exemplary people, Master Frankford, Matthew Shore, Young Geraldine, the long-suffering heroes who bend to the lash of fate. In an untoward situation they display sublime abnegation of self. In the relation of romance to realism, and in the nature of the realism itself, the other plays mentioned above differ from Heywood's play. *Wily Beguiled* and *The Merry Devil of Edmonton,* the latter one of the most delightful comedies of the period, are essentially romantic, the realism consisting of episodical scenes in the background. Even though avarice has instigated the inimical decisions of the parents in both cases, misfortune because of poverty or rank is not stressed. In neither play does a situation arise comparable in its import to the tavern scene or Old Forrest's arraignment of Old Harding in *Fortune by Land and Sea.* The poachers of *The Merry Devil of Edmonton,* the peasants of *Wily Beguiled*—Will Cricket, Peg, and Mother Midnight—afford charming pictures of English rural life in episodes introduced mainly as diversions. By them, however, the main plots are not motivated. Conversely, in the two other comedies, *The Roaring Girl* and *A Chaste Maid in Cheapside,* romance, subordinated to realism, is almost wholly lacking except as the nature of the theme itself suggests, of course, romance. That the spirit of romance is more clearly evident in *The Roaring Girl* than in *A Chaste Maid in Cheapside* is due, probably, to Dekker's collaboration with Middleton in the former play. What is prominent, in each play, is an involved plot of intrigues centered in a background reflecting contemporary manners. There is abundant color of middle-class London life: the atmosphere of London shops, the celebrations of high days and holidays—note the pictures of the gossips at the christening feast in *A Chaste Maid in Cheapside*—the conviviality of roysterers; but it is the wantonness of Mistress Gallipot, the hypocrisy of the Puritans, the limitations of Mrs. Yellowhammer's education, in a word, the follies of the Londoners that are chiefly exhibited for ridicule. From the midnight sports of Host Blague and his associates to Middleton's figures is a far cry. Equally removed is Heywood from both. With him the social conditions surrounding the characters make the issue, but the issue is such a serious one that the background is neither harmless amusement nor detached pictures of folly. The background motivates the action showing human happiness in the balance; under it all is the thinly veiled protest against social injustice. Directly and indirectly it appears as the theme of the play. *Fortune by Land and Sea* stands apart among the plays of the period developing the arbitrary-parent motive in its elaboration of the nature of the social background that makes possible the dramatic issues.

The Late Lancashire Witches

"The Late Lancashire Witches A well-received Comedy, lately Acted at the Globe on the Banke-side by the King's Majesties Actors. Written by Thom. Heywood, and Richard Broome" was published in 1634.[27] The running title of the play is "The Witches of Lancashire." Two entries for this play appear in the Stationers' Register. The first, dated October 28, 1634, is a record of the license to "Benjamin ffisher" for "a Play called The Witches of Lancashire etc."[28] The second, dated March 27, 1637, is a record of transfer of publishers' rights by the said Benjamin Fisher to "Master Young." In the list of books cited in the second entry "The witches of Lancashire" is number twenty-seven.[29] *Fortune by Land and Sea* and *The Late Lancashire Witches* are the two extant plays in which Heywood is known to have shared the labor of writing. Both plays were published without formal addresses, a circumstance to be accounted for partly by the fact of double authorship.

That *The Late Lancashire Witches* was inspired by actual events is evidenced by lines in the prologue and epilogue. Apologizing for the plot, the poet writes:

[27] *List of Plays,* Greg, p. 52.
[28] *A Transcript of the Registers of the Stationers' Company,* IV, 329.
[29] *Ibid.,* IV, 378.

> .... we are forc'd from our owne Nation
> To ground the Scene that's now in agitation;
> The Project unto many here well knowne;
> Those Witches the fat Jaylor brought to Towne.
> An Argument so thin, persons so low.
> Can neither yeeld much matter, nor great show.
> Expect no more than can from such be rais'd,
> So may the Scene passe pardon'd though not prais'd.
>   L. L. W. Prologue (Vol. IV, p. 169)

And again:

> Now while the Witches must expect their due
> By lawfull Justice, we appeale to you
> For favorable censure; what their crime
> May bring upon 'em, ripnes yet of time
> Has not reveal'd. Perhaps great Mercy may
> After just condemnation give them day
> Of longer life. We represent as much
> As they have done, before Lawes hand did touch
> Upon their guilt; But dare not hold it fit,
> That we for Justices and Judges sit.
> And personate their grave wisedomes on the Stage
> Whom we are bound to honour; . . . . .
>   L. L. W. Epilogue (Vol. IV, 262)

Direct evidence for the source of the play exists in one or both of two trials for witchcraft occurring in 1612 and 1633-34 respectively. Since the date and nature of the collaboration—as to whether *The Late Lancashire Witches* is an old play revived or the joint production of two men working simultaneously—depend upon the conclusions as to the sources used, there has been much discussion of the subject of sources. Recently, the question has been revived in two articles: "The Authorship of the Late Lancashire Witches"[30] by Professor C. E. Andrews and "Is the Late Lancashire Witches a Revision?"[31] by Professor Robert Grant Martin.

[30] "The Authorship of The Late Lancashire Witches," C. E. Andrews. *Modern Language Notes*, XXVIII, pp. 163-166.

[31] "Is The Late Lancashire Witches a Revision?" Robert Grant Martin. *Modern Philology*, Vol. V, pp. 253-265.

Professor Andrews notes that Fleay considers the play an old play of Heywood's written shortly after the 1612 trial and revived by Brome for the King's men in 1634. Fleay's conclusion is based chiefly upon the assumption that a woman of good birth, one Alice Nutter, found guilty with others at the 1612 trial, was the prototype for the character of Mrs. Generous and upon the similarity between the language used by Mrs. Generous, when she is brought to bay, and an account of the deposition of one of the defendants in the trial. These words, as Professor Martin quotes, are as follows:

> GEN. Resolve me, how farre doth that contract stretch?
> MRS. What interest in this Soule, my selfe coo'd claime
> I freely gave him, but his part that made it
> I still reserve, not being mine to give.
> GEN. O cunning Divell, foolish woman know
> Where he can clayme but the least little part,
> He will usurpe the whole; th'art a lost woman.
>
> L. L. W. (Vol. IV, p. 227)

> In the examination of James Device, one of the accused in the trial of 1612, he deposed that there appeared to him a thing like a browne Dogge, who asked (this Examinate) to give him his Soule and he should be revenged of any whom hee would: whereunto (this Examinate) answered, that his Soule was not his to give but was his Saviour Jesus Christ's, but as much as was in him (this Examinate) to give, he was contented he should have it.
>
> Crossley op. cit. sig H²verso.

In accepting Fleay's theory, Professor Andrews adduces further internal evidence for this opinion: "the obvious interpolation of an episode, an omission of one or two incidents that we are led to expect, and a mention in two places of names of witches or spirits inconsistent with the names in the rest of the play." The fact that Heywood was writing for the Queen's company in 1633 when the play was brought out by the King's men is added as proof against collaboration.[30]

In Professor Martin's discussion of the subject, the history of the arguments for both sides of the question is reviewed: the revision theory of Fleay, Ward, and Professor Andrews; the position of Professor Schelling and Professor Notestein. (Professor Schelling, without entering into details of analysis, bases the play upon the incidents of the trial of 1633; while Professor Notestein, in his treatise on witchcraft in England, affirms that "the main incidents and the characters of the play are so fully copied" from the testimony of the later trial "that a layman would at once pronounce it a play written entirely to order from the affair of 1634."[32]) Professor Martin himself has presented a strong case for the relation of the play to the incidents of the later trial and also for the pure-collaboration theory. In the critical examination he makes of the evidence bearing upon the source and the authorship of the play, he shows quite conclusively that while the poet was undoubtedly indebted to the account of 1612 trial for the original of Mrs. Generous, yet, the witches, the boy, and the incidents in the play concerning witchcraft follow the depositions of the trial of 1634. These elements are dramatized in the following parts of the play: "the boy and the greyhounds (II, III, IV), the boy's ride through the air with Goody Dickison (II, IV), the milk pail which obeys Moll's summons (II, VI), the witches' feast (IV, I), the boy's story of his fights with the devil (V, I), Peg's confession (V, V)." Corroborative evidence is furnished by an apparent allusion in the play to Prynne's punishment, which occurred early in 1634, to an introduction of new farthings (also an event of 1634), and to the time of the composition of the play. This last bit of internal evidence consists of the words of Generous in a casual reference to the hot weather of July and August. Professor Martin, inferring that the play was written in July or

[32] "Is the Late Lancashire Witches a Revision?" Robert Grant Martin, *Modern Philology,* Vol. V, p. 254.

August of 1634, between the time of bringing the accused persons to London and their trial, as indeed the Prologue intimates, feels that the language of Generous may not be wholly insignificant. Mainly, then, from the close parallelism between the characters and incidents of the witch scenes, on the one hand, and the narrative of the 1634 trial, on the other, and from several details of internal evidence, Professor Martin concludes that the play was written in 1634.

There appear to be no valid reasons for assigning the play to an earlier date. If the play is a revision, the original draft must have differed radically from the extant version; for, when the incidents plainly derived from the trial of 1634 are omitted, little remains of a play, either in central theme or action.

The main plot of *The Late Lancashire Witches,* that is, the Generous action together with the amusing episodes presenting the tiresome Whetstone and his tormentors Arthur, Shakstone, and Bantam, has been ascribed to Heywood by all the critics. A very sound argument for this decision rests on the fact that the erring-wife motive as treated in this play is entirely in the spirit of Heywood's employment of this theme in *A Woman Killed with Kindness, Edward the Fourth,* and *The English Traveller.* Mr. Generous, whose name attests his nature, is the hospitable Englishman pictured in Master Frankford and Master Wincott. Note too, Heywood's method of describing a character before his appearance:

> SHAK. .... are you resolv'd
>   Where we shall dine today?
> ARTH. Yes where we purpos'd.
> BANT. That was with Master *Generous.*
> ARTH. True, the same.
>   And where a loving welcome is presum'd.
>   Whose liberall Table's never unprepared.
>   Nor he of guests unfurnisht, of his meanes,
>   There's none can beare it with a braver port,

And keepe his state unshaken, one who sels not
Nor covets he to purchase, holds his owne
Without oppressing others, alwayes prest
To indeere to him any knowne Gentleman
In whom he finds good parts.

BANT. A Character not common in this age.
ARTH. I cannot wind him up
Unto the least part of his noble worth.
Tis far above my strength.

L. L. W. (Vol. IV, p. 172)

Like Heywood's "true gentleman," Mr. Generous would
reject the news of his wife's guilt brought by the faithful
servant Robin, another Nicholas; when he is forced to
believe the evidence of his senses he, too, is overwhelmed
with grief rather than rage; and he, too, struggles between
his convictions as to his clear duty and his strong affection
for his wife. In his ultimate action, he, like his prototypes,
has conquered self absolutely. If further evidence were
necessary to prove the comparatively late date of the writing
of this play, the character of Mrs. Generous could be cited,
for she is unlike Heywood's earlier conceptions of the erring
wife. Presented when she has already surrendered to guilt,
she recalls Mrs. Wincott, but she is more crafty and subtle.
When she is first detected in the thralls of witchcraft, she
keeps her head, and with ingenuity and force of will she
dissimulates to placate her husband; she takes refuge in
subterfuge when the network of evidence is spread around
her; she becomes indifferent when she perceives the inevitability of failure. To the end she exhibits neither the weakness of Mrs. Wincott nor the remorse of Mrs. Frankford
and Jane Shore. By turns unconcerned, wary, defiant as to
her fate, she flings her gauntlet at the feet of her accusers:

MRS. GEN. I will say nothing, but what you know, you know,
And as the law shall finde me let it take me!

L. L. W. (Vol. IV, p. 258)

The victim of error, she maintains her rôle with stoic indifference; but by virtue of her strength she is more attractive

than Mrs. Frankford, Jane Shore, or Mrs. Wincott. As the center, the inspiring force of the witches, she is presented in vigorous action; a vivid, alert creature, she moves in and out of the scenes; compared to her, Mrs. Frankford and Jane Shore are lay figures. In his creation of Mrs. Wincott, Heywood gave the first bare sketch of the erring wife who is absolutely responsible for her guilt; but the motivation of Mrs. Wincott is born not of strength but of an unmoral nature, and, as we have seen, she collapses when her guilt is laid bare. In Mrs. Generous he goes a step further; Mrs. Generous is consistently strong throughout the play.

A scene from this play is illustrative of Heywood's mastery of the technique of the effective scene. At the moment when Generous discovers that his wife is a witch, there is presented with consummate skill an entanglement of opposing forces: Robin is anxious to betray Mrs. Generous; Generous is horrified and grieved before the evidence confronting him; Mrs. Generous is desirous to escape the punishment hovering over her. All three are fencing vainly with themselves and with one another. In the ensuing conflict of emotions, Heywood reaches and sustains an intense dramatic moment, the climax of the play.

As Professor Martin points out, Professor Andrews' reason for assigning the Seeley story to Heywood and the Lawrence-Parnell story, as an integral part of the former, to the same hand rests upon the unconvincing assertion that Brome received his suggestion for *The Antipodes* from the Seeley story. This argument is based upon Professor Andrews' conclusions as to the date of the original version of *The Late Lancashire Witches* and the nature of its collaboration. Professor Martin's refutation of Professor Andrews' claim of the sub-plot for Heywood is so convincing that it may be accepted without further evidence. This part of the play, moreover, is marked by certain qualities in the nature of the theme and its general tone which point anywhere except to Heywood's hand. In the first place, we must remember that the tricks in Heywood's plays are not turned at the expense of the servants, the peasants, the clowns, or any of the humbler characters in the play. An apparent exception to this rule is the humiliation of Clem at the court of Mullisheg, but this bit of Elizabethan humor is an episode only forced in for amusement, the single instance of its kind in the plays. Nicholas and his fellow servants, Hobson's apprentices, Jockey, Hobson, Clem elsewhere, and the unnamed clowns are the instigators of merriment, shafts being levelled only infrequently at them. The rôle of Lawrence and Parnell is different. From the position they are given in the reversal of fortunes in the Seeley household to the exhibition of their own dilemma, they are the butts of hilarious ridicule. In tone, also, the humor is too broad for Heywood; although at rare intervals his dialogue reflects the license of his times, he is not innately coarse and would hardly have centered the turning point of an action in an incident such as that which worked the climax of the Lawrence-Parnell story. Again, in the entire group of Heywood's women none is characterized by the crudeness, the total lack of feminine modesty, which we observe in Parnell. The same cannot be said for Brome. In a word, the Lawrence-Parnell story bears no earmarks of Heywood's manner, while the Seeley story, essentially a burlesque, suggests the same hand that wrote *The Jovial Crew* and *The Antipodes*. As the witch scenes, featuring Mrs. Generous as the dominant force, are an integral part of the Generous action, Heywood in all likelihood wrote them. Brome, however, may have composed the songs.

A Warning for Fair Women

"A Warning for Faire Women containing the most Tragicall and Lamentable Murther of Master George Sanders of London, Merchant, nigh Shooters Hill; consented unto by his owne wife, acted by M. Browne, Mistris Drewry and Trusty Roger, agents therin: with thier severall ends. As it hath beene lately diverse times acted by the right Honorable the Lord Chamberlaine his Servantes." Thus reads the title page of this play published in 1599. It is a murder play founded upon a crime reported in full details by Holinshed (1577)[33] and Stow (1573),[34] and briefly summarized by Anthony Munday in *A View of Sundry Examples* (1580).[35] Simpson, who edits the play in his *School of Shakspere,* reprints an anonymous pamphleteer's version of the murder. In this narrative the bare details of the tragedy, as given by the chroniclers, are embellished by exhortations and moralizings, which lengthen the original account into a weighty, protracted sermon.[36] According to the Stationers' Register "A Warnynge for fayre women" was entered for the publisher William Aspley on the seventeenth of November, 1599.[37] Reminiscent in basic theme and in some details of situation of *Arden of Feversham, A Warning for Fair Women* unfolds in rapid action the temptation and fall of Mrs. Anne Sanders, who consents to the murder of her husband, and, with her co-partners in guilt, George Brown her betrayer, Mrs. Drury his agent, and Roger the servant, atones for the crime upon the gallows. In the presentation of the action the poet sketches in hastily Brown's seduction of Mrs. Sanders. There is one brief scene before Mrs. Sanders' doorway where the betrayer vaguely hints at his desires only to be repulsed firmly by the wife's loyalty to her husband; there is a momentary meeting

[33] *Holinshed's Chronicles of England, Scotland, and Ireland,* Vol. II, pp. 1865, 1866.

[34] Stow's *Annales,* p. 674.

[35] *A View of Sundry Examples* by Antony Munday, 1580, pp. 78-80.

[36] *A briefe discourse of the late murther of master George Saunders. . . . .* 1573. In Simpson's *School of Shakspere,* Vol. II, pp. 2?1-239.

[37] *A Transcript of the Registers of the Stationers' Company,* Vol. III, p. 151.

of the two after the murder has been committed. It is in the speeches of Tragedy, the Chorus, and in the dumb show that the first phase of Mrs. Sanders' emotional problem is put before us. In pantomime Chastity appears struggling with her enemy Lust; in the wake of the two is Murder; when Chastity finds she is overpowered she flees the stage leaving the field to her victors. We are given little opportunity to see Mrs. Sanders. In the background of the movement, of which she is in reality the subject, she moves as a shadow, only to emerge vitally as a pitiful creature in the closing scenes of the play. After she is arraigned for the murder, she is anything but passive in her futile attempt to escape the gallows. On the other hand, the pictures of Mrs. Sanders as housewife and mother are good. The lively dialogue between her and the merchants bringing their wares to her house and the scene in which she gently chides her little son, afford us glimpses of the frugal, dutiful housewife, the gentle, watchful mother. The first scene of the play is dramatically strategic—the adroit Mrs. Drury is quick to take advantage of Mrs. Sanders' momentary flare of anger and resentment at what she considers her husband's penuriousness—but it is also a delightful bit of contemporary life. The dialogue, the account given by Sanders' man of the busy morning in his master's life, the presentation of the thrifty merchant, Sanders himself, and the episode featuring Old John the farmer and Joan his maid constitute a wholesome atmosphere of Elizabethan middle-class life. The sympathetic portrayal of middle-class ideals both intensifies and relieves the tragic outline of the plot.

As a domestic drama developing the unfaithful wife motive, *A Warning for Fair Women,* we repeat, barely suggests the wife in the essential action of the theme. It is more striking as a murder play. In this respect it suggests, though in sharp contrast, *Arden of Feversham.* Before the action of the latter play begins, Alice Arden is already guilty of infidelity. It is her strong love for Mosbie that inspires her to be what she is, the alert force of the sordid plot; Mosbie is in reality her accomplice. In the hands of Brown, Mrs. Drury, and Roger, Mrs. Sanders is a puppet. Playing upon her unsuspecting nature, her superstition, and her innate weakness of character, they overcome her scruples and then execute the crime. Barring the scenes which are practically all atmosphere, the action centers in the efforts of Brown to secure the aid of Mrs. Drury and her entire willingness to be his accomplice, in the baffled attempts to perpetrate the murder and the details of the murder itself, and finally in the train of incidents in the wake of the crime. It is a shocking murder play rendered none the less so by the sombre figure of Tragedy and the gruesome nature of the attendant dumb shows. In purport the play is consistently ethical.

A Warning for Fair Women was published anonymously, having been acted by the Chamberlain's men. Recently it has been attributed by Professor Adams to Heywood upon its resemblance to Heywood's plays both in the prevailing tone and atmosphere of the play and in minor details of style.[38] In its rhetorical and verbal characteristics, in the wholesome ethics of the final judgment, in its simplicity, and in the realism of its atmosphere the play does suggest our poet. Some features, however, of its structure and sentiment are vastly different from what is found in any of Heywood's acknowledged plays. Heywood, as we know, delighted to use the Chorus and dumb shows in his early plays; in one of his late plays we find him reverting to the dumb show. In his method of employing these devices, he seems to have developed a systematic policy.· We are not speaking, of course, of his plays upon classic themes. In the drama of contemporary incident he has used the Chorus purely as a link bridging the chasm between different places of action

[38] "The Authorship of A Warning for Fair Women," Joseph Quincy Adams, Jr. *Publications of the Modern Language Association of America*, XXVIII, pp. 594-620.

and changes in characterization as in *The Four Prentices
of London,* and *The Fair Maid of the West;* connecting
two plots as in *Edward the Fourth (2);* or adding an episode as in *If You Know Not Me You Know Nobody (2).*
The dumb show unaccompanied by a Chorus may cover a
gap in the action as in *If You Know Not Me You Know
Nobody (1).* Moreover, the Chorus of Heywood does not
appear between the scenes of the plays which are domestic
drama—*A Woman Killed with Kindness, The English
Traveller, The Late Lancashire Witches,* and *Fortune by
Land and Sea.* Quite unlike Heywood's Choruses is the
Chorus of *A Warning for Fair Women,* appearing at the
beginning of each act, anticipating the atmosphere and events
of the act immediately to follow. In no sense is it needed
to bridge abrupt changes in place, time, characters, or sentiment or to connect unrelated elements of the consistently
unified plot. If it were omitted one would miss events in
the same thread of action; that is all. It remains then as an
integral part of the play constituting moreover a considerable
bulk of the total lines: 257 lines as opposed to 88 lines of
The Four Prentices of London, 17 lines of *Edward the
Fourth (2),* 27 lines of *If You Know Not Me You Know
Nobody (2),* 19 lines of *The Fair Maid of the West (2).*
In purpose and in spirit Heywood's Choruses are unlike the
Chorus of *A Warning for Fair Women.* Similarly, as
another note of inconsistency, the Induction presents diffi-
culties. In discussing the play, Professor Brooke writes,
"The prefatory dialogue in the *Warning for Fair Women*
and the epistle prefixed to George Whetstone's *Promos and
Cassandra* (1578) are probably the most important pieces of
dramatic criticism to be found in any English stage play
previous to 1600."[39] The point to be noted in regard to this
Induction is that its dialogue among the three characters
Tragedy, History, and Comedy is an argument upon the

---

[39] *The Tudor Drama,* C. F. Tucker Brooke. Boston, 1911, p. 360.

virtues of the main divisions of drama, the issues being defended upon aesthetic grounds. Tragedy says:

TRAG. I must confess you have some sparks of wit
Some odd ends of old jests scrap'd up together,
To tickle shallow unjudicial ears:
Perhaps some puling passion of a lover,
But slight and childish. What is this to me?
I must have passions that must move the soul;
Make the heart heavy and throb within the bosom,
Extorting tears out of the strictest eyes—
To rack a thought, and strain it to his form,
Until I rap the senses from their course.
This is my office.

W. F. W. (Induction 32-42)

Written in or before the year 1598, it preceded by a number of years Heywood's *Apology for Actors*. We recall, that in this treatise Heywood stresses the utilitarian aspects of the drama, defending his conclusion upon ethical grounds. We have seen how in writing his plays he kept before him apparently this point of view. It is hardly probable that he would have reverted from the broader to the narrower aspect. In harmonious flow of the blank verse, in simplicity of utterance the versification suggests Heywood's directness, but there is little or none of Heywood's repetitions of lines and the tone color is strikingly varied as compared to Heywood's occasional lapses into flat monotony. There are lines of poetic reach in this play scarcely to be attained by Heywood. That is, for sheer poetic beauty. The charm of Heywood's diction is in its unpretentious simplicity and sincerity, in the force of its genuine feeling. When the character is frail, he cannot express remorse in ennobled diction. In the lines below, quoted from *A Woman Killed with Kindness*, note how the poet has to resort to stringing out details, and parallelisms in phrasing to get effect. In contrast to this, mark the dignity of language and sentiment which a greater poet can put upon the lips of a character lacking the very virtues one finds in Mrs. Frankford. Heywood is more sincere in his characterization, but the poetry suffers:

ANNE (Frankford)

> I would I had no tongue, no eares, no eyes,
> No apprehension, no capacity.
> When do you spurne me like a dog? when tread me
> Under your feete? when drag me by the haire?
> Though I deserve a thousand, thousand folde
> More than you can inflict: yet once my husband,
> For woman-hood to which I am a shame,
> Though once an ornament: Even for his sake
> That hath redeem'd our soules, marke not my face,
> Nor hacke me with your sword: but let me go
> Perfect and undeformed to my Tombe.

W. K. K. (Vol. II, p. 139)

ANNE (Sanders) Shall I feare more my servants, or the world,

> Then God himselfe? He heard our trecherie
> And saw our complot and conspiracie.
> Our hainous sin cries in the eares of him,
> Lowder than we can cry upon the earth.
> A woman's sinne, a wives inconstancy:
> O God, that I was borne to be so vile!
> So monstrous and prodigous for my lust.
> Fie on this pride of mine, this pampered flesh!
> I will revenge me on these 'tising eyes
> And tear them out for being amourous.
> Oh, Sanders, my deare husband! Give me leave,
> Why do you hold me! Are not my deeds ugly?
> Let them my faults be written in my face.

W. F. W. (Act II, ll. 653-666)

One thing that strikes me as peculiarly odd about this play, in the light of any suggestion as to Heywood's authorship, is the absence of the philosophic strain, the brief meditative notes scattered by Heywood through all of his known plays. The theme of *A Warning for Fair Women* would lend itself easily to moralizing and reflection upon Heywood's favorite subjects for contemplation: fatalism, loyalty, the inevitability of punishment, the spirit of truth.

There is barely a line in the play even faintly expressive of the enlarged vision of life which sees the experience of individuals as manifestations of universal laws or general tendencies governing human thought and social life. Of course we are speaking of the actual words of the play and not of any ulterior didactic intention on the part of the author to be inferred from the unambiguous words of the title. The play carries with it its own message. But it lacks absolutely the verbal expressions of the meditative mood of Heywood.

Although Heywood produced plays without a clown, the comic element as relief is, as we have seen, regularly present. In the consistency of the tragic tone *A Warning for Fair Women* is almost Senecan. From Old John and Joan we might have expected lively dialogue, such humor as Hobs in *If You Know Not Me You Know Nobody* furnishes, but these peasants are in a strangely serious mood. Over them hangs the ominous shadow of impending murder. Slowly they walk along the road disturbed in mind as they recall fateful dreams of the night before and other unlucky omens that beset them. This atmosphere of gloom may scarcely be explained in the subservience of the poet to the tone of the theme, the facts of which were well known to the theatre-goers, but rather in the temper of the poet consistently, morosely serious. If this author was Heywood, who always mingled the gay with the grave, he displays here an attitude toward his art at variance with his characteristic mood.

I should like to believe that Heywood wrote *A Warning for Fair Women,* for the play bears the marks of sure workmanship, such as I should like to find in the work of a poet of Heywood's loftiness of purpose and kindly feeling. In no one of his known plays can I discover, combined, the artistic merits of this play: the swift action of the Senecan plot, the sustained harmony of thought to tragic theme, the uniform level of the verse. The thought of the Induction does not accord with Heywood's theory of the drama, nor

can we feel that Heywood's known plays were constructed
by one who ever considered seriously the artistic beauty of
his productions. Then too we look in vain through the
play for Heywood's pithy, philosophical sayings. If he
collaborated in the writing of this play, which, it is true,
displays his characteristic attitude toward contemporary life,
his share in the production was scarcely much. He may
have written a rough draft from a plot furnished him, while
another hand than his revised the play. This is the utmost
that I can believe as to Heywood's contribution to the authorship of *A Warning for Fair Women.*

How a Man May Choose a Good Wife from a Bad

This play is described upon the title-page of the edition
of 1602 as "A Pleasant conceited Comedie, Wherein is
shewed how a man may chuse a good wife from a bad.
As it hath beene sundry times Acted by the Earle of Worces-
ters Servants."[40]   Other early editions of this popular play
were published in 1605, 1608, 1614, 1621, 1630, 1634.[41]
There is no record of the play in the Stationers' Register
nor among the entries made by Henslowe for the Earl of
Worcester's company, these entries in Henslowe bridging
the period of time from August 1602 until the spring of
1603.   Because of its omission from the company's accounts
with Henslowe, Fleay[42] followed by Professor Swaen[43] concludes that the play must have been written before the
company went to the Rose, Henslowe's theatre, probably as
early as 1601.   If the Earl of Worcester's company was not
organized in London until 1602, performances being given
before that date in the provinces, *How a Man May Choose a*

[40] *List of Plays,* Greg, p. 13.
[41] *Ibid.*
[42] *A Biographical Chronicle of the English Drama.* Vol. I, p. 290.
[43] *How a Man May Chuse a Good Wife From a Bad,* edited by
A. E. H. Swaen, 1912. Introduction, VI.

Good Wife from a Bad may have been put on in Coventry, Leicester or Barnstaple, the principal known places of the company's itinerary between 1600 and 1603.[44] On the other hand the play may have been presented in 1602 at the Boar's Head in Whitechapel[45] where the company acted for a short time after its reorganization but before it began acting at the Rose in connection with Henslowe.

How a Man May Choose a Good Wife from a Bad is a domestic drama built upon the faithful-wife, prodigal-husband theme. As such it is related to a large group of plays of its type, the plots of which are characterized by certain constant features. These common elements are as follows: a faithful wife is deserted by her husband; the husband pursues a wild career; finally, the husband returns penitent to his wife to receive whole-hearted forgiveness. In actual development, however, the plays differ as the emphasis of characterization, situation, and action veers from the sufferings of the neglected wife to the escapades or degradation of the errant husband. *How a Man May Choose a Good Wife from a Bad* follows in its basic action the conventional lines of the treatment of the theme. A happy balance is preserved in the characterization of the principal figures in that the wife is not condemned to undergo indignity as Grissil does, and the husband does not drink to the dregs the draught of vice as is the case with Matthew Flowerdale of *The London Prodigal* and William Scarborow of *The Miseries of Enforced Marriage*. In the delightful portrayal of character through action Mrs. Arthur's fidelity is clearly seen; she chides Pipkin the clown for his half merry hints of Master Arthur's escapades; she defends her husband against the criticism of both father and father-in-law; she repulses Master Anselm who would woo her; she receives the courtesan graciously into

[44] *English Dramatic Companies,* I, p. 53; *Chambers Elizabethan Stage,* II, 225.
[45] *Elizabethan Stage,* II, 225, 444.

her home. Her suffering arises from the knowledge of her husband's indifference. Even after she learns of his attempt to take her life, her faith never wavers. The wayward Master Arthur also is consistently well drawn from the first scene of the play up to the moment of his repentance. In the refinement of his cruelty, he forces upon his wife the humiliation of entertaining her rival, but he lacks the brutality of Matthew Flowerdale, who takes his wife's dowry and then abuses her and his own father. Liveliness is sustained in *How a Man May Choose a Good Wife from a Bad* by the humor characters: the vacillating old Arthur, the complacent Old Lusan, the diffident Anselm, Fuller with the ready tongue, and Aminadab the pedant. Not less amusing is the waggery of Pipkin the clown. The play abounds in a veritable array of delightful characters, their appeal, however, being somewhat weakened by the author's clearly apparent efforts at studied character balancing.

The main thread of action and the episodes introducing the minor characters are developed in a setting, sympathetic in its realism to a slight degree, satiric for the greater part. There is a charming picture of Mrs. Arthur's domestic economy as well as of her patience. She is preparing to entertain the courtesan:

> MIST. AR. Come spread the Table: Is the hall well rubd,
> The cushions in the windowes neatly laid,
> The Cupboord of plate set out, the Casements stuck,
> With Rosemary and Flowers, the Carpets brusht?
> MAYD. I forsooth Mistris.
> MIS. Looke to the kitchen Mayd, and bid the Cooke take
> downe the Oven stove, lest the pies be burnt: here take
> my keyes and give him out more spice.
> MAYD. Yes forsooth Mistris.
> MIS. AR. Where's that knave *Pipkin,* bid him spred the cloth,
> Fetch the cleane diaper napkins from my chest,
> Set out the guilded salt, and bid the fellow
> Make himselfe handsome, get him a cleane band.

H. M. M. C. (1470-1482)

Satire, however, is the stronger note, but satire untinged with mockery or bitterness. Though the spirit is pure fun, delightful raillery, the poet holds up for sport the shallow pedantry of Aminadab's school-room, the sophistication of the law courts in Justice Reason's verbiage, the inconstancy of women and the hypocrisy of Puritanism in Fuller's recitals of his amours. The characterization of Mrs. Arthur is the only important element of the play capturing the sympathies of the poet. The subjects, nevertheless, of the satire are indicative of right thinking; virtue, simplicity, good faith, innocence are not the targets of the poet's shafts. Likewise, it may be noted that the musings into which the poet falls now and then are in direct accord with his satire. For instance:

> Money can make a slavering tongue speake plain.
> . . . .
> Gold can make limping *Vulcan* walke upright
> Make squint eyes look strait, a crabd face looke smooth
> Guilds Copernoses, makes them looke like gold
> Fils ages wrinkles up, and makes a face
> As old as *Nestors,* looke as yong as *Cupide.*
>
> 970-974

> O what are the vaine pleasures of the world,
> That in their actions we affect them so?
> . . . .
> What is vaine bewtie but an Idle breath?
> Why are we proud of that which so soone changes?
> But rather wish the bewtie of the minde,
> Which neither time can alter, sicknesse change,
> Violence deface, nor the black hand of envie,
> Smudge and disgrace, or spoile, or make deformed.
>
> 2325-2337

The action of *How a Man May Choose a Good Wife from a Bad* might occur anywhere. True it is that one hears a general allusion to London—

> A sweet dusk all London cannot yeeld

Pipkin vaunts his knowledge of

> The parson of *Fanchurch,* the parson of *Pancridge,*
>
> 1638-1640

and reference to the Exchange occurs a half dozen times or more in the play. But these allusions are too few to establish any local background for the action. One misses in the play also pictures of English life and manners.

The plot is a main thread woven in and out of episodical situations furnishing merriment. Integrally related to the main action is the Anselm-Mrs. Arthur action. Due to the constant movement of characters, there is much stage business, one cause probably of the continued popularity of the play. The dialogue is spirited—there are a few soliloquies and longer speeches, notably Master Fuller's long narratives of his amours and the reflection of Mrs. Arthur. In the straightforward, simple phraseology may be noted a liberal number of classicisms and familiar quotations. The rather scant imagery is restricted to direct comparison. Not the least significant characteristic of the versification is the quality of the tone color produced by the constant repetition of words, phrases and even sentences. These repetitions are not restricted to the recurrence of words in end-rhyme but appear in the overuse of the same expressions in single speeches or small groups of lines. Thus:

> MA. Why you Jacke sauce, you Cuckold, you whatnot,
> What am not I of age sufficient
> To go and come still when my pleasure serves,
> But must I have you sire to question me?
> Not have my will! Yes I will have my will.
>
> YONG. AR. I had a wife would not have usde me so,
> But she is dead.
>
> BRA. Not have her will, sir, she shall have her will,
> She saies she will, and sir I say she shall.
> Not have her will? That were a Jeast indeed,
> Who saies she shall not, if I be disposde
> To man her forth, who shall finde fault with it?
> What's he that dare say black's her eie?

Though you be married sir, yet you must know
That she was ever borne to have her will.
Splay.   Not have her will, Gods passion, I say still,
A women's nobodie that wants her will

2187-2203

Mist. Ar.   If you delight to chaunge, chaunge when you please,
So that you will not chaunge your love to me.
If you delight to see me drudge and toyle
Ile be your druge, because tis your delight,
Or if you thinke me unworthie of the name
Of your chast wife, I will become your maide,
Your slave, your servant, anything you will,
If for that name of servant and of slave,
You will but smile upon me now and then,
Or if as I well thinke you cannot love me,
Love where you list, only say but you love me.

252-261

Old Ar.   Your daughter is the wonder of her sexe,
Old Lu.   Are you advisde of that, I cannot tell
What tis you call the wonder of her sexe,
But she is, is she, I indeed she is.

98-101

This sort of verbiage makes up the dialogue as a whole, the play containing scarcely a page free from such repetitions, mannerisms suggesting the author's intention to secure thereby humorous effects. Thus marred by a device so patently artificial, the verse loses a natural charm and freshness which its simple phraseology and ease of flow might secure to it.

The source of *How a Man May Choose a Good Wife from a Bad* has been pointed out[46] as a story found originally in Cinthio's *Hecatommithi* III, 5. In all likelihood the poet was indebted directly, as Professor Baskervill suggests,[47] to an Elizabethan version of the Italian made by

[46] *How a Man May Chuse a Good Wife from a Bad.* Introduction, XIII-XLII.

[47] "Source and Analogues of *How a Man May Choose a Good Wife from a Bad.*" By C. R. Baskervill, *Publications of the Modern Language Association of America*, XXIV, 1909, pp. 711-730.

Barnaby Riche in his collection of tales entitled *Riche his Farewell to Militarie Profession* (1581).[48]

Several critics have assigned *How a Man May Choose a Good Wife from a Bad* to Heywood; namely, Fleay,[49] Swinburne,[50] and, recently, Professor Swaen[51] and Professor Adams.[52]   Professor Schelling says "There seems no reason for Fleay's assignment of this play to Heywood."[53]   Ward points out the similarities between Pipkin and Heywood's clowns but rejects the play because "such resemblances . . . . . are not evidence."[54]   Fleay's conclusion: "Certainly it is by the same author as *The Wise Woman of Hogsdon,*" is based upon the resemblance of Sir Aminadab's phraseology to that of Sir Boniface in *The Wise Woman of Hogsdon* and to the reference in *How a Man May Choose a Good Wife from a Bad* to one "Thomas," who, Fleay thinks, is Heywood himself.   More convincing is the evidence submitted by Professor Swaen and Professor Adams.   The former supports his theory by resemblances in situation and characterization to certain plays of Heywood, by Elizabethan sentiment and coloring, and by general characteristics of style.   Of similar nature are the arguments of Professor Adams, but he stresses, especially, the verbal and rhetorical elements of similarity between the two plays.   Much has been made of the points in common between this play and *The Wise Woman of Hogsdon*.   Professor Quinn, in the Introduction

---

[48] Reprinted for the Shakespeare Society, 1853.

[49] *Biographical Chronicle of the English Drama*, I, p. 290.

[50] *The Age of Shakespeare*, by Algernon Charles Swinburne, 1908, p. 247.

[51] *How a Man May Chuse a Good Wife from a Bad.* Introduction, VII.

[52] "Thomas Heywood and *How a Man May Choose a Good Wife from a Bad,*" by Joseph Quincy Adams, Jr. *Englische Studien*, XLV, 30-44.

[53] *Elizabethan Drama*, Vol. I, 331.

[54] *History of the English Dramatic Literature*, IV, 106.

of his edition of *The Faire Maide of Bristow*,[55] lists the analogues of the latter play, among which are *The Wise Woman of Hogsdon* and *How a Man May Choose a Good Wife from a Bad,* and points out the relatively closer identification of characters in *The Fair Maid* and *How a Man May Choose a Good Wife from a Bad,* as well as the general parallelism between *The Wise Woman of Hogsdon* and *The Miseries of Enforced Marriage.* But omitting the character rôles enforced by the theme itself and the dialogue of the pedants, I see little in *The Wise Woman of Hogsdon* that suggests *How a Man May Choose a Good Wife from a Bad.* As has been said, Heywood's treatment of the prodigal-son and faithful-wife theme in *The Wise Woman of Hogsdon* is distinctly unique; in *How a Man May Choose a Good Wife from a Bad* the conventional pattern is followed. Neither, to my mind, is there any similarity, except in outline rôles, between Young Chartley and Young Arthur, Mrs. Arthur and the Second Luce, or the fathers of the plays. Such a difference in characterization, though, has little significance for the question of the authorship of the play. We know that Heywood does not always repeat himself even when writing two plays upon the same theme. (Note the marked difference between Mrs. Wincott and Mrs. Frankford.) Then too, the correspondence in tone of the satire is clear. On the other hand, there is lacking in the play Heywood's lavish coloring of Elizabethan manners, the topographical allusions characteristic of all of his plays, even of those with un-English backgrounds. It is hard to conceive of a Heywood play laid in London—the mention of the Exchange makes that point clear—with barely a specific reference to the background always emphasized in the acknowledged plays. The artificiality of the dialogue and of the character grouping strikes another note in con-

[55] *The Faire Maide of Bristow,* edited by Arthur Hobson Quinn, 1902.

The play *Captain Thomas Stukeley,* published by Simpson in his *School of Shakspere,*[62] adheres to the facts of history in its presentation of the marvelous adventures of its hero in Ireland, Spain, Italy, and Africa. The favorite of fortune, Captain Thomas Stukeley achieves one victory after another until luck deserts him at the battle of Alcazar. Reckless, brave, magnanimous in a grandiose way, he is presented as the typical Englishman, dauntless at all times. In his career of glory our hero sees life in its magnificent reaches only. As he says:

> I must have honour; honour is the thing
> Stukley doth thirst for, and to climb the mount
> Where she is seated, gold shall be my footstool.
>
> Captain Thomas Stukeley 706-708

Spurred on by his overweening ambition, he is callous to the obligations of personal friendship and love. As he needs money to support his plans, he supplants his friend Vernon in the affections of Nell Curtis, the alderman's daughter, and, his wife's dowry once secured, he becomes deaf to the entreaties of wife and father and starts to conquer the world. In the presentation of Stukeley's domestic relations and his life in London together with his connection with Vernon, the poet introduces into the play two elements of importance: the one is a background of contemporary Elizabethan life, the other a strain of fatalism permeating the action; both serve in the characterization of the hero. Nell Curtis, her father, and her mother form a pleasing picture of a family circle: the hectoring, good natured father stirred by pride at the notion of a suitor's breaking his plighted word; the mother, ambitious for her daughter, but timid and conciliatory; Nell herself, dutiful, modest, with the courage however to say a word for her own happiness. The father does not willingly give his daughter to a

---

[62] *The School of Shakspere,* edited by Richard Simpson. Vol. I.

spendthrift. Against the mother's pleas for the "gentleman well born," he opposes his knowledge of the world:

> Passion of me wife, but I heard last day
> He's very wild, a quarreller, a fighter,
> Aye, and I doubt a spend-good too.
>
> Captain Thomas Stukeley 107-109

But in his ultimate consent to the match, he shows himself the indulgent father, prudent, wary, yet tender at heart. In the few lines of the dialogue of this scene the poet has deftly characterized the three and left with us a sketch of a delightful family group. In a more intimate manner still he has introduced the figures of London tradesmen; the mercer, the vintner, the cutler, the buckler, the fencer, and the tennis keeper, our hero's creditors, rushing in to get their pay when they hear of the fortunate marriage their debtor is about to contract. Among them, though, are no sharpers; they come for their own; they can detail their services: "Silks and Velvets," "tavern suppers," "quarts of wine," "bilboes, foxes and Toledo blades," "Broad lines bucklers, beside steel pikes," "tennis balls when the French ambassador was here," "fair linen" "forfeits and Vennyes given upon a wager at the ninth button of your doublet." Thus they approach Stukeley, and the good natured spendthrift, generous with his wife's dowry, satisfies them. In the dialogue of the traders is disclosed an entire vista of one side of Elizabethan life, the very breath of sport and pleasure.

The gentler emotions of our hero are smothered under his absorbing passion for honor and glory. In contrast to Stukeley is his unfortunate rival Vernon. Vernon loves Nell Curtis devotedly; in the nobility of his affection he relinquishes her that she may follow the dictates of her heart, but it is in no humble mood that he meets the lucky suitor. Like a nemesis he appears to anger his opponent wherever the latter is flushed with victory. Their final encounter is at the Battle of Alcazar. Reconciled just before the moment of their deaths they both bow to the power of destiny. In the words of Stukeley:

> Why Master Vernon, in our birth we two
> Were so ordain'd to be of one self heart
> To love one woman, breathe one country air
> And now at last, as we have sympathized
> In our affections, led one kind of life,
> So now we both shall die one kind of death. . .
>
> Captain Thomas Stukeley 2714-2719

The rôle of Vernon serves by way of contrast to picture Stukeley in stronger vitality—the meeting of the two, until the last scene, is always an occasion for the parade of Stukeley's fiery mettle; it sustains the human appeal in an action built solely upon the theme of ambition and adventures growing out of the thirst for honor; and it adds the note of fatalism.

From these elements then: a story of marvelous adventure displaying English fortitude and power, a sympathetic background of wholesome, Elizabethan, middle-class life, the subordination but not repression of the human element, and the thread of fatalism pervading the whole, the rather loosely woven play has been constructed. These salient points have been observed merely because they are related most closely to what we believe is distinctively characteristic of Thomas Heywood.

The structure of the plot is loose, constituting five successive motions, one may say, as the hero shifts from England to Ireland, to Spain, Italy, and Africa. Bridging one gap is a Chorus. The characterization is well done, Stukeley himself being presented with unusual firmness and clearness. A clown as such is lacking but Stukeley's page furnishes humor in the manner of the conventional clown, and the dialogue of the traders before Stukeley's appearance contributes much merriment. The dialogue is straight-forward and unaffected, devoid of much imagery. Scattered through the play are a few classical allusions, and there are many topical references. The verse on the whole is smooth, less than a hundred rhyming lines of the total 2556 verse lines; feminine endings and run-on lines are infrequent. Fleay,[63] Simpson,[64] Mr. Oliphant,[65] and Professor Adams[66] think that the play is the work of several hands. Further than this, Simpson has pointed out that two or three plays must have been laid under contribution in the piecing together of this hybrid composition. Several lines referring to scenes not in the present play give rise to this belief. To Professor Adams we are indebted for the suggestion that it was Heywood who wrote the Stukeley scenes, at least. Professor Adams has indicated also the general parallelisms between *Captain Thomas Stukeley* and Heywood's plays and has made a minute analysis of the phraseology of the play, finding here as in *A Warning for Fair Women* and *How a Man May Choose a Good Wife from a Bad* indications of the Heywood vocabulary.[66] The arguments adduced by Professor Adams for ascribing the Stukeley scenes in this play to Heywood are similar to those advanced for the other two plays. In this case, however, there appears to be stronger foundation for the conclusions, as Captain Thomas Stukeley seems to possess practically all of the characteristics that are peculiarly Heywood's: the loose plot, the idealization of English virtues as found among the middle class, a dominant note of patriotism, a colorful background of middle-class life, an element of humor, and a simplicity of style.

[63] *Biographical Chronicle of the English Drama.* Vol. II, p. 188.
[64] *The School of Shakspere.* Vol. I, p. 142.
[65] "Capt. Thomas Stukeley," by E. H. C. Oliphant. *Notes and Queries,* Series X, III, 1905, pp. 301, 342, 382.
[66] "Captaine Thomas Stukeley," by Joseph Quincy Adams, Jr. *Journal of English Germanic Philology,* XV, 1916.

CONCLUSION

We have seen that the outstanding features of Thomas Heywood's dramatic work are the presentation of wholesome types of Elizabethan men and women in a rich and varied atmosphere of Elizabethan life. A beautiful faith in his Englishmen, an unswerving loyalty to a belief in the essential virtues of his countrymen—in other words, his own enduring patriotism—inspired our poet to maintain a sympathetic attitude toward his creations, drawn generally from the middle class, an attitude as sincere as it is consistent. In his belief in man's better nature, however, he turns deliberately from the sordid conditions of life, and presents a realism tinged with idealism; there are no false lights in the background, but character is conceived as well-nigh faultless. But the poet has his lighter, gayer moods, moods furnishing a wholesome humor never entirely absent from any of his plays.

Heywood's contribution to Elizabethan drama seems quite clear. Influenced by his conscious purpose—*Aut prodesse solent, aut delectare*—he wrote a huge number of plays, the greater number of those that are extant dealing with contemporary English life. His realism is sympathetic, direct, in contrast to the satire of Ben Jonson, Chapman, Middleton, and Brome, who also drew their figures from Elizabethan London; but the kindly tolerance of Heywood's point of view and the unmistakable interest he shows in a class are not shared to any extent by his associates. By way of exception, Dekker and Rowley lose themselves in their pictures of homely life, but in neither case is the amount of their work comparable to Heywood's, nor is their attitude consistently serious. In sheer artistry the one has a poetic reach beyond the grasp of our poet, the other a dramatic vigor superior to Heywood's supreme efforts. Outranked in technique by his contemporaries whose chosen field of work was his also, Heywood, nevertheless, holds a position distinctively his own. The demand for successive editions of some of the plays while the memory of the performances was still fresh proves the popularity of the poet. Such was the response given to the challenge of sincerity, goodwill, and hearty humor consecrated to a wholesome ideal of everyday English life. Among the Elizabethans no other poet is so frankly and completely and consistently stirred by this sympathetic interest in the joys and woes of the ordinary man. From this point of view Heywood's plays should be studied in their relation, first, to the sentimental drama of the century following Heywood's own and, second, to the realistic drama of modern times.

Professor Ernest Bernbaum, in the introductory chapter of his book *The Drama of Sensibility,* writes: "The drama of sensibility, which includes sentimental comedy and domestic tragedy, was from its birth a protest against the orthodox view of life, and against those literary conventions that had served that view . . . . . . It wished to show that beings who were good at heart were found in the ordinary walks of life. It so represented their conduct as to arouse admiration for their virtue and pity for their sufferings. In sentimental comedy, it showed them contending against distresses but finally rewarded by morally deserved happiness. In domestic tragedy it showed them overwhelmed by catastrophes for which they were not responsible."[1] According to this definition the compassion of the playgoers is aroused by the spectacle of the innocent hero, who is, as it were, the sport of fortune. The characters, thus, are presented as lay figures that do not effect their own happiness or distress; but as paragons of virtue, as patient martyrs under affliction, they rise or fall through the force of attendant circumstances conceived as a malignant or propitious fate. As an inevitable consequence of this false conception of art,

---

[1] *The Drama of Sensibility,* Ernest Bernbaum, 1915, p. 10.

a theory ignoring the natural reactions of human nature to conditions promising happiness and to those tending to thwart one's well being, the distinctive feature of the characterization, situation, and atmosphere of sentimental drama is improbability.

It is far from our contention to claim for Heywood the conscious anticipation of a type, which was, as we know, a moral protest against the artificiality and general tone of Restoration drama. But in the creation of his characters, his individualized figures of domestic drama and the stock types of his comedy, we see the man in the ordinary walks of life raised to the dignity of a hero. His men and women are ennobled by their cardinal virtues: patriotism, loyalty, honesty, courage, shrewd common sense, together with essential goodness of heart and fineness of spirit. They are not lay figures, absolutely the sport of circumstances, but they are not masters of their own fate. Fortune rather than human will is the dominant force in the action. Professor Bernbaum, commenting upon the domestic tragedy of the Elizabethans, has noted the emphasis upon responsibility for wrong-doing, citing the virility of Alice Arden in contrast to the complete passivity of the central figures in sentimental drama. But Heywood's heroes and heroines, a long list of them—Master Frankford, Young Geraldine, Mr. Generous, Matthew Shore, Susan Mountford, the Forrests, Palaestra, and Scribonia—suffer through no guilt of their own; they are active only in the spiritual strength of their abnegation of self. Mrs. Frankford, though not innocent, falls because she lacks the strength to withstand an opposing force. Innately weak, she is at the mercy of fate. In the plays, in which the characters mentioned appear, *A Woman Killed with Kindness, Edward the Fourth, The English Traveller, The Captives,* and *The Late Lancashire Witches,* Heywood has made a contribution to that phase of sentimental drama that displays the helpless victim of circumstances. He has not, however, placed his characters in overwhelming situations which bring woes upon woes to the sentimental hero. Indiana, for instance, the heroine of Steele's *Conscious Lovers,* is the long-suffering heroine under misfortunes—the tragic death of her parents, the equally tragic death of her guardian, the unscrupulous plans of the heir-at-law, the hostile attitude of her lover's father. Beauty in distress, she is the true sentimental heroine who accepts in heroics the exquisite tortures of her destiny. Heywood stops far short of this refinement of cruelty, but to the extent that he has depicted undeserved suffering and has created his noble peasants and model tradesmen, he has stepped over the threshold of sentimental drama. This he has done in parts of all his plays of contemporary life.

More noteworthy, as clearly modern, is the underlying purpose of his work. It has been suggested that the repeated effort to characterize such noble types, to present in humorous as well as in serious aspects an entirely wholesome background of contemporary life, must have been born of a conscious aim. In living up to his aim, namely to evoke genuine sympathy for the ordinary man, he wrote purpose dramas. Surely his words voice this point of view:

> Hob. Now, alas, good soul!
> It melts my heart to heare him, and mine eyes
> Could weepe for company.—What earn'st a day?
> Taw. Little, God knows.
> Though I be stirring earlier than the larke,
> And at my labour later than the lambe,
> Towards my wife and childrens maintenance
> I scarcely earne me three pence by the day.
> Hob. Alas, the while, poor soules, I pitty them;
> And in thy words, as in a looking-glass,
> I see the toil and travell of the country,
> And quiet gaine of cities blessednesse.
> Heavens will for all, and should not we respect it,
> We are unworthy life........

I. Y. K. N. M. II (Vol. I, pp. 304-305)

In championing the cause of the ordinary man Heywood points forward to the realism of the social dramas of our own day. Because of his sense of proportion, his appreciation of balance, he has introduced the comic element into his plays to relieve but not obscure the seriousness of his mood. Meditative but not psychological, he has not sounded the depths of social misery. He has shown the brighter side of a dark picture to gain a sympathetic appreciation for the whole. Such a method illustrates, perhaps better than anything else, his wisdom as well as his art. Galsworthy, recalling Heywood, develops his plots as social studies, pleads for true charity, sympathy, above all, for justice for those who, he feels, rarely enjoy it. The centuries between the Elizabethan age and our own day have dignified the cause of the oppressed classes; Galsworthy can handle his problems directly as problems. But his underlying motive, the trend of his sympathies, the nature of his final judgment, which is always ethical, suggests the Elizabethan poet whose ideals were the same. Sterner in mood than Heywood, Galsworthy is the uncompromising student of modern life; he views social unrest and social misery as arising from the clashes of class distinction. In his plays there is nothing indicative of Heywood's gayer spirit that accounted for the charming pictures the Elizabethan has given us of English tavern life, the rollicking country dances, and other sports. It is alone the prevailing purpose of Heywood, rather than his method, that brings the two names together.

As to Heywood's place in the drama, critics are generally in agreement. When Dryden refers slightingly to "Heywood, Shirley, Ogleby" as "neglected authors,"[2] and Oldham, echoing Dryden's wit, says

> Quarles, Chapman, Heywood, Wither had applause,
> And Wild and Ogilby in former days;
> But now are damned to wrapping drugs and wares,[3]

[2] *MacFlecknoe*, John Dryden.
[3] *A Satire Concerning Poetry*, John Oldham.

we are simply reminded of the fact that, after the Restoration, Heywood's popularity, with that of other Elizabethan dramatists, had waned. From Langbaine to Professor Schelling the students of Heywood have agreed as to the poet's sincerity, his unwarped and kindly nature, his nobility of character. His contributions to Elizabethan domestic drama, and his colorful pictures of wholesome Elizabethan life, are appreciated not only for their enduring charm but as expressions of the poet's faith in man's better nature, and his own loyalty and patriotism. Lovers of Heywood have not denied the poet's faults—the limitations of his poetic genius and his carelessness in technique—but much has been forgiven for his wholesome ideals, his generous heart, and his kindly tolerance. The memory lingers fondly, I think, upon the long years of activity during which the poet never swerved from his ideal as voiced in his chosen motto, the years that brought scant return of appreciation, that witnessed little growth in the mastery of his art. That he was content to keep his faith in face of meagre reward argues that he had a great gift, not the creative inspiration of the great poet, but the patience and loyalty and strength of an utter fineness of spirit.

INDEX